Is There Always Value to Adversity?

Is There Always Value to Adversity?

Looking Beyond "What Doesn't Kill You Makes You Stronger"

ERANDA JAYAWICKREME

OXFORD
UNIVERSITY PRESS

OXFORD
UNIVERSITY PRESS

Oxford University Press is a department of the University of Oxford.
It furthers the University's objective of excellence in research, scholarship,
and education by publishing worldwide. Oxford is a registered trade mark of
Oxford University Press in the UK and in certain other countries.

Published in the United States of America by Oxford University Press
198 Madison Avenue, New York, NY 10016, United States of America.

Library of Congress Cataloging-in-Publication Data
Names: Jayawickreme, Eranda author
Title: Is there always value to adversity? : looking beyond "what doesn't
kill you makes you stronger" / Eranda Jayawickreme.
Description: New York, NY : Oxford University Press, [2026] |
Includes bibliographical references and index.
Identifiers: LCCN 2026001904 (print) | LCCN 2026001905 (ebook) |
ISBN 9780197515471 hardback | ISBN 9780197515495 epub | ISBN 9780197515501
Subjects: LCSH: Personality development | Suffering |
Resilience (Personality trait)
Classification: LCC BF723.P4 J39 2026 (print) | LCC BF723.P4 (ebook)
LC record available at https://lccn.loc.gov/2026001904
LC ebook record available at https://lccn.loc.gov/2026001905

DOI: 10.1093/oso/9780197515471.001.0001

Printed by Marquis Book Printing, Canada

The manufacturer's authorized representative in the EU for product safety is
Oxford University Press España S.A. of Parque Empresarial San Fernando de Henares,
Avenida de Castilla, 2 – 28830 Madrid (www.oup.es/en or product.safety@oup.com).
OUP España S.A. also acts as importer into Spain of products made by the manufacturer.

MIX
Paper | Supporting responsible forestry
FSC www.fsc.org
FSC® C103567

For Lisa, Micah, and Maya

Contents

Preface

The journey of writing this book has, in many ways, mirrored its subject matter—a process of challenging past beliefs and questioning assumptions I used to take for granted. It began with reflections on my personal memories, specifically the unresolved questions that arose from my childhood in Sri Lanka, but it has grown into a much larger project that has spanned the last fifteen years of my life.

My goal here has been to write a book that could speak to a wide audience: not only to my colleagues in psychology, but also to thinkers in philosophy, counseling, and religious studies, and indeed to anyone who has ever wrestled with these questions. These chapters aim to give you a sense of how I would teach this topic to my students (In fact, the lecture notes for my undergraduate seminar on post-traumatic growth, or PTG, formed the foundation for this text). To that end, I have woven together personal reflection, multidisciplinary scholarship, and empirical evidence in a way that I hope is both rigorous and readable. Chapter 5 is the most technical chapter, and may be of special interest to academic readers, but my hope is that each reader will find value in many of the chapters.

My writing frequently uses the specific language of personality science, grapples with theological concepts, and examines the methodological details that underpin psychological research. I have tried to provide clear definitions of these terms when I first introduce them, but I am aware that some of these terms may be unfamiliar. To make things easier, I have included a glossary at the end of the book.

1

Rethinking Growth

The Reality Behind "What Doesn't Kill You Makes You Stronger"

I was four years old when my family moved back to Sri Lanka from the United Kingdom in 1984. The country was on the cusp of a bloody quarter-century of insurgency and ethnopolitical violence.[1] Growing up in the 1980s and 1990s, I witnessed violence that still unsettles me when I think back to those experiences, though at the time it felt strangely routine. Bombs regularly tore through city centers, shifting daily life in an instant. My twin brother and I would stay home from school, sometimes for months at a time. We learned to monitor suspicious movements on buses, to keep tabs on checkpoints, and to stay alert to signs of danger. To some extent that vigilance lingers even now.

Against this backdrop, I have long been skeptical of the familiar cultural refrain—especially prevalent in the United States, where I've lived for nearly 25 years—that suffering can, and should, produce strength. Although the apostle Paul's letter to the Romans (5:3–5) promises that "suffering produces endurance, and endurance produces character, and character produces hope," my childhood experiences suggested a different reality. Many people around me were not stronger for their hardships, but were instead weary, resigned, and numb, finding it more difficult to hope and accepting the violence passively as karma or God's will. The idea that "what doesn't kill you makes you stronger"[2] felt disconnected from the challenges I saw. To me, it lacked authenticity.[3]

In August 2001, I moved to the United States for college and encountered a different set of messages about adversity from what I had experienced at home. Weeks after my arrival, the September 11 attacks shook the country, and leaders in New York spoke of the importance of standing strong, of emerging more determined and more resolved. I noticed an insistent optimism in those words: that some good would come out of tragedy. It appeared in political speeches, everyday conversations, and popular media, encouraging everyone to "rally 'round the flag."[4] This belief permeates contemporary US life, from motivational talks to memoirs to national narratives of resilience. The appeal is clear: Adversity becomes an opportunity for growth, a furnace for character.

This *triumph-through-adversity* mindset, while a defining feature of American culture,[5] exists elsewhere. Conversations with Chinese colleagues and students revealed that adversity's benefits may be framed communally, as suffering that strengthens family or societal bonds. One student in my seminar noted that while an American redemption narrative might focus on an individual's resilience and comeback, a narrative in China might emphasize how family and community pulled together, how individuals made sacrifices for the collective, and how the experience reinforced the broader community and country. Many religious traditions, from Buddhism to Islam, likewise highlight moral and spiritual opportunities in hardship. Patience, wisdom, and compassion are said to develop under suffering's tutelage.[6]

Yet from my vantage point, such narratives often felt ill-fitting. Many people, whether in the United States or Sri Lanka, remained exhausted or traumatized. Others did not see an "opportunity" at all, but a punishment for transgressions in this or a past life. This book begins from that observation and asks: Does hardship inherently produce growth, or do we simply prefer to believe it does? And, crucially, what does psychological research reveal about change after trauma, and should we trust it?

The Need to Scrutinize the Idea of (and Evidence for) Growth Following Adversity

When I talk to the media about my research, I emphasize that adversity[7] *can* sometimes inspire moral or psychological growth and that social support is often pivotal: Sharing an experience within a community can help people make sense of it.[8] At the same time, believing or claiming that one has grown may function as a coping strategy (positive reframing or reappraisal), restoring a sense of control and meaning without necessarily reflecting genuine change in character. This distinction between perceived and actual change is central and will recur in the chapters that follow.[9]

Reflecting on Sri Lanka's civil war also made clear that detachment or numbness can be a survival strategy.[10] In war or post-conflict settings, people may persevere by normalizing horror, or they may emerge embittered or petrified by their experiences. Consider three individuals who lose their homes in a natural disaster. One channels energy into rebuilding and community organizing, reporting a newfound sense of purpose. A second focuses on day-to-day survival, emotionally detaching to manage overwhelming stress. A third finds solace in faith, viewing the event as a test of spiritual endurance and turning to prayer and acceptance. A single storyline of positive change flattens these divergent outcomes.[11]

There are also exceptional figures—Martin Luther King Jr., Nelson Mandela, Malala Yousafzai, Mahatma Gandhi—who refused despair and responded to adversity with courage, challenging injustice at great personal risk. Such examples show that adversity can spark moral depth for some. But I kept circling the tension: Why is adversity an opportunity for growth for certain people but a relentless struggle for others? The more I engaged these questions, the more I saw how context, social resources, cultural expectations, and personal values shaped the aftermath of hardship. I also realized, as a psychologist now settled in the United States, that the empirical evidence for growth was not as strong as many assume.

The Credibility Crisis in Research on Post-Traumatic Growth

In the 1990s, clinical psychologists Richard Tedeschi and Lawrence Calhoun introduced the term *post-traumatic growth* (PTG) to describe positive psychological change people report following adversity. Their early work identified five domains:[12] improved relations with others, new possibilities, perceived personal strength, spiritual growth, and an enhanced appreciation of life. PTG is widely reported: A recent review estimated that about 52 percent of trauma-exposed individuals report at least moderate growth.[13]

At first glance, these findings seemed to confirm the cultural narrative that adversity fosters change. Yet, as interest in PTG increased, so did skepticism about its empirical underpinnings.[14] How do we know that growth has occurred, and how do we measure it? Many studies rely on assessment tools like the Post-Traumatic Growth Inventory (PTGI). As I discuss later, critics note that such measures often reflect subjective perceptions shaped by cultural forces and measurement issues rather than authentic change.[15] These limitations blur the line between coping (through finding silver linings in adversity) and authentic changes in character. Mixed findings on well-being compound the problem: Some individuals report better mental health, while others show enduring struggle despite claiming growth. Together, these issues challenge dominant narratives about adversity's positive effects.

Does Growth Always Follow Suffering?

A central claim of this book (perhaps obvious to some of you reading this) is that suffering alone does not guarantee change. Where growth occurs, it likely results from active processes, such as reflective practices (e.g., journaling, therapy, meaning-making), social support (e.g., communal gatherings, peer networks), and intentional behavioral changes (e.g., setting new goals, recalibrating priorities).[16] Without supportive resources, people may continue to struggle. Whether people adapt or suffer is often dictated by contextual factors such as environment, culture, and socioeconomic conditions.[17]

Importantly, the assumption that adversity is a stepping-stone to development is not universal. I remember my mother's quip once when I was trying to explain my research to her: "Bad things are called bad for a reason; why would you expect something good from it?" Western individualistic cultures often idealize personal triumph. Other cultures emphasize communal healing and interdependence. Still others may frame suffering as the result of actions in this life or a past one.[18] Religious beliefs matter as well, with many traditions seeing suffering as a path to wisdom or enlightenment (although, as I discuss in Chapter 3, there is substantial variability within traditions).

Ethically, framing adversity as a "gift" or pressuring survivors to find silver linings can be harmful, particularly in contexts of systemic injustice, where long-standing patterns of disadvantage are created by institutions, policies, and norms that distribute power and resources unevenly. Encouraging people experiencing chronic homelessness due to economic inequality to "find the gift" in their situation minimizes the structural forces at play. While resilience of course has value, these narratives risk obscuring the need for affordable housing, job creation, and social support. Ultimately, discussions about growth can shift responsibility from societal structures to individuals, letting systems off the hook while burdening those already struggling.[19]

Why This Book?

This book interrogates both the belief that adversity typically leads to growth and the psychological research that appears to support this view, and, in my view, it does so differently from prior examinations.

First, unlike popular accounts that celebrate PTG, this book integrates philosophical inquiry, religious accounts, and a critique of empirical research to offer a more clear-eyed view of adversity's possible benefits. Second, rather than focusing solely on academic psychology, it situates "growth" within broader philosophical, religious, and cultural contexts. By tracing how different traditions, from Stoicism to Judaism, from Western individualistic narratives to more communal frameworks, conceptualize suffering's value, I show that what counts as growth is neither universal nor culturally neutral. Third, this work directly confronts methodological problems that others minimize or ignore,[20] examining the gap between perceived and authentic change and urging more rigorous approaches.

Fourth, unlike accounts that treat growth as a purely individual phenomenon, this book emphasizes how social structures, cultural narratives, and systemic inequities shape both exposure to adversity and recovery pathways. By highlighting research on collective dimensions of adaptation, I expand the conversation beyond individualism. Finally, while many books focus primarily on recommendations for fostering growth, this one also addresses the ethics of imposing redemptive expectations. By acknowledging multiple valid responses—including stability, acceptance, and ongoing struggle—this book aims to support survivors without pressuring them to grow.

Through these lenses, the goal is not to debunk the *possibility* of growth, but to build a more credible, evidence-based, and ethically responsible account of when, how, and for whom change occurs. By challenging oversimplified narratives while honoring authentic experiences of growth, I hope to provide a framework that respects both the potential for change and the diversity of human responses to suffering.

Rethinking the Narrative: A More Credible Approach

My personal journey and academic work—reflecting on Sri Lanka's violent past, responses to tragedies like 9/11, the pressure many felt during the COVID-19 pandemic, and the US political climate as I finish this book in the fall of 2025—lead me to a set of questions. First, does suffering truly build character, or is that an appealing myth supported by our cultural milieu? And even when people report positive change, do these claims reflect measurable differences in character? Second, if PTG occurs, what does it look like under careful, methodologically sound research? Too often, flawed methods inflate growth claims, and so we should be cautious about simplistic redemption stories. Third, does adversity genuinely strengthen virtues such as compassion or wisdom, or might these qualities be fostered more effectively through gentler means?[21] Fourth, and finally, does an excessive focus on individual growth obscure the essential roles of communities and relationships? My experiences in Sri Lanka and research on American conceptions of PTG highlight the limits of individualistic frameworks and the importance of *shared* struggle, solidarity, and support. Together, these questions form the heart of this book, challenging assumptions about adversity's value and offering a more realistic account of human development.

Re-examining the narrative that adversity inevitably leads to growth, I argue for several shifts. Most importantly, while genuine growth can occur, it is not predestined. Many people report feeling strengthened, yet many others experience enduring distress or stagnation. Recognizing this variability is crucial; we should resist romanticizing suffering or demanding meaning in every misfortune. Such expectations can contribute to shame or guilt among survivors[22] and can make us less empathetic toward those struggling. A more compassionate understanding of varied responses can help us better support people.

Interpretations of growth must also account for culture, social context, and economics. Rather than assuming a universal trajectory toward redemption, we should understand growth within diverse frameworks and traditions. With this variability in mind, our methods must distinguish perceived growth—how people feel they changed—from *authentic*, observable shifts in beliefs, behavior, relationships, or well-being. Longitudinal, multimethod studies (e.g., studies that employ a combination of assessment methods beyond people's own self-reported beliefs) are essential.

If our individual and collective aspirations include growth, what role should trauma play? The assumption that trauma can frequently be a catalyst for moral or psychological development deserves scrutiny. Research increasingly suggests that resilience, wisdom, and appreciation of life can develop through everyday experiences, not solely through adversity. Acknowledging this allows us to support diverse post-adversity paths—recovery, resilience, acceptance, coping—without prescribing one.

These shifts matter both for our science and for how we respond to suffering. When a friend loses a job, do you immediately urge them to "find the silver lining"? When you face setbacks, do you feel pressure to emerge "stronger"? Sometimes the most compassionate response is to simply acknowledge suffering with care.

Roadmap of What Lies Ahead

This book follows a deliberate arc, moving from experience and theory to methods and practice. Each chapter aims to build a balanced account of whether—and how—adversity can change us for the better. Chapter 2 examines philosophical perspectives, contrasting classical traditions such as Stoicism with contemporary accounts, to define what meaningful growth entails before it can be measured. Chapter 3 extends this lens to religious traditions, showing how cultural and spiritual contexts shape what "counts" as growth and why Western models may reflect particular, non-universal assumptions. Chapter 4 explores how people construct their narrative identity after adversity, and how cultural master narratives may mask evidence of genuine change. Chapter 5 applies these insights to a critical review of PTG research, revealing how measurement practices have distorted our understanding of this phenomenon. Chapter 6 discusses more credible evidence for personality growth following adversity, distinguishing between change in narrative identity, goals and values, and dispositional traits; I also draw on Whole Trait Theory to explain how growth following adversity could plausibly occur. Chapter 7 translates these insights into practice, outlining ethical, culturally sensitive interventions that create conditions for growth without presuming or pressuring it. Chapter 8 ties the arguments in this book together to make the case for a more balanced approach to PTG that honors both the possibility of change and the diversity of human responses to suffering.

The phrase "what doesn't kill you makes you stronger" resonates because it promises redemption in the wake of hardship. However, while some do experience positive change, adversity is neither a guaranteed catalyst nor inherently beneficial. An evidence-based lens can better pinpoint conditions under which people flourish after adversity and help us support varied paths in ourselves and others, whether toward recovery, resilience, acceptance, or endurance. Ultimately, I hope this book helps you decide whether adversity makes people stronger or whether that comforting belief conceals more than it reveals. By examining philosophical traditions, religious and spiritual perspectives, and modern psychological findings, we can move beyond a simplistic mantra. Some people, with sustained effort, emerge with renewed clarity or depth; many remain caught in suffering or find only partial relief. None of these paths is inherently "wrong." What matters is capturing the interplay between adversity and human functioning—with its complicated, context-dependent outcomes that resist a single story.

I learned early on that horrors like war can break people's spirits, galvanize moral courage, and lead to everything in between. From my vantage point as a child raised in Sri Lanka who now lives in the United States, I see countless public claims of "redemption." As the chapters ahead suggest, the truth lies in the slow, uneven ways some recalibrate their lives, in the difficulties that linger, and in the occasional examples of genuine and striking growth.

2

Conceptual Considerations I

Philosophical Foundations of Post-Traumatic Growth

While the cultural narrative that "what doesn't kill you makes you stronger" permeates contemporary discussions of adversity, this belief didn't emerge in a vacuum. Its roots extend deep into Western philosophical traditions, from Aristotle's virtue ethics to Friedrich Nietzsche's distinctive embrace of adversity. To understand—and evaluate—the modern concept of post-traumatic growth (PTG), here I provide an overview of these philosophical foundations. How have different thinkers across centuries conceptualized the relationship between suffering and character development? What assumptions about human nature and moral development underlie the belief that adversity can be transformative? By exploring these philosophical perspectives in this chapter, I'll identify some conceptual tools for evaluating our current understanding of PTG.

The Elusive Definition of *Growth*

As I mentioned in the previous chapter, my formative experiences in Sri Lanka in the 1980s and 1990s fostered skepticism about claims that adversity typically has an upside. While I don't know for certain what motivated me to study the nature of PTG, it's possible that these early encounters shaped my interest in the broader philosophical question of whether there is value to suffering. Many years later, in 2014, I returned to northern Sri Lanka to conduct interviews with Tamil survivors of the conflict. At a clinic in Vavuniya, I sat face to face with individuals whose lives embodied the complexity of trauma. One survivor described a transient existence, with the treatment center being her only stable refuge. Thinking I was a medical doctor, she kept asking about the medications she had been prescribed and wanted a second opinion about her treatment. Another recounted enduring hardship while maintaining a sense of moral clarity and an almost vibrant sense of optimism, despite her family's wartime displacement and their bleak prospects for a secure future. Yet another quietly expressed resignation about the fate of her "disappeared" child. She kept talking about her son and asked for my help in locating him.[1] That evening, as we drove away in the gathering darkness, I struggled with the stories I'd encountered. I was left to grapple anew with an ancient philosophical question: How do you face up to life when life itself is stacked against you?[2]

These deeply unsettling conversations offer a critical vantage point for examining the philosophical foundations of PTG. The concept of "growth" more broadly—whether moral, psychological, or spiritual—has long been a focus of heated discussion. This complexity deepens with the idea of PTG, which suggests that adversity can drive meaningful positive changes in one's character. However, the field faces significant definitional and methodological challenges. Philosopher Michelle Panchuk[3] points out that scholars have voiced multiple reservations about the ways PTG studies define their core concepts, employ their methods, and about whether their findings can be reliably replicated. Similarly, the philosopher Christian Miller questions whether PTG can even be coherently defined.[4] Indeed, psychologists Jonathan Adler and Ted Schwaba point out that researchers currently lack an agreed-upon standard for identifying PTG.[5]

In essence, claiming growth after adversity requires three fundamental components that complicate both its empirical assessment and personal evaluation. First, any assertion of growth necessitates a criterion against which to measure progress: some standard of "good" or "better" that allows one to credibly claim being substantially "better off" for having experienced trauma. For example, if a person claims to have become "more empathetic" after experiencing a serious illness, a clear criterion will need to clarify *whether being more empathetic is a constituent of growth.*

Second, as health psychologists Howard Tennen and Glenn Affleck argue, it is important to distinguish between authentic, enduring change and ephemeral or illusory improvements that may feel significant but lack substantive, long-term impact.[6] Without this distinction, temporary coping strategies or self-enhancement might be misinterpreted as enduring change. For example, feeling a temporary surge of euphoria and a desire to "live life to the fullest" in the immediate days after surviving a dangerous situation would be an ephemeral improvement. Enduring change might be evidenced by consistent engagement in new, meaningful activities or a sustained shift in daily priorities much later, long after the initial emotional intensity has subsided.

Third, culture and collective ethics profoundly shape what counts as growth in different contexts.[7] What Western individualistic societies value as positive change (personal autonomy, self-actualization) may differ markedly from what more collectivistic cultures (e.g., in India, Sri Lanka, China, and other East Asian cultures) prioritize (communal harmony, role fulfillment). For example, after losing a limb in an accident, an individual living in a highly individualistic Western context might define growth as regaining physical independence and pursuing new athletic challenges (emphasizing autonomy). In a more collectivistic society, growth might be defined by the individual's ability to accept support gracefully, find new ways to contribute to their family or community despite limitations, and strengthen relational bonds (emphasizing acceptance and role fulfillment).[8] These three requirements—clear criteria for what growth is, distinction from illusory beliefs about growth, and cultural variation in what constitutes growth—form the conceptual foundation for any meaningful discussion of PTG.

Here, reviewing different philosophical perspectives can help clarify what counts as growth, how adversity might bring it about, and what its unique role in personality formation is. I next explore classical roots of growth through adversity (e.g., adversity as a test of character vs. adversity as a forge for the development of character), then move to modern philosophical voices, and consider relational critiques that emphasize collective well-being. I then pose key questions about adversity, virtue, and how cultural contexts shape the meaning of PTG.

Classical Perspectives on Adversity and Growth

Aristotle's Crucible of Virtue

In Aristotelian thought, adversity can be a test that fosters the development of moral virtues such as courage (*andreia*) and endurance. Aristotle contends that living well (*eudaimonia*) arises from practicing virtues over time, and often under pressure or challenge.[9] Thus, adversity is not inherently good, but it may create conditions under which fortitude, prudence, or generosity can flourish. This idea resonates with contemporary perspectives on the value of suffering: Adversity can dismantle complacency, forcing people to reevaluate priorities.[10] If we accept the Aristotelian view, growth post-trauma reflects a more mature or refined expression of virtues—for instance, a deeper sense of courage.[11]

For Aristotle, virtue is developed through practice and tested in the context of real-life challenges. In the *Nicomachean Ethics*, he suggests that a person's true character and excellence (*aretē*) become evident when confronted with misfortune. A person's character exhibits itself most clearly in adversity, and a good character helps them handle adversity in the best possible way. Aristotle maintains that a truly virtuous and prudent person accepts whatever fate brings with grace, consistently chooses the noblest course of action, and lets their excellence shine even in the worst misfortunes.[12]

To take one example, consider two university leaders facing an economic downturn. One, who has not cultivated the ability to make thoughtful decisions in challenging circumstances—in other words, prudence—might make rash decisions, blame others, or collapse under pressure. The other, having practiced prudence, might carefully analyze the situation, make difficult but fair choices to protect the university and its faculty and employees, and maintain their integrity. The experience of adversity did not create prudence in the second leader; it provided the stage upon which their virtue was revealed and became effective. In other words, a virtuous individual maintains their integrity and dignity under duress, turning adversity into *an occasion* to exercise virtues like courage, patience, or justice.[13] Adversity itself does not automatically create virtue on this account; rather, it reveals and rewards virtue.

It should be noted, however, that Aristotle acknowledged that significant adverse "external events," such as extreme poverty, serious illness, or the loss of loved ones, can impede the achievement of eudaimonia. Indeed, some adversity may not have an upshot, offering no opportunity for virtue development, but only suffering. The idea that all adversity can be a crucible for growth ignores the reality of trauma for many people.

Stoic Readiness for Adversity

Stoicism similarly frames adversity as integral to forging a resilient character.[14] Practicing acceptance of events beyond one's control and cultivating emotional discipline prepare the Stoic for inevitable hardships. Although modern notions of growth following adversity typically emphasize positive change (e.g., appreciation of life, new possibilities), the Stoic tradition underscores that systematic mental training fosters equanimity when adversity strikes. The Stoic philosophers of ancient Greece and Rome, including Epictetus, Seneca, and Marcus Aurelius, built on the idea of thriving under adversity by radically reframing what is "good." For Stoics, virtue (especially wisdom, justice, courage, and self-control) is the only true good, and people should as a result be indifferent to external hardships except insofar as they provide a stage to practice said virtue.

Resilience, in the Stoic sense, comes from accepting what we cannot control and focusing on our own will and rationality. Epictetus famously advised in Chapter XXIV of the *Discourses* that when trouble comes, one should view oneself as an athlete matched against a strong opponent: "Difficulties are what show men's character. Therefore, when a difficult crisis meets you, remember that you are as the raw youth with whom God the trainer is wrestling."[15] On this account, hardship is a form of training for the soul: a chance to strengthen one's moral fiber by exercising endurance and rationality.

Marcus Aurelius similarly wrote that things outward "cannot touch the soul," which resides in an impregnable "inner citadel" of virtue.[16] According to Stoicism, adversity brings moral clarity: It forcefully differentiates what is under our control (our choices, values) from what is not (illness, loss, others' actions). Such perspectives have enjoyed a renaissance in popular culture in recent years.[17]

Indeed, Stoic acceptance resembles the psychological construct of secondary control coping, which involves accepting and accommodating (rather than pushing back on) changes in one's life.[18] Consider a student who fails an important exam and initially experiences distress. Stoic acceptance, akin to secondary control, would involve acknowledging the reality of the failure without succumbing to despair, and then focusing on what *is* controllable: analyzing what went wrong, developing better study habits, and preparing for a future attempt. The growth here is the enhanced self-discipline and realistic focus prompted by the initial failure. Crucially, and as I noted earlier, Stoicism clarifies that adversity does not automatically yield virtue; one must engage deliberately in "preparation exercises" to transform adversity into progress, such as developing a form of deep acceptance or fatalism toward the past (but not the future).[19] In other words, growth comes from accepting what you can't control and mastering what you can—specifically, your own mind and its reaction to adversity.

But is acceptance the only virtuous path in response to adversity? Specifically, is acceptance (as an indicator of growth) always the optimal outcome, or can a *lack* of acceptance form the catalyst for meaning that prompts moral development? To take one example of an alternate response to acceptance, Stoic accounts have cautioned against anger due to its capacity to override reason.[20] As Epictetus notes in Chapter 20 of the *Encheiridion*:

> Remember that it is not the offensive or abusive person that insults you, but the judgment about them that they're insulting. So, whenever someone provokes you to get angry, know that it is your opinion that angers you. Therefore, first of all try not to be abducted by the impression, since if you take some time and delay responding, then you'll master yourself more easily.[21]

However, others have pointed out anger's adaptive and moral functions, especially in the context of adversity and injustice. When people face wrongful harm or witness moral violations, anger can serve as a signal that something is deeply unjust and needs to change. As the philosopher Martha Nussbaum[22] has observed, when the oppressed get angry, it is taken to signal that a) they recognize the wrong done to them, and b) that anger can also motivate protests of such wrongs. In this sense, anger provides moral clarity: It draws attention to violations of values, signals our commitment to justice,[23] and can energize that individuals to take a stand.

One could therefore argue the Stoic perspective focuses on individual anger and thus overlooks the value of anger for sparking collective moral action and societal growth. Indeed, such anger has sparked social movements, suggesting that adversity might galvanize moral or interpersonal growth at the collective level.[24] History offers many examples of anger fueling social movements, from the civil rights movement in the United States, spurred by anger at racial oppression, to contemporary movements like #MeToo, and to the *aragalaya* movement in Sri Lanka,[25] where people's anger at long-tolerated challenges led to collective action. However, Nussbaum[26] cautions that anger can become a vengeful and destructive attitude, and the philosophers Agnes Callard[27] and Olúfémi Táíwò[28] have both recently argued that anger can have a corrupting influence on one's character. Perhaps one way to square these perspectives is that this emotion, when channeled constructively and dynamically with acceptance in response to setbacks and obstacles, can become a source of courage and empowerment, especially for the marginalized.

Existential Perspectives on Adversity

Existential philosophy provides an important perspective for understanding how individuals grapple with adversity and the struggle to find meaning in suffering.[29] A central theme of existentialism is the acknowledgment that suffering is intrinsic to the human condition, compelling us to confront fundamental questions about purpose, meaning, and morality. The French philosopher Albert Camus, for instance, viewed life's ubiquitous suffering and apparent absurdity not as something to be passively endured, but as a profound challenge requiring active engagement, urging us to affirm life's value even amid great pain and ambiguity.[30] Arthur Schopenhauer noted that engaging with suffering was a primary purpose of existence and held the potential to make people better appreciate their privileges and further foster empathy, patience, and tolerance toward others who are suffering.[31] Similarly, the psychiatrist and philosopher Karl Jaspers argued that adversity could be a gateway to what he termed "existential authenticity," encouraging individuals to rise above daily trivialities and connect deeply with life's essential truths.[32]

Nietzsche, whom I mentioned briefly at the beginning of this chapter, offers one of the most influential existentialist perspectives on suffering and personal change. Nietzsche's provocative assertion in *Beyond Good and Evil*—that adversity provides "the discipline of suffering," creating conditions for human enhancement—reflects his belief that true personal growth emerges from courageously facing and affirming life's challenges ("*amor fati*"):

> You want, if possible—and there is no "if possible" more insane than this—to abolish suffering. . . . Well-being as you understand it —that is not a goal, to us it seems like the end! A state that immediately makes humans ridiculous and contemptible —that makes their destruction desirable! . . . That strength cultivating tension of the soul in misfortune, its shudder at the sight of great ruin, its inventiveness and courage in enduring, surviving, interpreting, exploiting misfortune, and whatever it was granted in terms of profundity, mystery, mask, spirit, cunning and greatness: has all this not been granted through suffering, through the discipline of great suffering?[33]

Nietzsche argued that by engaging with adversity and actively choosing responsibility for our responses, we become more resilient, authentic, and capable of creating meaning, even in a seemingly indifferent world.[34] Indeed, going back to our earlier discussion of anger, on this view taking responsibility for our responses to adversity—by advocating for justice, for example—can provide meaning to our lives. In Nietzsche's view, the embrace of hardship is constitutive of what he called *Selbstüberwindung* (self-overcoming), and suffering functions as a necessary precondition for greatness. In other words, adversity can be worth the suffering it causes.

However, Nietzsche's perspective that the strongest people are those who have suffered the most also raises tensions when applied to PTG: Does the expectation of personal change risk romanticizing suffering, failing to recognize ongoing injustice, or marginalizing people who are not strong enough to choose such responses and benefit in this way? Such a view may also lead people to romanticize suffering rather than take steps to alleviate it. The way people afflicted by tuberculosis in Europe during the nineteenth century were romanticized as more artistically sensitive and authentic because of their state of suffering and proximity to death is one telling example.[35,36]

Modern existential perspectives provided by the philosopher-psychologist Emmy van Deurzen[37] and the philosopher Mara van der Lugt[38] build on these philosophical foundations, arguing for frameworks that help individuals accept life's inevitable paradoxes and navigate both adversity and joy as intrinsic and simultaneous aspects of the human experience (as van der Lugt puts it, the pessimism along with the optimism). Of note, the idea of a "dual attitude"—the ability to hold both positive and negative experiences concurrently[39]—echoes Buddhism's recognition of *dukkha* as unavoidable (see Chapter 3), as well as the Chinese concept of *yin-yang*.[40] Going back to the example of social movements, such a perspective may lead to more constructive actions when encountering challenges and setbacks.

Contemporary Philosophical Voices

In recent decades, philosophers have examined how adversity can shape moral and psychological development. In this section, I briefly discuss three contemporary perspectives that have made substantial contributions to the discussion of how life events can impact our character: Ian Kidd, myself and Michael Brady, and L. A. Paul.

Ian Kidd: Exemplars, Moral Growth, and Practical Wisdom

The philosopher Ian Kidd[41] proposes that adversity can reveal "exemplars": individuals who embody moral growth, emotional resilience, and practical wisdom in the wake of profound challenges. Through observing or emulating such exemplars, survivors themselves can integrate new moral insights. Kidd has argued that narratives of moral exemplars—that is, people who embody exceptional moral qualities—often feature adversity as a crucible for their growth, and that we should explicitly recognize this. We should further leverage the human tendency to look to people of high status for guidance to create the expectation that one *can* experience growth after adversity. He makes the case that accounts of exemplars should include their struggles and hardships, as these experiences are crucial to their moral development and can inspire others.

For example, returning to the heroic figures I mentioned in the first chapter—Martin Luther King Jr., Nelson Mandela, Mahatma Gandhi, and Malala Yousafzai—we admire not only their achievements or virtues but also the way they overcame profound adversities (imprisonment, disability, violence) to cultivate those virtues. Including adversity in exemplar narratives serves several moral functions, according to Kidd: It increases our admiration for the exemplar's resilience, enables more effective emulation (we see a path we too might follow when facing difficulties), and affirms deep truths about the human condition—namely, that suffering and fragility are part of life, but can be met with courage and wisdom.[42] For example, a young person facing community violence might read about Malala Yousafzai's response to being shot by the Taliban. Learning not just of her survival, but of her process—her fear, her determination, her continued advocacy for education despite ongoing threats—provides a more relatable and actionable model than simply hearing "Malala stood up for girls' education." In other words, her story provides a pathway to courage that seems more attainable.

Kidd's philosophical perspective bridges ethics and psychology: It suggests that stories of growth through adversity are pedagogically valuable. By learning how moral exemplars grew from their trials, we glean insights that can inspire and teach others how to navigate their own struggles. This challenges simplistic notions that virtue is only for the fortunate; according to this view, moral excellence often arises *because* of hardship, not despite it. However, one question that remains unanswered here is whether adversity shifts specific virtues. This was one issue that motivated my own collaborative philosophical work, which I describe next.

Brady and Jayawickreme: Precision in Defining Growth

My collaboration with the philosopher Michael Brady began in the wake of a meeting I co-organized in New York in 2017, which focused on the conceptual murkiness of PTG research. We have argued that claims about "virtue development" or "positive change" risk becoming nebulous if the nature of the change one expects remains underdefined.[43] We press for conceptual clarity by both distinguishing between stable trait changes (such as changes in dutifulness or humility) and short-lived coping gains and clarifying what it means for change to be "positive," a question that, as we will see, can shift across cultures or historical moments.[44]

This demand for precision is important for several reasons. From a philosophical perspective, it is important to specify the criteria for normative development and how we distinguish illusions of growth (e.g., fleeting feel-good perceptions to relieve distress) from lasting psychological change. As I noted earlier in this chapter, Miller[45] has highlighted how existing definitions of PTG leave crucial ambiguities unresolved. He identifies four main concerns: (1) The criteria determining what constitutes "positive" change remain unclear, posing a risk of subjective or culturally biased interpretations; (2) it is uncertain whether PTG should require comprehensive positive change across multiple psychological domains, or if isolated changes on specific traits suffice; (3) current definitions blur the distinction between PTG itself (e.g., specific traits) and its psychological outcomes (e.g., well-being, mental health), complicating empirical and theoretical analyses; and (4) the temporal durability of positive changes necessary to qualify as true growth is inadequately addressed (e.g., how long should the change last for before we decide that someone has grown?).

This critique highlights the need to define PTG precisely, with clear criteria that distinguish lasting change from brief psychological shifts. Such conceptual clarity is vital for credible empirical work and practical utility of PTG theory. Viewing PTG through a character-formation perspective changes the focus from self-reported improvement to verifiable moral, emotional, and behavioral growth. Adversity then becomes an opportunity—though not a guarantee—for building virtue. Specifying which virtues matter, and why, is crucial to avoid common theoretical and methodological problems in PTG research.

Brady and I collaboratively advanced a philosophical approach to PTG, especially focusing on how to define and measure *growth* in meaningful terms. We note that the idea of benefiting from adversity has been around for much longer than the psychological term *post-traumatic growth*, permeating cultures, religions, and philosophies. However, psychological research that employs certain methods (often brief self-report surveys asking people how they changed), though prolific, may not capture real, lasting growth. We argue that philosophy can help put PTG research on firmer theoretical footing by clarifying what counts as genuine growth and how it might be observed. One key insight we offer is to conceive of PTG in terms of virtue development, which could be externally measured or verified, rather than relying solely on a person's subjective assessment.

In addressing this theoretical deficit, there are six conceptual constraints that any adequate account of growth must satisfy:

- PTG must refer to actual change, not merely perceived or self-reported change. It would not be enough to feel that one has become stronger following adversity; you need to manifest that strength in daily life more so than before the adverse event.
- Growth must be conceptually distinct from mere recovery or resilience; it represents change beyond pre-adversity functioning.
- Growth differs from various coping mechanisms, which are primarily aimed at managing demands or reducing negative emotions from traumatic events.
- Growth must constitute significant or meaningful positive psychological change, not merely fleeting or trivial improvements. Rather than simply stopping to smell the flowers more, growth would manifest in terms of greater commitment to helping.
- The change must be unambiguously positive. While increased cynicism in the wake of an interpersonal adversity may be perceived as growth by some (e.g., becoming more "street-smart"), a more unambiguously positive change would involve greater discernment in future relationships.

- Growth must result non-accidentally from trauma; there needs to be a clear causal connection between the traumatic experience and the subsequent growth, such as developing greater patience and appreciation for health as a direct consequence of and reflection upon recent surgery.

We examined several prominent psychological frameworks in light of these constraints. The clinical psychologists Richard Tedeschi and Lawrence Calhoun's five-dimension approach (appreciation of life, personal strength, new opportunities, relating to others, and spiritual change)[46] offers a rich empirical foundation, but struggles to establish whether these changes are viewed as equally valuable across different cultural contexts. The clinical psychologists Stephen Joseph and Alex Linley's conception of growth as an increase in domains of psychological well-being, such as meaning, purpose, and personal growth, better captures growth's positive nature, but may include changes that are too short-term to constitute meaningful growth.[47] Thinking of growth in terms of positive personality change provides a promising explanation of the causal connection between trauma and growth (see also Chapter 6),[48] but it would be important for defining PTG to clarify which "positive" personality changes should count as growth.

Virtues—understood as excellences or stable dispositions that make one an excellent person—provide both the right theoretical fit and the appropriate normative standard for assessing positive change after trauma.[49] They represent excellence in being "for the good" both intentionally (in desire, emotion, and feeling) and causally (in reliably bringing about that good). The life of former South African president Nelson Mandela is arguably a clear instance of virtue development through adversity: his twenty-seven-year imprisonment for anti-apartheid activism reoriented him toward reconciliation rather than retribution following his release and led to the dismantling of the political apparatus of the apartheid regime in the country.

In each domain, virtue provides the appropriate standard by which genuine growth can be distinguished from mere coping or illusory change.[50] By grounding PTG in virtue development, we offer a philosophically robust criterion that can help resolve the field's long-standing struggle to define and measure genuine growth after trauma. In other words, to be credible, *growth* must be defined as actual, lasting, and unambiguously positive change in character.

Brady's own *Suffering and Virtue*[51] explores how undergoing suffering can cultivate specific virtues; for example, facing illness might lead one to develop patience and fortitude, or experiencing loss might deepen one's capacity for empathy. He emphasizes that certain valuable qualities emerge through trials and might not surface without them. On this view, adversity truly contributes to personal excellence when it leads to demonstrable growth in virtue or character. Empirically, it would be important for researchers to design studies that look for behavioral or long-term changes—such as increased generosity, wiser decision-making, or greater integrity under pressure—as evidence of PTG. It is also important to acknowledge that illusory growth is possible—people might believe they've grown even if their personality hasn't meaningfully changed (more on this in Chapter 5).[52]

L. A. Paul: Transformative Experiences

The philosopher L. A. Paul[53] similarly argues that certain life experiences can be "transformative" because they fundamentally change us in two crucial ways. First, these experiences are *epistemically* transformative—they provide knowledge about what the experience is like that we simply couldn't have accessed beforehand, creating a form of understanding accessible only through direct experience (This was certainly true in my own life when I became a parent in 2019). Second, and perhaps more significantly for our discussion of PTG, transformative experiences are *personally* transformative—they fundamentally alter our preferences, values, and sense of self. In other words, we come to see both the world and ourselves differently after such events, often leading to shifts in what we care about and how we orient our lives. In her book about the final days of Sri Lanka's civil war, *Still Counting the Dead*, journalist Frances Harrison highlights the story of the Catholic nun Sister Ignatius, who was caught in the middle of the conflict. She both gained visceral knowledge of what displacement and daily fear was like and was challenged to face up to the war's horrors with increased courage and a determination to bear witness to war crimes.[54]

This dual epistemic and personal change helps explain why trauma may stimulate profound changes in worldview and identity. Notably, this perspective emphasizes the unpredictability of such changes: people cannot fully grasp how a major event (traumatic or otherwise) will shape them until after it occurs. This resonates with PTG, where some individuals discover significant shifts in worldview, priorities, and personal identity. However, because the outcomes of transformative experiences are unknown beforehand, it is not clear how one can reliably predict who will experience positive changes, how profound those changes will be, and even if they end up being a "positive" experience.[55,56]

Paul's work raises some interesting philosophical and psychological tensions when applied to PTG. Central among these is the epistemic problem: Can we genuinely know whether we have "grown" from adversity if our very perspective and standards for evaluation shift after trauma? Paul argues that transformative experiences radically alter our knowledge of what life is like, leaving individuals possibly unable to meaningfully compare their "before" and "after" selves.[57]

Further complicating matters is the identity problem: If trauma profoundly reshapes an individual's values, preferences, and overall sense of self, the pre- and post-trauma selves might differ so radically that assessing "growth" becomes conceptually problematic. Since the person evaluating the change is no longer the same as the one who experienced the trauma initially, growth comparisons risk becoming meaningless. This unpredictability also leads to a decision-making paradox. If transformative change inherently reshapes a person's values and perspectives in ways that cannot be anticipated, it will be hard for individuals to rationally choose such a challenging experience on the assumption that doing so would lead to change.[58] It also bears mentioning here that people only rarely volunteer to undergo extremely adverse or traumatic experiences.[59]

I also think that Paul's framework highlights one ethical risk: To the extent that our societal structures and norms support such experiences as understood from her framework, beliefs about the positive value of such experiences may impose "redemption pressure" on people who have experienced adversity.[60] As the philosopher Rebecca Chan notes, "More subtle conceptual structures shape and limit the way we form our self-identities. These injustices are obviously bad in themselves, and they also interact with transformative experience in a way that furthers the injustice."[61] Similarly, the philosopher Elizabeth Barnes[62] argues that certain identities may be seen as more plausible, supported, and "available" in specific contexts, which may not always be helpful to everyone. The pressure to conform to a specific "redemptive" identity may cause survivors who do not perceive meaningful positive change from a challenging choice (e.g., quitting a job, leaving a religious community, becoming a whistleblower) to experience shame or guilt. This expectation to "make meaning" from suffering can thus harmfully pressure people who may have no choice but to conform to a redemption narrative, potentially increasing distress rather than alleviating it. In validating this narrative, the loved ones of people experiencing adversity may also inadvertently exacerbate their suffering.

Some Key Questions

Drawing on these classical, contemporary, and relational critiques, let me highlight several overarching questions that researchers must address to advance our understanding of PTG. First, can wisdom be cultivated in the absence of hardship? While classical thinkers suggest adversity can expedite virtue development, virtues can also arise through positive modeling and reflective practice. PTG theories should clarify what unique conditions adversity supplies for developing specific virtues.[63] Second, which virtues matter most, and in which contexts? Cultural contexts and historical epochs prioritize different virtues (e.g., care vs. dutifulness, as we'll see in our discussion of Jewish theological traditions in Chapter 3), requiring PTG research to remain sensitive to these variations when defining what constitutes "positive" change. Third, when does adversity truly *cause* growth? Disentangling post-event illusions or coping strategies from genuine moral or personality change presents significant empirical challenges.

Many traditions imply that wisdom—defined as a reflective, compassionate understanding of life—often arises from overcoming trials. For example, people frequently refer to elders who have "seen so much" as being wise. In some of our qualitative work in Sri Lanka asking about characteristics of wise people, elders were frequently nominated.[64] Empirical research has begun to examine whether experiencing adversity is associated with gains in wisdom-related qualities (such as perspective-taking, emotional regulation, and openness to life's uncertainties), although the current evidence suggests that adversity may not lead to such positive changes.[65]

It could be that certain kinds of hardship teach specific lessons one might not otherwise learn. Yet, it is also possible to learn such lessons vicariously or through milder challenges. For example, one might argue that while hardship can accelerate or deepen wisdom, a person could also cultivate wisdom through education, empathy, and critical self-reflection in the absence of extreme trauma. In addition, if adversity promotes virtue, are those virtues universal or culture specific?[66] PTG research will need to avoid cultural bias in settling on a single monolithic definition of *growth*, as different cultures sometimes emphasize different explanations for and functions of adversity.[67]

This question also relates to the authenticity of PTG. Specifically, these explanations for the function of adversity may primarily serve as a salve to help people cope with and manage the ubiquity of suffering, rather than as a roadmap for change. Indeed, a persistent critique in the field is that what people report as growth may in many cases be a psychological coping strategy (self-deception, denial, or reframing)[68] that may help the person feel better but doesn't correspond to lasting change. For example, someone might claim "everything happens for a reason, and I've grown from this" very soon after a trauma—but is that genuine growth, or is it an attempt to *impose* meaning to avoid despair?

Toward a Philosophically Grounded View of PTG

From Aristotle and the Stoics to contemporary perspectives such as L. A. Paul, Ian Kidd, and my work with Michael Brady, philosophical inquiry suggests that suffering does not automatically guarantee growth. Instead, adversity can function as a mechanism for moral, emotional, and existential shifts—*but only if* certain conditions (e.g., supportive communities, virtuous exemplars, and a willingness or ability to learn) align.

A virtue-oriented approach to PTG addresses key normative concerns, clarifying that not all changes qualify as growth. Emotions may catalyze or counter moral or social impetus (e.g., anger). Finally, cultural considerations caution against an overly individualistic orientation: Growth may be evidenced by increased solidarity, collective moral responsibility, or acceptance of personal responsibility.[69] For many, the key to growth following adversity may lie in forging deeper connections and communal flourishing.

Adversity is a ubiquitous (albeit unwelcome) presence in our lives; yet, as the perspectives above illustrate, it *may* have the paradoxical potential to catalyze growth and insight. Philosophically, thinkers from Aristotle to the present day have recognized that the meaning and value of adversity lie in our response to it—in the virtues we forge, the meanings we make, and the communities we build in its aftermath. Here, I'll note four key insights.

First, growth is multifaceted. It can mean moral development (as Aristotle and the Stoics emphasized) or newfound resilience and wisdom (as contemporary voices like Brady and Kidd discuss). Second, adversity is not inherently beneficial; it is *potentially* beneficial. Many of these perspectives note that suffering in itself is not good; what can be good is how humans manage to face up to suffering. Third, philosophical reflection can enrich our understanding of PTG by clarifying its nature. Additionally, by making clear predictions and incorporating specific outcomes related to virtue or wisdom, scientists can test claims about whether and how adversity can lead to changes on specific, theoretically plausible outcomes.[70] Philosophical analyses also provide a critical lens to examine these claims (e.g., what do we consider a good outcome after trauma?).[71] Fourth, context and culture matter. One clear implication is that growth does not happen in isolation. An interdisciplinary approach to PTG must consider not just the individual psyche but also social support systems, cultural narratives about suffering, and structural conditions.[72] This will be a focus of our discussion in Chapter 4.

In subsequent chapters, I use these philosophical insights to sharpen the questions psychologists should ask—about which outcomes matter, what evidence would count as genuine change, and how context and culture condition the likelihood of growth. By bearing in mind both classical and contemporary discussions of the value of adversity, I have sought to establish a conceptual foundation for PTG—one that requires clarity, normative grounding, and cultural sensitivity to ensure that what we term *growth* is more than a simple reframing of trauma.

3

Conceptual Considerations II

Religious Foundations of Post-Traumatic Growth

The philosophical frameworks I discussed in Chapter 2 provide some conceptual clarity for understanding the potential for growth through adversity. However, they represent only one dimension for understanding how humans have interpreted suffering throughout history. For many people worldwide, religious and spiritual traditions have offered powerful frameworks for making sense of hardship. These traditions—from Christianity's redemptive suffering to Buddhism's concept of *dukkha*—provide both explanatory systems and practical guidance for navigating adversity. Notably, they frequently contextualize individual suffering within broader communal or spiritual narratives.

In this chapter, I examine how diverse faith traditions conceptualize the relationship between suffering and change, revealing both striking parallels with philosophical approaches and some key divergences. This exploration will identify some key narratives related to understanding adversity while highlighting how different religious traditions shape what counts as "growth" after trauma. Recognizing the distinctions and overlaps between these two perspectives offers critical insights into how cultural and philosophical assumptions shape our expectations and experiences of adversity.

Indeed, growing up in multiple religious traditions in Sri Lanka—Buddhism dominant in the culture on my father's side of the family, Catholicism on my mother's side, and Anglicanism in my formal education—I witnessed how different theological frameworks offered distinct interpretations of suffering. I remember the Christianity lectures at Trinity College in Kandy—religious instruction was part of the standard curriculum. One day, around age twelve, I found myself troubled by a lesson on suffering and divine justice. After class, I approached my teacher privately and asked her why the God of the Old Testament seemed so stern and willing to inflict suffering, while the God depicted in the New Testament appeared kinder and more compassionate. Her response was somewhat hesitant and inconclusive (specifically, "To be honest, I have no idea"), leaving me to wonder why a loving deity would allow or even mandate suffering.

As I grew older, I would also puzzle over how Buddhism—a religion that centers the principle of *ahimsa*, or non-violence—could also undergird a violent form of nationalism.[1] This early confusion planted seeds of curiosity that continued to grow, leading me to question the ways religious traditions interpret adversity. As we'll see, religious teachings—from Christianity's concept of redemptive suffering to Buddhist interpretations of *dukkha*, to Islamic notions of divine tests, to feminist Jewish emphases on collective resilience—present the experience of suffering as a potentially meaningful but also morally complex phenomenon.

"Why Religion?"

When the scholar of religion Elaine Pagels published *Why Religion?*,[2] readers encountered both an award-winning scholar of early Christianity[3] and a grieving mother and wife. Pagels's losses—the death of her young son, followed soon after by the sudden death of her husband—initially led her to spiral into despair. However, as she notes in her memoir, she used her expertise in early Christian texts to process and interpret her own trauma. In doing so, Pagels demonstrated how religious frameworks can provide sources of resilience during profound suffering. Throughout her memoir, Pagels describes feeling unmoored, uncertain how the intellectual frameworks she had built as a scholar could explain what she had been through. As she notes at the beginning of her book:

> More than twenty-five years ago, when the death of our young child, followed soon after by the shocking death of my husband, shattered my life, I never imagined that I would ever write about what happened. Those losses left a crater that loomed as large as the Grand Canyon, which I could not enter, and in which I could see hardly anything, like a black hole in space.[4]

Yet, as the book progresses, she discusses how the texts and traditions she had studied for decades offered a language and structure through which she could interpret her suffering, grapple with unanswerable questions, and find a measure of solace. For Pagels, grief opened the door to a deeper understanding of ancient Christian stories—those in both canonical Gospels and Gnostic sources—and illuminated the age-old human quest to make sense of tragedy. Another pertinent example involves the writings of St. Ignatius of Loyola.[5] In this way, *Why Religion?* supplies a case study of how religious or spiritual frameworks can facilitate a shift from despair to resilience and renewed meaning. Quoting the apocryphal Gospel of Thomas in reference to her struggle, she notes: "If you bring forth what is within you, what you bring forth will save you. If you do not bring forth what is within you, what you do not bring forth will destroy you."[6]

Of note, Pagels's path was not one of uncritical faith, but an interplay between doubt, anguish, inquiry, and yearning for comfort. Indeed, she strongly rejects simplistic notions of meaning and growth and reacts negatively to suggestions from others that she should explore possible lessons from her loss. Her experience here highlights how the pressure of simplistic growth narratives can compromise our ability to thoughtfully support our family members, friends, colleagues, and fellow community members who are suffering in the wake of adversity:

> After Mark's death, someone reaching for something "nice" to say assured me that surely his death would teach us some "spiritual lesson," so that we could "find meaning" denied to more fortunate parents like herself. I was furious, speechless with anger. *Schadenfreude*, I thought: she's congratulating herself on her own good luck at our expense, and she doesn't even realize it. Doesn't she know that suffering can shrivel hope, break hearts? Even if she hadn't just spouted a sentimental cliché, how *dare* she suggest that any benefit to us could possibly be worth a child's life. *Find* meaning?[7]

Over time, however, the Christian rituals, prayers, and gatherings gained personal relevance in her mourning. By engaging with them from a place of vulnerability and spiritual struggle, Pagels experienced the potential for this spiritual knowledge to transform sorrow into connection—connection to lost loved ones, to a tradition spanning centuries, and to others in her community who also sought hope. Readers witness how this engagement led to a shift in her perspective: the reconfiguration of identity, the deepening of relationships, and the gradual emergence of a sense of grace.

Sacred Narratives of Suffering and Growth

I had the opportunity to present with the philosopher Eleonore Stump at a conference in 2018, and her *Wandering in Darkness: Narrative and the Problem of Suffering* offers another glimpse of how Christian narratives can foster deeper trust and relationship with the divine amid trauma. Stump[8] suggests that growth emerges more from *how* one relates to God in suffering—via second-person "intimacy" and empathetic engagement—than from any abstract theodicy that attempts to explain why God permits evil. As she notes in relation to her discussion of the Book of Job in the Old Testament:

> It is a mistake, then, to characterize God's speeches to Job as demonstrating nothing but God's power over creation. The speeches certainly do show God's power; but, equally importantly, they show God in second-person connection to all his creatures. He relates to everything he has made in this second-personal way; and in such second-person interaction, God deals as a parent with his creatures.[9]

As with Pagels's writings, Stump's work shows that religious texts and traditions can serve as catalysts for personal change, although they can also raise fresh questions about guilt, blame, or responsibility, which may lead to crises of meaning. (C. S. Lewis's crisis in the wake of his wife's death, described in *A Grief Observed*, is one famous example).[10]

As she notes in her introduction, when Stump decided to write *Wandering in Darkness*, she chose a method that might seem unconventional in a philosophical landscape often dominated by logical arguments and abstract theodicies. Rather than rely exclusively on reasoned propositions, Stump turned to stories—biblical narratives like those of Job, Abraham, Mary of Bethany, and others—to shed new light on the question of evil and divine goodness. Her central insight was that suffering is best understood not only through theoretical explanations but also through an empathetic immersion in the experiences of real or imagined persons.

For Stump, a difference exists between asking, "Why does God allow suffering?" in the abstract, and considering the experience of someone who grapples with heartbreak, loss, or trauma. In *Wandering in Darkness*, she explores how individuals in biblical narratives relate to God's presence (or perceived absence) in their darkest moments. By delving into the distinct experiences and emotional reflections of these scriptural figures, she opens a window onto their lived experience as recounted in their stories—and onto the ways in which a loving God might remain intimately involved even when the reasons for suffering remain unclear.

This narrative approach has interesting implications for post-traumatic growth (PTG). Stump suggests that genuine intimacy with God—what she calls a "second-person experience" of the divine—can transform suffering from an isolating burden into a context for a stronger relational union. As a result, she moves beyond the "why" question and focuses on the "how": *How* might a person's woundedness become the very place where they encounter love, compassion, and, ultimately, healing? Rather than propose a definitive solution to the problem of evil, Stump offers a discussion of how growth can emerge through trust, relationship, and sustained attention to the stories of those who have suffered before us.[11]

The examples of Pagels's memoir and Stump's scholarly exploration of suffering foreshadow a central theme of this chapter: People worldwide have long grappled with suffering and have leaned on the tools of religion to frame it as a catalyst for moral or spiritual growth—a forerunner to what psychologists today call PTG. Yet each tradition also carries tensions: Religious discourse can console or oppress, can spur growth or exacerbate guilt, can challenge injustice or reinforce harmful structures. I next explore these tensions across Christianity, Buddhism, Islam, and Jewish theological perspectives.

Christian Views: Redemptive Suffering and Soul-Making

A central Christian motif is the notion of redemptive suffering. In the Epistle to the Romans (5:3–5), St. Paul writes that "suffering produces endurance," which in turn "produces character, and character produces hope." This has shaped centuries of Christian theology, suggesting that hardship—whether persecution, loss, or personal tragedy—can be part of a salvific process. As the Canadian historian and former political leader Michael Ignatieff notes, "From knowing despair . . . we come to know what hope actually is, and it is the memory of despair that can make us fight so hard to live in hope."[12] The philosopher and theologian John Hick's soul-making theodicy broadens this idea, arguing that adversity refines virtues like patience or humility, gradually shaping souls fit for communion with God.[13] More specifically, the soul-making theodicy posits that adversity and suffering have inherent value because they can facilitate moral refinement and spiritual development. This perspective suggests that hardship, rather than being purely destructive, functions as a necessary catalyst for the growth of virtues such as patience, humility, and resilience.

However, embracing this narrative without critique raises serious ethical concerns. Glorifying adversity risks romanticizing pain and could inadvertently justify oppressive circumstances or impose unrealistic expectations of change on those enduring adversity.[14] Thus, while soul-making narratives acknowledge the potential for moral growth through the experience of adversity, they must be handled with care and sensitivity to the dangers of obscuring systemic injustice or placing undue burdens on individuals who do not perceive growth in their suffering.

Panchuk's Critique: Religious Trauma and the Problem of Evil

The philosopher and religious scholar Michelle Panchuk has written extensively on how religious beliefs, communities, and power structures can themselves *cause* or exacerbate trauma, particularly in cases of different forms of harm that can be inflicted in religious contexts.[15] Building on the work of Miranda Fricker,[16] she clarifies how victims of abuse might misidentify their experiences as "discipline" or "divine punishment," often leading to victim-blaming or internalized shame.[17,18]

She also connects religious trauma to the *problem of evil*—the philosophical challenge of reconciling a good and omnipotent God with seemingly gratuitous suffering. Religious trauma, she argues, is a poignant instance of suffering perpetuated within the very institutions that claim to heal and protect. Evaluating classical theodicies (e.g., free will, soul-making) in light of this trauma reveals their potential to perpetuate harm by urging survivors to see their suffering as divinely mandated or spiritually redemptive.

In her monograph *Religious Trauma*, Panchuk[19] explores the phenomenon of religious trauma, focusing on how religious factors, such as concepts, discourse, and power structures, can shape the experience and interpretation of trauma. She argues that a survivor of such trauma may miscategorize their experience due to religious discourse; she labels this as a *first-order misclassification*.[20] For instance, a survivor of abuse might misinterpret their experience as discipline due to a religious framework that normalizes such harmful behaviors, or a congregant regularly pressured to make large donations they cannot afford is told this is "sowing seeds for God's blessing" and comes to believe their financial strain is a holy sacrifice.

Second-order misclassifications occur when individuals correctly identify the type of action but misunderstand its higher-order type due to religious interpretations.[21] For example, survivors of sexual assault might misinterpret their experience as something for which they should feel shame or guilt before God, rather than recognizing it as an act for which they bear no responsibility. Or, returning to the example in the previous paragraph, the congregant correctly identifies the pressure to donate as exploitative but, due to teachings on unquestioning obedience to religious leaders, misinterprets their internal resistance or resentment as a spiritual failing on their part, leading to guilt rather than appropriate boundary-setting. Such misclassifications can lead to victim-blaming and perpetuate the cycle of abuse.

Panchuk also critiques how religious institutions often use theological explanations to justify or reframe suffering. She discusses how some faith traditions teach that suffering leads to moral purification (e.g., Christian notions of redemptive suffering) while others position suffering as a test of faith. These frameworks can provide meaning to adherents, but also risk invalidating their pain or discouraging them from seeking justice and change.

One of the most significant claims in *Religious Trauma* is that religious institutions themselves must be held accountable for the harm they perpetuate, rather than taking advantage of religious and cultural beliefs about redemption and placing the burden on survivors to "grow" from their suffering. As she notes, "Popular culture paints the person who 'bounces back' or is especially resilient in the wake of trauma as morally superior to those who do not, but personal merit has little to do with one's vulnerability to the long-term effects of trauma".[22] If systemic religious trauma is a key factor in shaping suffering, then challenging the institutional norms—rather than solely engaging in individual psychological work—is necessary for genuine recovery to occur.

The concept of religious trauma complicates the optimistic narrative that suffering invariably produces spiritual growth. Survivors of religious abuse frequently encounter pressure—often implicitly reinforced by religious teachings—to interpret their experiences as spiritually beneficial or as opportunities for personal change.[23] However, such pressure can severely undermine survivors' psychological well-being, forcing them into self-blaming or spiritually oppressive frameworks. This reveals a paradox: Frameworks meant to foster moral or spiritual progress may instead deepen trauma, particularly when they fail to acknowledge systemic injustice and power imbalances within religious communities.

Panchuk's work highlights that justice here involves confronting and rectifying such power imbalances, rather than obscuring them behind rhetoric of redemption or divine testing. An ethical danger arises when religious institutions or discourses push survivors toward a redemptive narrative, suggesting that their suffering inherently serves a divine or moral purpose. Far from facilitating authentic healing, this expectation can entrench toxic structures, silence victims, and obstruct genuine accountability. Thus, identifying growth in contexts of religious trauma requires a careful reconsideration of narratives that frame adversity as inherently valuable. Instead, a more ethically and psychologically sound approach involves validating survivors' experiences, addressing systemic harm, and fostering communal practices that prioritize justice and healing over expectations of redemption.

Buddhism: *Dukkha* and the Path to Enlightenment

Buddhism begins with the premise that life is pervaded by *dukkha*—variously translated as suffering, dissatisfaction, or stress. Far from inducing despair, this recognition is intended to prompt a turning point toward compassion and wisdom. As outlined in the Four Noble Truths, acknowledging *dukkha* motivates practitioners to follow the Noble Eightfold Path and develop wisdom and compassion for all beings.[24]

In Buddhism, suffering holds a paradoxical place: It is unequivocally an affliction to be ended, yet it is also the very starting point and motivator of the spiritual path. The Buddha's teaching famously begins with the recognition of suffering and ends with its eradication. Gautama Buddha's first sermon announced the Four Noble Truths, the foundational framework of Buddhist doctrine: (1) the truth of suffering (*dukkha*)—that life in conditioned existence is permeated by unsatisfactoriness and sorrow; (2) the cause of suffering—driven by craving and attachment (*taṇhā*) grounded in ignorance (*avidyā*); (3) the cessation of suffering—that freedom (*nirvāṇa*) is possible; and (4) the path leading to the cessation of suffering—the Noble Eightfold Path of ethical living, meditation, and wisdom. A famous (and apocryphal) Buddhist saying encapsulates this attitude: "I teach only two things: suffering and the end of suffering." This reflects that while Buddhism aims to eliminate suffering, the direct confrontation with suffering is the entry point to enlightenment. Notably, this perspective is similar to Nietzsche's concept of *amor fati* discussed in Chapter 2.

The Six Perfections

Many Mahayana Buddhist traditions detail the Six *Pāramitās* (Perfections): generosity, morality, patience, joyful effort, concentration, and wisdom. These perfections act as a structured path toward moral and spiritual growth. Philosopher of religion Emily McRae highlights how recognizing suffering can be a critical pivot for developing these qualities.[25] She further explores the Tibetan Buddhist monk Tsongkhapa's five "good qualities" of suffering:

- Suffering provides motivation for liberation by highlighting pleasure's impermanence and the primacy of moral development. For example, the decline of one's career might lead one to realize the impermanence of worldly success, motivating a deeper search for meaning beyond material achievements.
- Hardship dispels arrogance by revealing human vulnerability. So, a champion athlete suffering a career-ending injury may have their arrogance dispelled as they confront their physical vulnerability and dependence on others for care.
- Recognizing suffering's origins in harmful actions encourages the avoidance of wrongdoing. A parent experiencing the loneliness that results from their own past selfish actions might recognize the harm caused, motivating them to avoid such behavior, cultivate more considerate habits, and reconcile with their family.
- The desire to escape suffering cultivates virtue through ethical and compassionate behavior. For example, facing a long period of health challenges, one might be motivated to cultivate virtues like patience and compassion to manage the hardship.
- Personal suffering generates compassion by fostering empathy for others' experiences, reinforcing compassion as a moral ideal. A person who has endured a painful career setback might develop profound compassion for others experiencing similar challenges, as they understand the depth of others' distress in that situation.[26]

McRae's discussion of the six perfections (*pāramitās*) offers an ethical and psychological roadmap for how suffering can be used as a mechanism for growth, emphasizing that mindset and discipline shape the trajectory of suffering's impact. Two of these perfections—enthusiasm (*virya*) and meditative concentration (*dhyana*)—highlight the volitional component of change following adversity.

Buddhism presents a distinctive approach to adversity, framing suffering as both an inescapable aspect of human existence and a critical entry point for spiritual insight and compassionate development. While Western psychological accounts of PTG frequently emphasize strengthened individual resilience or newfound personal meaning, Buddhist teachings often highlight interdependence and the potential dissolution of rigid, self-centered identities. Philosophers like McRae argue that deliberately engaging with suffering can foster virtues such as patience, humility, and compassion, yet they caution against assuming these benefits emerge automatically.

However, endorsing Buddhist narratives also carries risks: An excessive emphasis on personal acceptance or spiritual detachment could unintentionally minimize the significance of social and systemic injustices that perpetuate suffering. Indeed, this ethical system views suffering as a consequence of one's own actions, sins, or spiritual debts (i.e., *karma*).[27] Thus, while Buddhism contributes valuable insights into how adversity may catalyze ethical and spiritual maturity, practitioners and researchers alike should be wary of narratives that overstate individual acceptance at the expense of recognizing—and actively addressing—the societal roots of trauma.

Pema Chödrön: *When Things Fall Apart* and Compassionate Insight

The Buddhist nun Pema Chödrön stands as a prominent Buddhist voice on responding to suffering in the Shambhala tradition in the United States. Her book *When Things Fall Apart*[28] is a key text in the American Buddhist literature. Chödrön's teachings on facing up to suffering center on several principles: She advocates "leaning into pain" through mindful acceptance rather than escaping suffering, suggesting that facing discomfort directly provides insight into our habitual reactions; she emphasizes the value of recognizing impermanence and letting go, showing how understanding that all conditions eventually change can reduce attachment-based suffering; she presents self- and other-directed compassion as essential, framing personal struggles not as punishments but as gateways to deeper empathy; and she promotes humility and openness by challenging our desire for certainty, encouraging vulnerability and curiosity as important foundations for genuine resilience.

Chödrön's approach resonates with the idea of PTG in that suffering can become a catalyst for deep introspection and change. However, she is clear that growth arises from a willingness to meet pain with compassion, self-reflection, and a spirit of nonjudgment:

> When we protect ourselves so we won't feel pain, that protection becomes like armor, like armor that imprisons the softness of the heart. We do everything we can think of not to feel anything threatening. We try to prolong feeling good about ourselves. Looking at color pictures in magazines of people having fun on the beach, many of us earnestly wish that life could be that good.
>
> When we breathe in pain, somehow it penetrates that armor. The way we guard ourselves is getting softened up. This heavy, rusty, creaking armor begins to seem not so monolithic after all. With the in-breath the armor begins to fall apart, and we find we can breathe deeply and relax. A kindness and a tenderness begin to emerge. We don't have to tense up as if our whole life were being spent in the dentist's chair.[29]

This open and self-compassionate stance stands in opposition to arguably more "unsentimental" accounts of Buddhism (such as the Theravada tradition, the oldest surviving school of Buddhism grounded in the ancient Pāli Canon), as well as a kind of Stoic-inspired "redemption pressure" that can burden trauma survivors with the expectation that they *must* emerge stronger. It also reflects the importance of an intentional willingness to face up to suffering (an insight that will emerge again later in Chapter 6).

Islam: Testing, Purification, and Eternal Perspectives

In Islam, hardship is frequently interpreted as a test of faith—a trial from God that, when met with patience (*ṣabr*) and trust in God (*tawakkul*), fosters moral purification. Qur'anic narratives and prophetic traditions often remind believers that worldly life is transient, and so enduring trials can lead to eternal reward.

The Qur'an states, "We will certainly test you with a measure of fear and hunger and loss of wealth, lives, and fruits—but give good tidings to the patient" (Qur'an 2:155). Another verse promises that "Verily with hardship comes ease" (Qur'an 94:5–6), implying that adversity is not permanent and that God will provide relief and reward to those who endure with patience. Prophetic sayings amplify this perspective. The Prophet Muhammad is reported to have said, "Whenever God wills good for a person, He subjects them to adversity." In other words, hardships are interpreted as a sign of God's favor, providing an occasion for the believer to earn spiritual merit and purification. Another hadith in the *Sahih al-Bukhari* states, "No fatigue, nor disease, nor sorrow, nor sadness, nor hurt, nor distress befalls a Muslim, even a thorn that pricks him, except that Allah expiates some of his sins for it." This encapsulates two oft-repeated themes in Islamic thought on suffering: expiation and elevation. Suffering can expiate (atone for) one's sins, purifying the soul, and it can elevate one's spiritual rank in the eyes of God.[30]

An illustrative example from the Islamic tradition is the story of Job (Ayyūb), a prophet common to the Judeo Christian faith traditions well known for his immense trials. The Qur'an presents Job as a model of patience: After affliction with loss of wealth, family, and health, Job remains steadfast and calls out, "Truly adversity has touched me, but You are the Most Merciful of the merciful" (Qur'an 21:83). God rewards Job for his unwavering faith by restoring him, thus reinforcing that trials are temporary and serve to distinguish the truly patient and faithful.[31]

Islam offers a compelling narrative similar to the Christian tradition that frames adversity as a test (*ibtilā'*) designed to strengthen faith, patience (*ṣabr*), and moral purification.[32] Such perspectives can significantly bolster personal resilience, providing believers with meaning and purpose during hardships, as patience and reliance on God (*tawakkul*) are seen as morally commendable responses that can refine character and deepen spirituality (Qur'an 8:46; 31:17). However, while Islamic teachings on perseverance and moral improvement through trials offer meaningful avenues for personal growth, such trials are not only individual matters: The Qur'anic mandate of *zakāt* and the Prophet's creation of welfare endowments (*waqf*) signal that *ṣabr* (patience) should be joined with active, communal responsibility to relieve communal hardship and rectify injustice.[33]

Jewish Perspectives: Collective and Relational Dimensions

The Hebrew Bible (*Tanakh*) offers a number of paradigms for making sense of suffering. In many instances, suffering is seen as a punishment for sin or a means of divine discipline (especially at the collective level—the Deuteronomic theology links Israel's fortune to its covenantal obedience). Yet the Bible also shrouds the reasons for suffering in mystery: The Book of Job pointedly challenges the notion that all suffering is deserved. Job is a righteous man who undergoes intense undeserved suffering, and while he initially insists on questioning God's justice, he eventually encounters God in the whirlwind and comes to an acceptance of the limits of human understanding.

This tradition of challenging God is a hallmark of the Jewish relationship with adversity. The patriarch Abraham argued with God over the fate of Sodom, saying, "Shall not the Judge of all the earth do justice?" (Genesis 18:25), effectively holding God to God's own standard of justice. The very name Israel (*Yisra'el*) is often rendered "one who strives with God," after the night-long struggle of Jacob (Abraham's grandson) with a divine messenger (Genesis 32:22–32).

How is this "wrestling" relationship between God and those who suffer characterized? Much of the Jewish theological writings over the last seventy-five years have focused on making sense of this relationship in the context of the Holocaust. For example, in *Faith after the Holocaust*, the rabbi and theologian Eliezer Berkovits grapples with the theological challenge it poses, offering a distinctive Jewish response to how faith can exist after such unprecedented evil.[34] One of his arguments centers on the "hiding of the face" (*hester panim*), a biblical concept where God seemingly withdraws his presence from the sufferer.[35] Berkovits argues that God's self-limitation is paradoxically necessary for human freedom and moral responsibility. He contends that God must partially withdraw to allow humans genuine moral choice, even though this creates the possibility for evil. Berkovits rejects both simple theodicies that try to explain away suffering and the notion that the Holocaust proves God's nonexistence. Instead, he maintains that authentic faith must confront the reality of suffering while still affirming God's ultimate justice. Interestingly, Berkovits criticizes Christian theological responses to the Holocaust and argues that only Judaism, with its history of wrestling with God through suffering, can provide a meaningful framework for faith after such catastrophe. He emphasizes that Jewish faith is not about blind acceptance, but about continuing to question and engage with God even in the face of tragedy: "Redemption itself is a continuous process and is never final in this world."[36]

However, the religious scholar Melissa Raphael,[37] in her article "The Price of (Masculine) Freedom and Becoming," offers a feminist theological critique of Eliezer Berkovits's approach to post-Holocaust theology.[38] Where Berkovits constructs his argument around the traditional concept of *hester panim* (the idea that God's presence is sometimes hidden from direct human perception, even though God is in fact always present), Raphael challenges the fundamental premises and implications of this theological framework. At the heart of Raphael's critique lies her objection to Berkovits's preservation of a distinctly masculine conception of God. She particularly challenges Berkovits's emphasis on divine omnipotence and his explanation that God's self-limitation was necessary for human freedom. She sees in this framework a questionable prioritization of power as the defining divine attribute. This approach to theology, she suggests, remains trapped within patriarchal conceptions of relationship, where power—even when voluntarily limited—remains the central dynamic between God and humanity. In contrast, Raphael's approach emphasizes presence, relationship, and care as primary divine attributes.

The most significant divergence between these theologians appears in their understanding of how divine presence manifests during the Holocaust. While Berkovits focuses on God's withdrawal or "hiding," Raphael proposes that God was in fact present in Auschwitz—in the small acts of compassion and human dignity between prisoners. She particularly emphasizes the relationships of care among women prisoners, seeing in their maintenance of humanity amid systematic dehumanization a manifestation of divine presence.[39] These relationships, Raphael argues, challenge traditional notions of power and sovereignty that feminist theology has long questioned: "Characteristic of its period, the post-Holocaust free-will defense is articulated wholly without reference to gender difference in Jewry's suffering and without reference to the gendered nature of autonomy."[40] Through this lens, what appears as divine absence in Berkovits's framework becomes a different mode of divine presence in Raphael's.

This reconceptualization carries some important ethical implications. Raphael argues that Berkovits's explanation, despite its theological sophistication, ultimately risks *justifying* suffering rather than fully confronting its reality. By placing suffering within a cosmic framework of divine self-limitation and human freedom, Berkovits creates a theological structure that, while intellectually rigorous, may distance us from the concrete reality of human suffering by emphasizing a "masculine" ethics where God's inaction during the Holocaust is justified because if "God exercised his power in preventing the Holocaust he would have impeded 'man's' becoming."[41] Raphael's feminist theological approach, by contrast, emphasizes embodied care and the maintenance of human dignity as divine attributes manifested even in the context of extreme suffering.

Essentially, Raphael's critique shifts the theological question altogether. Rather than asking "Where was God's power during the Holocaust?"—a question that leads inevitably to conceptions of divine hiding or absence—she instead asks, "How was God's presence manifested in relationships of care amid suffering?" This reframing, which arguably echoes the rabbi Harold Kushner's argument in *When Bad Things Happen to Good People*,[42] opens new possibilities for understanding divine action not primarily through power and intervention but through presence and relationship. In doing so, Raphael offers a theological vision that speaks powerfully to contemporary feminist concerns about an overtly masculine and individualist approach to thinking about adversity, while providing a distinctive response to the enduring theological challenges posed by the Holocaust.

Raphael's tradition of feminist Jewish theology centers the idea that adversity is a collective and relational issue; indeed, traditional Jewish narratives, like the Exodus story, emphasize communal redemption.[43] Feminist voices contend that if a theology of suffering fails to address all perspectives, it risks perpetuating harm. Raphael builds on this tradition of wrestling with injustice, but extends it to address collective and systemic forms of suffering, particularly those related to patriarchal structures. She argues for a view of growth that is validated through communal well-being and social change, not just individual virtue or spiritual development.

Indeed, the dominant ideal of PTG, developed primarily by Western researchers, arguably reflects assumptions similar to Berkovits's framework. It emphasizes individual agency, heroic overcoming, and personal change—values aligned with traditionally masculine, individualistic conceptions of growth. This approach, like Berkovits's theological perspective, inadvertently centers power (in this case, personal agency to rise above suffering) as the primary metric of successful adaptation. The implicit message becomes that real growth means emerging stronger and more self-determined through individual triumph over adversity.

Raphael's alternative vision—finding divine presence in acts of care and the maintenance of human dignity amid systematic dehumanization—offers a parallel framework for thinking about PTG (See Chapter 6 for a related discussion). Her emphasis on relational care rather than individual power suggests that genuine growth can also manifest through enhanced capacity for connection, compassion, and communal healing. Just as Berkovits's theology preserves traditionally masculine attributes of divinity (power, sovereignty, self-limitation), dominant PTG frameworks may privilege specific socially sanctioned responses to adversity (stoicism, individual agency, instrumental control) over other valid responses.

From Sacred Texts to Lived Reality: The Case of Rwanda

The theological frameworks discussed so far provide important scripts for individuals, but they can also function as collective ideologies that shape entire communities in the aftermath of collective adversity. To see this in action, let us turn to the case of post-genocide Rwanda, where religion has played a dual role in both healing and potentially obscuring deeper injustice.

Building on her collaborative PhD project with Nicki Hitchcott's Rwandan Stories of Change project (conducted in partnership with the Aegis Trust and the Genocide Archive of Rwanda), the francophone scholar Caroline Williamson's[44] research on PTG in post-genocide Rwanda offers an important contribution to our understanding of the role of religion in communal growth.[45] This work clarifies a gap in PTG research by examining collective responses to trauma and the complex interplay between individual and group identity in post-conflict societies. Traditional approaches to PTG have predominantly focused on cognitive processes at the individual level, and Williamson argues that these approaches fail to capture the social dynamics that shape collective responses to trauma. Her research provides evidence for distinguishing between individual and collective PTG, as these processes operate at different levels and may sometimes work at cross-purposes.

Williamson developed her theoretical framework by drawing on the psychologist David Bakan's[46] account of fundamental human motivations—agency (focusing on self-oriented goals) and communion (focusing on other-oriented goals)—as well as the narrative personality psychologist Dan

McAdams's conceptualization of narrative identity (a person's internal story; more on this in the next chapter).[47] She posits that, just as trauma experienced by an individual can destabilize a person's sense of autonomy and relatedness, trauma experienced collectively undermines a group's ideological belief system by disrupting their drive for agency and communion. Consequently, for collective PTG to occur, these drives must be satisfied at the group level.

Williamson critiques previous attempts to conceptualize collective PTG, which have often equated enhanced group cohesion and collective identity with positive change. This perspective is particularly evident in analyses of American responses to the 9/11 attacks, where increased patriotism and social cohesion were interpreted as positive outcomes (similar to my assumption about the 9/11 attacks, which I discussed in the introduction).[48] However, such responses may be more accurately understood as processes of intergroup differentiation, encompassing both in-group enhancement and out-group derogation. While in-group enhancement (strengthened bonds among group members) may be perceived positively by those within the group, it typically co-occurs with harmful out-group derogation (in the case of the 9/11 attacks, Muslims and Arabs), making it problematic as a conceptualization of genuine collective growth. The Rwandan context provides a compelling case study where these intergroup dynamics are particularly salient. In post-genocide Rwanda, the government's narrative of unity and reconciliation, while appearing to eliminate ethnic divisions, continued to enact subtle forms of intergroup differentiation that maintain power imbalances between Tutsi and Hutu communities.

Williamson employed discourse analysis of survivor testimonies from a Rwandan archive to examine how collective PTG manifests in real-world contexts. This approach is particularly well suited for investigating ideological processes, as it allows researchers to analyze what is presupposed or implied by speakers, gaining insight into their underlying belief systems. By examining patterns of shared belief across multiple testimonies, she was able to identify the various ways in which survivors conceptualize their group identity and intergroup relations in the aftermath of genocide.

Narratives from Rwandan genocide survivors were categorized into four response patterns based on their pursuit of agency and communion. The first group pursues neither motive, instead submitting to the dominant ideology while maintaining ethnic divisions. She quotes from the testimony of the genocide survivor FM, who says, "For me, Hutus are ruthless animals. They still have that wickedness in their hearts. They are still hurting me, and that makes it hard for me to forgive them."[49] The second group seeks communion without agency, prioritizing reconciliation while remaining subordinate to governmental authority. The survivor RSM fits into this group: "Forgiving is possible. For example, myself, I have already forgiven, even though no one has asked me for forgiveness, I have forgiven all those who participated in the killing."[50] The third group demonstrates agency without communion, actively resisting governmental authority while rejecting reconciliation efforts. The survivor EN thus says: "Now, just because the Government says, 'Reconcile,' then we reconcile because there's no choice. What would you do? Nothing. If they say, 'Let's unite,' we unite. But it's not real."[51] Finally, the fourth group integrates both qualities, simultaneously seeking autonomy from governmental constraints and meaningful reconciliation with other ethnic groups. The survivor GM is a clear example of this group:

> If a person acknowledges his fault, he admits his sin genuinely and from the heart, then he is already being punished. It will always affect him and there is no greater punishment than the guilt in someone's heart. If it comes from the heart when a person says to me, "Forgive me, I was involved in the killing of your sibling, your parent. . . ." I would understand. I would forgive him because the burden he carries in his heart is enough of a punishment.[52]

She argues that this fourth response represents "genuine" collective PTG, as it enables the group to satisfy both fundamental motivations while developing a new, more adaptive shared understanding of their social reality.

Notably, these findings align with a qualitative study we ran on resilience and PTG among survivors of the 1994 Rwandan genocide.[53] Using a "bottom-up" thematic coding approach with open-ended questions, we explored how growth and resilience were understood in this post-conflict setting. Strikingly, participants described both resilience and PTG primarily in terms of environmental resources rather than individual psychological traits. The four most frequently cited were education, family, financial means, and work. This emphasis stands in sharp contrast to dominant Western models, which often highlight personal psychological changes, such as increased inner strength, deepened spirituality, or greater appreciation for life.

This contextual focus likely reflects the profound societal disruption caused by the genocide, which led to the collapse of infrastructure and social institutions. More than 80 percent of healthcare workers and 50 percent of teachers were killed, buildings were destroyed, and survivors lived in poor conditions with limited access to education and health services.[54] In this context, the ability to secure basic resources such as education, family support, financial stability, and employment became essential ingredients to both resilience and growth.

In this study, we also observed considerable overlap between characteristics associated with resilience and those associated with PTG. Unlike theoretical models that distinguish between these constructs (with *resilience* typically conceptualized as maintaining stability and *growth* as positive change), the study suggests that in the Rwandan context, these processes may be harder to disentangle. This finding has implications for how we conceptualize and measure these constructs across different cultural contexts. Overall, Rwandan conceptualizations of both resilience and PTG were more focused on restoring social connections than on individual psychological change.

Williamson[55] followed up by examining the role of religion in collective PTG, drawing a crucial distinction between religion and other PTG domains: Whereas self-perceptions of growth are individual-focused, religious beliefs function as ideologies. Ideologies are not confined to individuals; they are socially shared sets of beliefs that shape identity at multiple levels. Williamson observed that religious beliefs can have paradoxical effects on collective growth. At the individual level, they may offer existential comfort, providing survivors with meaning and purpose that aid coping. Yet at the collective level, these same beliefs can reinforce narratives that ultimately work against the group's interests.[56]

For example, Williamson found that some survivors were reluctant to condemn the crimes of priests who collaborated with the perpetrators (*génocidaires*), viewing them as sacred figures despite their complicity in violence. Notably, this reluctance to condemn the actions of priests resonates with our discussion of religious trauma earlier; this reluctance may be considered a first-order misclassification.[57] Similarly, some survivors interpreted the current government's position of forgiving perpetrators in religious terms, giving spiritual legitimation to a political regime. In these cases, religious ideology inhibits survivors' collective pursuit of agency and communion by preventing them from seeking truth, justice, and genuine reconciliation. However, she also observed that religious beliefs can promote collective growth when they inspire self-transcendence—motivating survivors to prioritize a higher purpose over their individual needs. Some survivors channeled their religious faith toward forgiveness and reconciliation (i.e., communion) or toward a sense of collective mission to reshape Rwandan society (agency).[58] As the survivor IM noted:

> As a Christian, I will forgive them with no regrets. For instance, I pardoned Papa Dido.... In that way, we became good friends, we get on well as Christians and we go to church together. I am also willing to forgive Paul as there is no way the dead can come back to life. If I knew that killing would bring back the person I lost, I wouldn't hesitate to do it. But I prefer to give out my forgiveness in order to save my soul.[59]

These findings offer several important insights about communal PTG. First, collective PTG occurs primarily at the *ideological* level, involving socially shared beliefs and representations about the world. Second, whereas individual PTG involves rebuilding cognitive schemas, collective PTG requires the development of new social narratives, a process Williamson describes as the social equivalent to schema change. Additionally, enhanced group cohesion immediately following trauma likely represents a defensive response rather than genuine growth, which requires time and effortful collective meaning-making. Finally, ideological systems like religion can simultaneously provide individual existential comfort while maintaining collective illusions about the value of adversity, complicating growth processes at the group level.

This framework has implications for post-conflict societies such as Rwanda (and Sri Lanka, for that matter). It suggests that facilitating positive social change requires addressing both *horizontal* relations (between different groups in society) and *vertical* relations (between survivors and those in positions of power). Creating spaces where survivors can develop counter-ideologies that promote both agency and communion is essential for genuine collective growth. However, this process faces significant challenges, particularly in contexts where elites control access to public discourse and employ strategies to maintain ideological control. In Rwanda, the government's restrictions on free speech and emphasis on a particular narrative of unity make it difficult for survivors to develop alternative interpretations of their experiences that might better serve their collective interest. It seems that in the wake of terrible trauma, religious beliefs in Rwanda are a double-edged sword: They can provide comfort to individuals while also reinforcing narratives that prevent the community from seeking true justice and agency.

Guilt, Shame, and the Danger of "Not Growing Enough"

Religious frameworks often encourage introspection and repentance, which can be healing or paralyzing. Survivors of trauma, especially religious trauma, may feel profound guilt if they do not experience change. Thus, religious teachings that tie righteousness to "growth through suffering" can create unrealistic expectations. A more thoughtful approach recognizes that not all forms of trauma yield growth, and that suffering within oppressive contexts cannot be "overcome" by personal effort alone.[60]

Let me return briefly here to my discussion of Michelle Panchuk and Eleonore Stump. In her article "What Doesn't Kill Me Makes Me Stronger? Post-Traumatic Growth and the Problem of Suffering," Panchuk[61] criticizes how Stump[62] employs PTG research in her defense of God's permission of suffering. Panchuk cites research on how trauma fundamentally disrupts a person's sense of self and capacity for relationships—precisely the aspects of psychic integration that would be necessary for a closer relationship with God on Stump's account.

Her critique proceeds to address several significant concerns with the PTG literature itself. Relevant to the current discussion, she observes that growth in PTG research is evaluated atomistically rather than holistically—in other words, people who have experienced positive changes in one area of their life (e.g., spirituality) are assumed to have "grown" overall, without considering whether they have experienced negative changes in other life domains (e.g., relationship quality).[63] This makes it difficult to determine whether reported improvements in specific domains reflect genuine holistic flourishing of the person.

She also considers the ethical implications of applying PTG research in philosophical and theological contexts. Specifically, she argues that Stump's application of PTG research risks inappropriately blaming trauma survivors for their continued suffering, since Stump notes that one reason why a person may not grow in the wake of adversity is their own free choice.[64] This application may reinforce cultural pressures that already marginalize those who experience persistent negative effects from trauma. She cautions against treating PTG findings as unambiguous evidence that suffering typically promotes the kind of psychic integration that enables a closer relationship with God. Theoretical frameworks for understanding suffering need to remain accountable to the lived experiences of trauma survivors, *including* those whose trauma has not led to growth or has resulted in lasting harm.

Common Threads and Key Differences

The discussion of different religious traditions in this chapter reveals a number of common threads in how they perceive the value of adversity, as well as important differences rooted in their distinctive theological frameworks. Let me attempt to summarize them here.

Suffering as a Test or Trial

Most traditions view adversity as a kind of examination or proving ground for the human spirit. In Christianity and Islam, this idea is explicit: God tests the faith of believers through hardships, as with Job's trials or the Qur'anic assertion that "We will certainly test you with a measure of fear and hunger and loss of wealth, lives, and fruits—but give good tidings to the patient." In Judaism, while less theologically emphasized as a "test" from God, the concept of *nisayon* shows that trials can reveal the depth of one's commitment.

In Buddhism, without a single testing deity, the "test" is more naturalized: Life itself, through *karma* or *samsara*, presents continual challenges that test one's wisdom and equanimity. Across the board, adversity is seen as something that can bring out virtue, courage, faith, and patience in a person. Where traditions differ is in who/what is testing and why. For Abrahamic faiths, a personal God who loves the person is ultimately behind the test, either allowing it or directly sending it for a greater purpose. In Buddhist thought, the tests are built into the cosmic moral order or natural law (*karma*, impermanence) rather than a personal divine will.

Suffering as Discipline or Purification

A closely related theme is that adversity can purify or refine an individual, much like fire refines gold. Christianity uses this metaphor (For example, 1 Peter 1:7 compares trials to a fire that can foster faith). Islam, too, sees suffering as expiating sin and purifying one's soul. Buddhism doesn't frame it in terms of sin, but encountering suffering is what purges ignorance and ego, leading one to renounce attachments—a purification of consciousness. Thus, many traditions agree on a cathartic function of adversity: It strips away illusions, selfishness, or moral flaws. The difference here lies in what is being purified (sin, ignorance, imbalance) and the role of grace versus effort in that process. For instance, Christianity and Islam would add that divine grace or forgiveness operates alongside the person's endurance, whereas Buddhism leans toward personal effort and insight doing the work of growth.

Suffering and Moral Character Development

Virtually all traditions assert that facing adversity can cultivate important virtues. Patience, compassion, resilience, faith, humility—these are commonly extolled as the fruits of suffering well met. In Christianity, perseverance in trials leads to hope and character (Romans 5:3–5). Islam elevates *ṣabr* (patience) and *tawakkul* (trust) as outcomes of enduring hardship.[65] Judaism highlights *ometz lev* (courage) and *emunah* (faithfulness). Buddhism specifically emphasizes compassion—one understands others' suffering by knowing one's own suffering, generating empathy. Across cultures, then, adversity is seen as a virtue training ground. One key difference may be which virtues are most emphasized (e.g., compassion is central in Buddhism, obedience to God's will in Abrahamic faiths). That said, these traditions share the common view of virtue being developed through trials.

Finding Divine Presence in Suffering

Many religious perspectives converge on the idea that God or the sacred is especially close to the sufferer. Christians believe that God Incarnate suffered with them (Christ on the cross), so in pain, one can intimately unite with Christ. In Islam, while God is not said to suffer, God is "with the patient" (Qur'an 2:153) through his mercy. In Buddhism, the presence is not of a personal deity but of Buddha-nature or deeper insight emerging in moments of pain. This shared notion can be understood as the *sacralization* of the experience of suffering: Hardship can become a locus of encounter with the sacred. I remember Good Friday commemorations in Sri Lanka's west coast (the country's so-called "Catholic Belt") featuring reenactments of the crucifixion as a marker of this sacralization each year, particularly at the historic Duwa Passion Play in Negombo.

Highlighting the Communal Dimension

All traditions stress that suffering is not merely an individual experience, but something that happens within and is addressed by community. Religious communities provide support systems, from the Christian church or Islamic ummah rallying around those in need, to the Buddhist sangha providing counsel and compassion. This notion of shared suffering does show up in multiple traditions. The apostle Paul said, "If one part of the body suffers, all suffer with it" (1 Corinthians 12:26), reflecting the idea of solidarity. Buddhism's compassion principle similarly sees all beings as interconnected: One's suffering is ultimately tied to the suffering of all. This communal outlook creates value in adversity by generating empathy and altruism in others—hardship can bring people together in ways prosperity might not. A clear commonality is the moral imperative to help those who suffer—every tradition has charity and care as a high commandment.

That said, Williamson's work discussed earlier points toward the possible downsides of such a communal perspective on PTG. For example, the doctrine of karma in Buddhism can lead to lay beliefs that focus on fatalism or blame. When suffering is viewed solely as the result of past actions, it may foster a lack of compassion or social indifference, suggesting that the poor deserve their circumstances or that the sick are merely reaping karmic consequences. I will confess to experiencing such views from people in Sri Lanka; attributing people's misfortunes to their actions in past lives is (unfortunately) a dominant cultural belief in many parts of the country.

Buddha's teachings emphasize empathy and aid. Buddhism's first precept, refraining from harming living beings, naturally extends to alleviating suffering. Yet when viewed through a purely karmic lens, some might resign themselves or others to suffering, believing interference disrupts cosmic justice. Some contemporary Buddhist teachers warn against this misconception, framing karma as *empowerment*—your actions matter—rather than deterministic fate. The Buddhist monk Thich Nhat Hanh's "engaged Buddhism"[66] insists that wisdom and compassion necessitate involvement in social justice and peacemaking, not passive observation of others' suffering as predetermined karma. Similarly, the Dalai Lama, while affirming karma's reality, advocates for compassionate action toward those who suffer.

Ultimate Transcendence of Suffering

Interestingly, nearly every tradition also holds out an ultimate state in which suffering is overcome, suggesting that adversity's value is instrumental and temporary. In Christianity, heaven is free from suffering; in Islam, Paradise has no pain; Judaism anticipates a Messianic Era of peace; Buddhism has *nirvāṇa* (the cessation of all suffering or *dukkha*). This shows a shared *telos*: Suffering is not eternal. It's either a means to an end (soul-making until heaven, purification until *moksha*, etc.) or a problem to be solved by spiritual evolution or divine deliverance. Thus, all traditions, despite valuing what suffering can teach, ultimately long for a state where those lessons are learned and suffering no longer exists.

Suffering, Meaning, and the Tension of Injustice

Across these diverse religious traditions, a consistent theme emerges: Adversity may hold transformative potential. Christianity's notion of redemptive suffering teaches that hardship can refine one's character, echoing the apostle Paul's assurance that endurance through trials fosters spiritual hope. Similarly, Buddhism invites practitioners to mindfully transform *dukkha*—the inherent dissatisfaction of existence—into compassion, wisdom, and spiritual awakening. Islam offers another framing, portraying adversity as divine testing (*ibtilā'*) that, when faced with patient trust, leads to moral purification and spiritual elevation. Feminist perspectives in Judaism, in contrast, emphasize that suffering is best understood and addressed through collective liberation and social justice rather than through individual redemption alone. Despite their distinct frameworks, these traditions converge in recognizing that adversity has the potential to catalyze profound personal and spiritual growth.

Yet precisely because these narratives valorize adversity, a challenge emerges: Emphasizing the spiritual or moral potential of suffering risks obscuring its systemic roots or placing undue pressure on survivors. When individual virtues such as patience or acceptance become norms, there is a real danger of blaming those who do not experience—or demonstrate—growth. As Panchuk and others caution (and echoing our discussion of Stoicism and anger in Chapter 2), religious communities can inadvertently reinforce oppressive dynamics by encouraging survivors to see their pain as spiritually necessary or divinely ordained, neglecting the real social injustices underlying suffering. Similarly, Raphael insists that genuine healing demands more than individual change; it requires communal liberation from oppressive structures. Finally, Williamson's work highlights the fact that religious worldviews can both provide existential comfort and potentially reinforce unequal power dynamics.

Ultimately, the voices explored in this chapter collectively urge caution against uncritically embracing the idea of adversity as inherently redemptive. As Stump notes, "Suffering can contribute to spiritual regeneration and growth; but it cannot guarantee them."[67] True meaning-making, they suggest, must occur alongside active efforts toward justice, structural change, communal support, and authentic empathy. Only then can adversity's potential benefits be genuinely realized without perpetuating harmful illusions or reinforcing existing injustices.

Religious traditions show that adversity can indeed function as a crucible for profound change. But as we turn to PTG research more explicitly in the next chapters, we must remain mindful that, in many cases, religious accounts also call us to communal responsibility—repairing not just individual souls but broken systems as well. By marrying these insights with psychological frameworks, researchers can better capture the complex reality that suffering may yield wisdom and resilience but should not be idealized as universally redemptive.

4

Narratives of Suffering–Story or Reality?

The religious frameworks explored in Chapter 3 highlight a key insight: Our understanding and interpretation of adversity are fundamentally shaped by the stories we tell about it. Whether through Christian redemption narratives, Buddhist concepts of change through mindful acceptance of the ubiquity of suffering, or Islamic perspectives on testing, purification, and community support, religious traditions offer powerful templates for constructing meaning from suffering. Indeed, contemporary American culture has reworked the ideal of Christian redemption into idioms of self-actualization, redemption, and heroic innovation, preserving the basic plotline—that adversity is an opportunity for growth—even as the explicit theological links fade into the background.[1]

This represents one example of how sacred narratives feed into secular ones, shaping cultural expectations about what it means to suffer "well" and reinforcing normative pressure to convert hardship into moral progress. In this chapter, we'll examine how personal narratives of suffering are shaped by dominant cultural narratives,[2] and attempt to answer the question: When we tell stories of growth after trauma, are we describing reality or following a script?

The Stories We Tell About Adversity

As noted in the introduction, during the 1980s, the Sinhalese-majority Sri Lankan Army battled Tamil separatists seeking an independent homeland in the north and east, while in the south, Marxist revolutionaries fought violently to overthrow the government. Such violence was impossible to ignore. I have vivid memories (shared, I should note, by many other Sri Lankans of my generation) of how our daily school commute in the late 1980s routinely took us past the lifeless bodies of young men and women who had been publicly executed the previous evening—in many cases, either beheaded or trapped in a set of rubber tires that were doused in fuel and set alight—for being on the "wrong" side of the insurrection. I struggled, even then, to reconcile the belief that adversity inevitably strengthens one's character with the stark reality of lives brutally cut short and families permanently scarred by trauma.[3]

Though I have lived in the United States for over two decades now, these childhood memories resurfaced vividly when I recently read the author Shehan Karunatilaka's Booker Prize–winning novel *The Seven Moons of Maali Almeida.* Karunatilaka[4] portrays his characters' suffering with a bleakly humorous, sometimes nihilistic realism—a stark contrast to the optimistic, often redemptive narratives prevalent in American culture. His characters inhabit a grim afterlife described as "Just Like Here But Worse," offering no easy redemption or comforting conclusions. These memories complicate any presumption that suffering can reliably lead to benefits. Is the hopeful narrative of growth so prevalent in American culture genuinely helpful, or might it obscure deeper truths about suffering? Do such narratives provide an important salve, or can they sometimes mask the uncomfortable truth of enduring pain and injustice?[5]

Think for a moment about a major challenge in your own life. What narrative framing did you find yourself reaching for to make sense of it? Was it one of redemption? Endurance? Tragedy? Human beings are inherently storytellers. We make sense of our lives by arranging our experiences into narratives with beginnings, middles, and ends. In the face of adversity, this storytelling impulse often leads people to seek meaning and even positive significance in their suffering. Traumatic or challenging events can shatter one's assumptions about the world, and constructing a coherent story can help restore a sense of order and purpose. Often, individuals in the West narrate their suffering in redemptive terms—that is, they frame a bad experience as ultimately leading to good outcomes such as personal growth, wisdom, or renewed faith. Even the Holocaust survivor and psychiatrist Viktor Frankl observed that suffering may cease to be perceived as suffering once meaning has been found in it.[6] By finding meaning or redemption in pain, people transform their trauma into a story of survival and improvement, which can make unbearable events psychologically bearable. This meaning-making is a core component of recovering well from adversity. For example, in her memoir *Love You Hard*, the public-school teacher Abby Maslin writes about the changes their family experienced in the wake of managing her husband TC's recovery from traumatic brain injuries caused by being the victim of violent assault:

> TC and I are still easing into these new identities. He is more spontaneous than I remember him before. More interested in the twists and turns of fatherhood and our little family than he is in career success. He is also gentler. . . . I, meanwhile, am listening in to learn. I am paying attention to the way the world works for other people. I am noticing injustice in every corner and feeling a grave responsibility to make use of each of my days.[7]

We all tell stories about who we are; this is our narrative identity. Narrative identity researchers in personality science posit that our sense of self is formed by the autobiographical stories we construct.[8] This approach to understanding personality emerged in the 1980s and 1990s as researchers recognized that trait approaches alone couldn't capture the richness and meaning of human lives. While traits describe what a person is generally like (e.g., extraverted, conscientious), narrative identity reveals how a person makes sense of who they are, how they became that person, and where they believe they are headed.

According to McAdams, narrative identity is a person's internalized life story—an evolving narrative that brings together reconstructed past experiences, perceived present reality, and anticipated future to provide life with unity, purpose, and meaning. These stories are not merely factual accounts of events, but interpretive constructions that selectively emphasize certain experiences while downplaying others. In McAdams's view, life stories do not simply *reflect* personality; they represent a distinct *level* of personality. This means that understanding someone fully as a person requires knowing not just their general patterns of behaviors and the major goals but also the story they tell about their life journey.

Several key features distinguish narrative identity:[9] Temporal coherence arranges life events in meaningful sequences with beginnings, middles, and ends, unlike traits that merely describe general tendencies. Causal connections allow the storyteller to create explanatory links between events, establishing how past experiences shaped who they became. Thematic integration weaves central themes such as agency, communion, and redemption throughout the narrative, providing consistency and meaning. Cultural and social influence shapes our stories through available cultural plotlines, expectations, and feedback from others who help co-construct our narratives. Finally, dynamic revision emphasizes that life stories are not fixed but continually evolve as new experiences are integrated and older ones reinterpreted through shifting perspectives and understanding.

In the context of recovering from adversity, narrative identity becomes particularly important. Traumatic events often disrupt a person's ongoing story, creating a "narrative rupture"—a point where the old story no longer fits.[10] Adversity can "shatter" existing narratives, prompting a revision that may include a newfound sense of meaning or growth. The work of rebuilding narrative coherence after trauma involves making sense of the event in a way that preserves or restores a sense of meaning and purpose.

Narrative identity researchers highlight how different narrative patterns relate to well-being outcomes. They identify two contrasting narrative sequences:[11] redemption sequences, which represent a movement from negative to positive, where suffering or failure leads to growth, insight, or positive change; and contamination sequences, characterized by a movement from positive to negative, where good events or expectations are spoiled by subsequent disappointments.

Research consistently shows that people who construct redemptive narratives tend to report higher subjective well-being, greater life satisfaction, and better mental health outcomes than those who tell primarily contamination stories.[12] For example, in one longitudinal study, adults who described difficult life events with themes of suffering leading to positive change showed better psychological adjustment over time than those who did not include such themes in their narratives. Importantly, this association holds even when controlling for personality traits and general optimism, suggesting that the narrative pattern itself contributes uniquely to well-being.

The personality psychologists Dan McAdams and Jennifer Pals[13] further argued that a positive, growth-oriented narrative can contribute to psychological well-being and resilience. In other words, telling a story of "I struggled, but it made me who I am today" can bolster one's sense of self as capable and meaningful. It can also create a sense of coherence in oneself: Someone who has successfully navigated a difficult divorce and is now in a happy new relationship might retrospectively describe their former marriage as "entirely miserable from day one," even if, at the time, there were also periods of happiness and contentment. This narrative reshaping makes their current happiness seem like a triumph and their escape from the past marriage a clearer "growth" step. The study of narrative identity also reveals important developmental patterns. While children begin constructing simple stories about themselves in early childhood, the capacity for full autobiographical reasoning typically emerges in adolescence and continues to develop throughout adulthood.

Yet my work with the philosopher Michael Brady, which I discussed in Chapter 2, reminds us that it is important to carefully distinguish between narratives that genuinely reflect changes and those that may primarily represent coping strategies or self-enhancement, given the distinctly subjective nature of one's construed sense of identity. Of course, even if some stories of growth involve selective memory or reconstruction, their psychological benefits may still be authentic. However, there is an important caveat: Not everyone is equally able or inclined to either craft or benefit from these redemptive narratives. Factors such as personality traits (particularly openness), narrative skills, cultural contexts, and social support likely influence whether such stories translate into genuine psychological change. Thus, while the construction of such narratives can indeed be a pathway to genuine recovery and resilience, researchers and practitioners should be careful about conflating this narrative coherence with changes in one's dispositional thoughts, feelings, and behaviors. We should acknowledge the diversity of individual experiences and guard against expectations that pressure survivors to show growth where little or none genuinely exists.

The Scripts We Are Given: Redemption as a Master Narrative

In Western cultural contexts, redemption narratives in which one endures adversity and emerges improved are ubiquitous. From personal biography to media portrayals, these arcs follow a recognizable pattern of personal struggle leading to a triumphant outcome. McAdams[14] labels these narratives as "redemptive life stories," where negative episodes transition into a positive resolution. Notably, such narratives have their origin (in part) in Christian conceptions of the value of suffering, which we discussed in Chapter 3.

Why do people so often narrate hardship as a growth experience? One reason is psychological coping: Casting oneself as a survivor who gained something from trauma can restore a sense of control and hope.[15] When someone's life "story" is disrupted by tragedy, creating a redemptive narrative helps to repair identity and optimism. Another reason is the influence of cultural scripts or master narratives. Every culture provides shared story templates about suffering and redemption that guide how individuals understand their own misfortunes. In many Western societies, there is a strong cultural script encapsulated by the saying "what doesn't kill you makes you stronger." This idea—that hardship can lead to strength—is a widely endorsed master narrative of resilience and redemption, at least in the United States.[16]

A classic American redemptive narrative might be the rags-to-riches story, where an individual born into poverty, through sheer grit and overcoming numerous obstacles (e.g., lack of education, discrimination), achieves great financial success and community respect. The initial hardship is framed not as a deficit but as the critical event that forged their character. One clear example of such a narrative is former US President Bill Clinton's 1992 speech at the Democratic National Convention in New York:

> I never met my father. He was killed in a car wreck on a rainy road three months before I was born, driving from Chicago to Arkansas to see my mother. After that, my mother had to support us, so we lived with my grandparents while she went back to Louisiana to study nursing. . . . Before I was big enough to see over the counter, I learned from [my grandfather] to look up to people other folks looked down on.[17]

Around the world, storytellers have long relied on such redemption arcs—narrative trajectories in which initial suffering ultimately leads to a positive outcome or moral uplift. In Western contexts especially, the redemptive story is a dominant master narrative with deep historical and cultural roots. As discussed in Chapter 3, Christian theology frames suffering as a path to salvation; literature and pop culture abound with heroes who "hit bottom" only to rise stronger. In modern life, redemption narratives dominate in the stories of celebrities and sportspeople who excel despite multiple obstacles. Indeed, professional sports create particularly clear redemption narratives (fall from grace leading to punishment or exile, and then a subsequent triumphant return). These are often carefully managed by media teams and shaped by commercial interests.[18] Finally, some may even manufacture such stories in order to gain sympathy and attention.[19]

McAdams used the term "redemptive self" to describe how many Americans construct their life stories: Overcoming hardship is portrayed as central to becoming a better, more successful person. McAdams and colleagues found that midlife American adults who scored high on generativity (caring for others and contributing to society) often told life narratives featuring redemption sequences—bad events that were turned to good—as opposed to "contamination" sequences where good events turned bad.[20] In short, narratives of redemption are seen as the adaptive, even heroic, way to respond to life's trials.

These narratives of redemption—stories that frame adversity as a pathway to profound personal growth—hold powerful cultural appeal, encouraging individuals to view their suffering as meaningful and transformative. Such redemption scripts offer significant psychological benefits, empowering survivors to reframe trauma in ways that foster hope, resilience, and a renewed sense of agency. As discussed in Chapter 2, stories like those of Nelson Mandela or Malala Yousafzai exemplify how adversity can catalyze extraordinary moral or psychological development, providing powerful exemplars who inspire others to imagine similar potential within themselves.

High-profile stories, such as the "Miracle on the Hudson" plane crash survivors on US Airways Flight 1549 in 2009 proclaiming newfound appreciation for life, or Oprah Winfrey's public reflections on childhood trauma, are emblematic of redemption narratives. I should also note that many survivors do embrace this culturally sanctioned redemption arc. For instance, as discussed in the preceding chapter, interviews with genocide survivors in Rwanda found that some men framed their trauma as motivating a *shared sense of national identity and unity* (a kind of collective redemption), while some women emphasized *personal empowerment and communion with others* as positive outcomes of their suffering.[21] These individuals actively adopted growth narratives, aligning their personal stories with themes of strength, optimism, and communal rebuilding. In Western contexts, one can find countless examples of adoption: cancer survivors describing themselves as stronger for the experience, or veterans saying that facing up to trauma made them appreciate life more, and so on. Such stories often gain media attention and social praise, reinforcing their power.

However, people in different cultures make sense of and see the possible value of adversity in different ways. The cultural psychologist Richard Shweder[22] noted that people around the world may explain suffering in many ways, including biomedical (a problem to be solved/cured), interpersonal (e.g., supernatural experiences, abuse), sociopolitical (oppression), psychological (e.g., frustrated desires), astrophysical, stress/environmental, and moral (e.g., transgressions, karma) explanations. These cross-cultural differences highlight the importance of understanding different types of moral reasoning that shape how suffering is understood across multiple perspectives and provide an important counterpoint to the primarily Western philosophical traditions discussed here (e.g., the Stoics, Aristotle).

While American cultural narratives often portray adversity and post-traumatic growth (PTG) as deeply individual experiences, other cultures may emphasize a communal understanding of suffering and resilience. Rather than seeing trauma solely as an individual's personal burden or a private path toward growth, these communities frame adversity as a shared experience that requires collective action and communal support. This perspective underscores that growth from trauma isn't merely a personal endeavor but is deeply intertwined with social context and interpersonal interaction. Indeed, certain forms of moral and psychological development, such as empathy, solidarity, or activism, fundamentally depend on interpersonal connections and community relationships. These socially rooted virtues highlight that meaningful change often emerges through social interplay rather than (a stereotypically philosophical ideal of) solitary introspection alone. Thus, in cultures where adversity is viewed primarily as a community concern, healing and growth may be seen as collective rather than strictly individual responsibilities.[23]

For example, following a community-wide natural disaster, a Western narrative might highlight individual "heroes" who single-handedly rescued others or rebuilt their lives through personal determination. In contrast, a more communal narrative, perhaps found in some East Asian or Indigenous cultures, might focus on how the entire community came together, how traditional collective rituals were used for healing, and how shared resources and labor led to the group's recovery, emphasizing "we grew stronger together" rather than "I became stronger." Recognizing this cultural variation provides a valuable corrective to the dominant Western narrative of individual redemption, emphasizing instead a communal dimension to resilience and healing that incorporates attention to systemic conditions and shared experiences.

Additionally, as discussed in Chapter 3, the philosopher and religious scholar Melissa Raphael[24] critiqued traditional Jewish theological accounts of suffering for focusing too narrowly on a "masculine" form of individual change, potentially ignoring the relational or communal dimensions of healing. If adversity arises from systemic injustice or communal crises, growth might involve rebuilding collective solidarity and social trust—less about one's personal strengths and more about strengthening our shared moral fabric. Most discussions of PTG focus on the individual: for example, how *my* character has deepened, or *my* life has improved in meaning after *my* adversity. Raphael's relational critique challenges such an individual-centric approach, arguing that growth should also be understood in relational and collective terms. Indeed, even narratives of redemption can take communal forms: Malala Yousafzai's post-shooting advocacy weaves her personal resilience into a collective fight for girls' education. Such examples highlight that redemption is not necessarily purely individual nor purely universal—cultural and social contexts shape these arcs.

Trauma and recovery are often shared experiences, rather than solo journeys. Humans are inherently social, and adversity frequently affects not only the person at the center of it but also their family, friends, and community. For example, an earthquake is experienced collectively by a community; the grieving and rebuilding process involves collective effort and can lead to positive communal changes (e.g., stronger social bonds, improved disaster response systems). More broadly, Western-centric notions of PTG risk overlooking how healing and growth happen through relationships and within cultural communities. One aspect of this critique is the importance of communal healing. Many cultures emphasize that after trauma, individuals heal by reconnecting with others—sharing their story, receiving communal recognition, and perhaps participating in rituals or communal remembrance.

This has led some researchers to discuss the possibility of "collective" growth, as I discussed in the context of post-genocide Rwanda in Chapter 3. Indeed, cross-cultural studies have identified collective growth as a dimension of positive change in some non-Western samples. In more collectivistic cultures (e.g., Japan and parts of Latin America), people may report that following a communal tragedy, there were *societal* positive changes (e.g., greater social cohesion, spiritual renewal of the group), not just changes within individuals.[25]

Redemption Pressure: The Double-Edged Sword of Master Narratives

However, there is a significant risk inherent in the cultural expectation of redemption: Such narratives can mask the complexities of lingering distress and ongoing struggles. By implying that one "should" grow stronger after adversity, these scripts unintentionally marginalize those who experience persistent trauma or who find no redemptive meaning in their suffering. Moreover, redemption scripts often obscure systemic injustices by individualizing the experience of growth, suggesting implicitly that if individuals do not achieve the culturally expected change, it reflects personal failure rather than structural conditions or inadequate societal support. Thus, while redemption narratives can inspire powerful personal growth, they may hide other trajectories and blind people to the recognition that not all suffering neatly resolves into uplifting narratives of change.

I should say here that for many trauma survivors, crafting a redemptive narrative can be genuinely empowering. These narratives can encourage survivors to reframe adversity positively and allow them to reclaim authorship of their life story, to say "I am not defined by what hurt me but by how I overcame it." Such narratives can provide emotional relief, a sense of meaning and purpose (e.g., "I went through this to learn X or to help others"), increased perceived control,[26] and increased self-worth. They can also attract social support, as people tend to admire and gravitate toward stories of triumph over adversity. In this way, redemptive narratives often serve as a psychological resource, fostering adaptive coping and well-being.[27] Research links redemptive story themes to positive outcomes like well-being, emotion regulation, and even health behaviors (e.g., staying sober).[28]

However, as noted in the example of Rwanda in the previous chapter, redemption narratives can also be constraining, even oppressive, when they become rigid expectations. The cultural mandate that you must find the "silver lining" may invalidate those who are not ready or able to reframe their pain positively. It can create a silent burden: Survivors may feel *compelled* to present an "inspiring" front, effectively performing PTG to satisfy others, while privately struggling. This pressure can inhibit genuine emotional processing—one might suppress grief or anger because it doesn't fit the redemption script.

The personality psychologist Kate McLean[29] offers a theoretical framework for understanding how master narratives—culturally dominant stories about what constitutes a "good" or "admirable" life—impact individual identity development. She emphasizes that Western societies strongly valorize resilience and self-improvement, fueling a "pressure" to grow after adversity. Consequently, individuals may feel compelled to narrate their experiences in a redemptive way, even if their internal reality is more ambiguous or marked by ongoing distress.

McLean's work on master narratives and identity provides a compelling framework for understanding the social forces that shape personal identity. Her work emphasizes how master narratives can constrain or enable individual growth. These themes connect directly to our discussions in Chapters 2 and 3 about how philosophical and religious frameworks for understanding suffering both enable and potentially restrict growth.

In this account, master narratives can influence people's own reports of PTG, as I noted when reviewing the philosopher L. A. Paul's work on transformative experiences in Chapter 2. For instance, people may unconsciously reshape their memories or interpret their past selves as "weaker" to validate a stronger present identity (more on this in the next chapter). Also, while Western narratives emphasize individual heroism, other more communal cultures may place greater focus on communal or relational resilience, highlighting interdependence over individual triumph as a positive outcome.

However, it is possible for people to resist or "rewrite" dominant redemption narratives. Some survivors do not identify with the standard "I overcame" arc, preferring stories of acceptance, endurance, or collective solidarity. Recognizing such counter-narratives is critical for a balanced understanding of adversity and growth. McLean explains why cultural scripts can be both empowering (by providing hope) and constraining (by limiting which stories are deemed acceptable):

> The directives inherent in these stories mean that there is the possibility of not aligning with expectations. For those who don't fit the bill, these master narratives can exclude, shame, and deny membership or community participation. And these narratives are most likely to deny inclusion to those who are the most disempowered, least privileged, or least likely to benefit from the status quo. Those in power tend to like power, and want to maintain their position in the hierarchy. And one way to do that is to perpetuate particular stories to maintain an inequitable status quo that benefits those in power.[30]

McLean and the developmental psychologist Moin Syed[31] argue that cultural master narratives strongly guide how individuals interpret adversity. In Western societies, heroic narratives of overcoming adversity abound, encouraging "I overcame" stories.[32] In more collectivistic contexts, a similar event might be narrated more as a communal journey, emphasizing moral responsibilities or shared solidarity rather than an individual's personal triumph. Consequently, PTG self-reports might reflect whichever cultural narrative is dominant in an individual's context.

Personal experiences of trauma and growth are deeply embedded in social contexts and master narratives. If one's culture has a master narrative of redemption, individuals are likely to interpret their experience through that lens—sometimes to their benefit. Given that, master narratives may provide a helpful language and framework for individuals. For example, US veterans returning from war might tap into a broader cultural narrative of the "wounded warrior" who finds meaning through sacrifice.[33] This can help them make meaning of their experience (i.e., personal growth through service). Collective narratives can also offer social support: When a whole community shares a story of resilience ("Boston Strong" after the 2013 marathon bombing in that city, for instance), individuals feel bolstered by a communal spirit. Their personal narrative of overcoming is reinforced and validated by those around them, which in turn strengthens their sense of growth.

That said, it is important to distinguish between cultures that emphasize communal healing and those that emphasize individual changes. As discussed in Chapter 3, some religious traditions (such as specific traditions in Buddhism and Islam) emphasize communal responsibility over individual triumph. In those contexts, a person might downplay personal change and highlight communal recovery in their story because that's what is valued and understood by others. Conversely, in the United States, someone who only spoke about communal aspects ("my family got closer") and not about how *they* changed might be prodded for more information ("Yes, but how did *you* grow from this?"), reflecting culture-specific expectations.

The Social Costs of Non-Redemptive Stories

While redemption stories can be inspiring, they also pose risks when normalized to the point of coercion. If the cultural or religious message is that adversity *must* result in growth, survivors may feel pressured to appear resilient, even when they remain in pain. These dynamics parallel the religious scholar Melissa Raphael's critique (Chapter 3) of spiritual frameworks that treat suffering as something to face up to in a "masculine" way, perhaps not dissimilar to Nietzsche's famous dictum. Consider also the historian Elaine Pagels's reaction to suggestions that she should explore the silver linings from the loss of her son, Mark. Such messages can harm our ability to show up for others who are suffering with compassion and kindness.

In one study, McLean and her colleagues[34] asked people to rate narratives of people who had experienced six types of traumatic experiences. Those who told stories with a redemptive ending—for example, "This terrible thing happened, but I overcame it"—received positive ratings from listeners. If a narrative did not provide an uplifting or redemptive ending (e.g., following a narrative of being in a car accident, "Since then, I have had flashbacks about the headlights coming toward me, and am still terrified to drive"), it was not rated as positively. This finding seems to underscore the fact that in American culture, the redemptive story is paramount. Listeners expect a tale of inspiration when hearing stories of adversity; when they instead hear lingering pain or ambiguity, they may become uncomfortable or dismissive. The social message to survivors is clear: *If you've suffered, you're supposed to come out of it a better person.*[35] This likely puts some trauma survivors in a double bind: They not only carry a painful story but also discover that telling it honestly (without a positive twist) fails to get them acceptance or validation. People who can't redeem their traumas feel they cannot tell their story and get acceptance from people.

In this regard, let's consider two employees laid off during a company downsizing. Sara tells colleagues, "This layoff was a shock, but it's given me the push I needed to finally start my own consulting business—it's a blessing in disguise!" This redemptive story is likely to elicit positive social feedback. William confides, "I'm devastated by this layoff; I feel lost and anxious about the future, and I don't see any good coming from it." In line with this study's findings, William might find listeners becoming uncomfortable or offering platitudes, as his non-redemptive story doesn't fit the preferred cultural script, potentially making them feel even more isolated.

You can test this finding in your own life by taking a moment to notice how others respond the next time you share your struggles. Do they seem uncomfortable unless you add a positive spin? This discomfort reveals our cultural bias toward redemption narratives. If you wish, you should also consider giving yourself permission to tell stories that resist and push back against dominant narrative scripts.

Can We Distinguish Reality from Stories?

Life narratives of growth following adversity are a fascinating and complex phenomenon at the intersection of psychology, culture, and storytelling. While narrative change is important, how do we know when a redemptive narrative reflects authentic personal changes rather than conformity to a cultural narrative? Given this challenge, to what extent should we promote redemptive narratives? Knowing their double-edged nature, professionals and support networks might wonder whether it's helpful to encourage a trauma survivor to focus on "finding the positive."[36]

The consensus in the contemporary literature is that authenticity and timing are key.[37] Early on post-adversity, when pain is acute, pushing positivity can backfire; the individual may need space to express their suffering without a bow tied around it. As time passes, and if the individual shows inclination, gently supporting them to identify any personal growth or meaning can be beneficial. It's not about imposing a narrative, but about helping people recognize growth *if it's there* and reinforcing it. Also, validating that *not* everyone experiences growth is crucial. Empowerment comes from allowing people to narrate their life honestly and construct meaning in a way that rings true for them.

Redemptive narratives are powerful and psychologically beneficial in many contexts, yet they risk substituting cultural beliefs for genuine inner change. By integrating narrative identity approaches with robust, longitudinal methodologies to examine shifts over time, we can better discern the true ubiquity of PTG.[38] Ultimately, the challenge remains to honor the healing value of stories without conflating them automatically with lived change. They may indicate PTG, but not always. Sometimes the narrative is a faithful reflection of positive change—a sign that the person has genuinely transformed their outlook, priorities, or behavior after trauma.[39] Other times, the narrative is perhaps ahead of the reality: a hopeful script one tells while actual change is still forthcoming, or may never fully match the story. And sometimes, the narrative is more a product of cultural narrative pressure or a coping illusion than an organic outcome of trauma.[40]

The ideal of growth following adversity (as both a scientific construct to evaluate and as an idea that resonates with people) is an indicator of the human capacity for meaning-making in the wake of adversity. Many people can talk about how they successfully thrive in the wake of hardship; they find new strength, deepen their relationships, and discover purpose. But this story of growth is not necessarily indicative of growth itself. Indeed, one challenge, as researchers who are also human beings, is that we must listen to these stories with both admiration *and* discernment.

By appreciating the role of narrative identity, understanding the influence of master narratives, and evaluating the strength of the link between stories and outcomes, we gain a more comprehensive view of why the idea of PTG feels so compelling. That said, as noted in our discussion of philosophical conceptions of growth in Chapter 2, it's important to think of positive change not only in terms of stories that may feel empowering, but also in terms of living out those stories in a fulfilling and authentic manner—that is, experiencing growth that plays out in daily life.

5

Post-Traumatic Growth

A Research Reality Check

The power of redemptive narratives and their cultural entrenchment nevertheless raise a critical question for researchers and practitioners alike: How can we distinguish between the dominance of such narratives and genuine change? If cultural scripts encourage survivors to frame their experiences in terms of growth, what does this mean for the validity of self-reports of post-traumatic growth (PTG)? What kinds of challenges do these powerful redemptive narratives pose to unbiased, scientific study of PTG? These questions bring us to the heart of current empirical research on PTG and to the methodological challenges that have plagued the field. In this chapter, we'll conduct a thorough "reality check" on PTG research, examining measurement approaches, study designs, and the gap between perceived and actual change.

The Challenge of Measuring Growth

As I've explored in earlier chapters, accounts of PTG often promise hope, redemption, and positive change after adversity. But how strong is the empirical research that supposedly validates these claims? To illustrate this, let me begin with a study I conducted in 2013 with my colleague Laura Blackie, the counselor Niranjala Somasundaram at the Family Rehabilitation Centre, and Wake Forest undergraduate student Victoria Britt among Tamil war widows in the eastern Sri Lankan town of Trincomalee.[1]

The civil war in Sri Lanka, which was deeply shaped by long-standing ethnic-political tensions,[2] inflicted profound trauma on countless civilians, especially members of the Tamil minority. Tamil women faced severe hardships—losing family members, enduring violence, and often unexpectedly becoming breadwinners. Given Sri Lanka's traditionally rigid gender norms, these women emerged as change agents, reshaping their roles and challenging societal expectations. Yet we wondered: Would adopting a redemptive narrative—framing their trauma as meaningful and growth-promoting—support their psychological well-being?

Drawing from life story interviews conducted in collaboration with Sri Lanka's Family Rehabilitation Center, we initially found that half of the women reported redemptive narratives around their traumatic experiences. Many were actively challenging traditional norms and supporting others in their community. However, despite the frequent and consistent identification of redemption in these narratives by local Tamil-speaking research assistants, stories of redemption showed no meaningful relationship with well-being among these war-affected women.

Now, this was a small study—around forty participants. That said, it does challenge the notion that redemption narratives reliably predict better psychological outcomes. Could it be that cultural differences impact how we talk about our experience with trauma? If so, how do we make sense of people's self-reports of their own growth or change? PTG has become a key framework in psychology to describe the positive psychological changes that can emerge from adversity. The appeal of PTG is intuitive; it suggests that hardship can foster deeper appreciation for life, greater personal strength, and even spiritual change. However, this crucial question persists: How do we know whether people are in fact growing rather than just believing they are?

As I noted in the introduction, many PTG studies rely on self-reported assessments, such as the Post-Traumatic Growth Inventory (PTGI), which asks individuals to reflect on how adversity has changed them. Yet memory is fallible, and perception does not always align with reality. Longitudinal research indicates that individuals who report the most growth are not necessarily those who exhibit measurable personality change. Some even show high PTG alongside significant distress, suggesting that perceived growth may sometimes function as a coping strategy rather than a marker of authentic change.

The field has been remarkably uncritical in its acceptance of self-reported PTG, despite well-established problems with retrospective assessment. This uncritical stance stems from multiple factors: the intuitive appeal of redemptive narratives, researchers' professional investment in the construct, the relative ease of administering questionnaires compared to more rigorous methods, and a cultural climate that celebrates stories of overcoming adversity. These factors create a perfect environment for accepting methodologically problematic evidence at face value, a problem that extends beyond PTG research to psychology more broadly.

Indeed, one explanation for this uncritical stance toward current research on PTG is the fact that the narrative of growth following adversity is culturally fluent (e.g., the idea "just feels right" because it is in line with dominant cultural beliefs) in many research contexts (especially the United States), potentially lowering the threshold for accepting evidence and reducing skepticism toward methods like the PTGI. The cultural psychologist Daphna Oyserman[3] discusses the cultural fluency of specific ideas in the context of the idea of possessing a "growth mindset" (believing abilities are malleable), which is highly culturally fluent in the United States, likely because it aligns with core American values of individualism, self-creation, and the "pull yourself up by your bootstraps" narrative. This fluency may contribute to its widespread popular acceptance, potentially overshadowing methodological critiques or inconsistent findings. This charge can similarly be made against research on PTG.

The fundamental assessment problem in PTG research may be explained in the following way: When someone claims on a questionnaire that "My trauma changed me for the better," researchers cannot determine whether this represents authentic personality change, a coping narrative, a cultural script, or some combination of these. The central question becomes not just *whether* growth occurs, but *how* we can measure it in ways that distinguish genuine change from socially influenced self-perceptions.

Let us next examine the empirical foundations of PTG research, addressing key methodological concerns and the persistent gap between perceived and authentic growth. I will put you in the "hot seat," as it were, and walk you through why current assessments of PTG should not be taken at face value. I explore how stronger methodological designs—longitudinal studies, experience sampling, and informant corroboration—can move the field forward, and why these approaches are essential for establishing the validity of PTG as a scientific construct. In doing so, I'll contextualize this discussion considering the recent credibility revolution in psychological research.

What Are the "Deadly Sins" of PTG Research?

In *The Seven Deadly Sins of Psychology*, the cognitive neuroscientist Chris Chambers[4] offers a stringent critique of methodological and systemic flaws in psychological research using the metaphor of the seven deadly sins, which in his telling are *bias*, *flexibility*, *unreliability*, *data hoarding*, *corruptibility*, *internment* (i.e., restricted access to research articles), and *bean counting*.

Specifically, he argues that confirmation bias (the tendency to seek out evidence that supports one's own beliefs), the use of questionable research practices and poor methods, resistance to open science practices (such as data sharing and open access publishing), and a focus on quantity over quality in publishing research on the topic have significantly compromised our field's ability to advance credible research. In my view, PTG research exemplifies many of these "sins" in alarming ways, creating a perfect storm of scientific vulnerabilities.

Current research systematically reinforces culturally appealing narratives about adversity fostering growth while minimizing null findings, reflecting researcher bias toward redemptive interpretations of suffering. This confirmation bias is enabled by hidden flexibility in research practices: cross-sectional, retrospective designs using poor-quality assessments, coupled with theoretical vagueness that allows researchers to selectively focus on growth self-reports while minimizing contradictory evidence (e.g., low levels of concordance with measured change on PTG-relevant characteristics over time, association with increased levels of distress). The resulting hype generated by this research distorts public and academic understanding, highlighting dramatic change stories while obscuring the (more common) experiences of partial recovery or continued struggle. Perhaps most troublingly, this skewed representation can reinforce prejudice by implicitly blaming survivors who fail to demonstrate growth, suggesting that continued distress reflects personal inadequacy rather than a normal trauma response.

The field's "bean-counting" approach of focusing on quantity over quality and publishing ever more studies on the topic using retrospective assessments (as opposed to more time- and resource-intensive longitudinal studies)[5] compounds these problems by reducing complex human experiences to simplistic numerical scores on methodologically suspect self-report measures, while the steep increase in PTG publications over the past fifteen years[6] rewards positive findings over null results, regardless of methodological quality. Together with the general unreliability of weak study designs that focus solely on retrospective self-reports of growth, these interlocking failures of "sins" have created a body of literature that fundamentally misrepresents how people in fact respond to adversity, undermining both scientific understanding and ethical support for trauma survivors.

Perhaps a root cause of the poor state of PTG research is that the subject matter—growth from adversity—aligns with a culturally appealing redemption script that can overshadow rigorous inquiry.[7] Indeed, when I first began studying PTG as a graduate student, I was struck by how readily other researchers in the field seemed to accept retrospective self-reports at face value. The reason was likely because the dominant redemption narrative was so compelling that researchers, participants, journal editors, and the public all have reasons to prefer stories of growth over accounts of stagnation or decline.

Why does this matter? Beyond important issues of scientific integrity, there are practical implications. If interventions, therapies, or public health messages are built on a shaky empirical foundation, they may inadvertently harm those they aim to help. Survivors may be pathologized for not experiencing growth, or resources may be misdirected based on inflated expectations of positive change.[8]

The State of PTG Research

Given the cultural power of redemption scripts, how have scientists tried to measure growth scientifically, and how have they gone wrong? As I noted earlier, the PTGI remains the dominant tool in PTG research,[9] despite fundamental problems with its methodology. The PTGI asks individuals to rate how much they have changed as a result of trauma across five domains: relating to others, new possibilities, personal strength, spiritual change, and appreciation of life. This approach suffers from critical flaws that call into question the validity of the entire PTG research enterprise.

The Central Problem: What Are We Measuring When We Measure Growth?

The PTGI and similar retrospective instruments suffer from several interconnected limitations that fundamentally undermine their validity; see also Ford et al. (2008).[10] Retrospective bias creates a foundational problem, as participants simply cannot accurately remember their pre-trauma selves, making "change" assessments inherently subjective and leaving claims of improvement without objective reference points in the absence of pre-trauma baseline measures. A person completing the PTGI five years after a serious illness may struggle to accurately recall their level of "spirituality" before the illness, potentially misremembering it as lower than it was, thus inflating perceived spiritual change. Compounding this issue, positive illusions may lead people to claim growth as a psychological coping strategy to maintain a sense of control or meaning after disruptive events.[11] The psychologists Shelley Taylor and David Armor[12] demonstrated that such self-protective cognitive adaptations are common responses to threat, functioning adaptively regardless of their accuracy. So, to return to an example from Chapter 4, an individual who experienced a difficult divorce might report growth in "personal strength" because believing they are stronger helps them cope with feelings of vulnerability, even if their objective coping skills haven't demonstrably improved.

Cultural scripts further distort self-reports, as narratives that valorize resilience and redemptive create implicit pressure to report positive change, with cultural frameworks particularly promoting "what doesn't kill you makes you stronger" stories that generate demand characteristics in research settings. In other words, in a society that heavily promotes the ideal of "what doesn't kill you makes you stronger," one might feel an implicit pressure to endorse items like "I can do better things with my life," aligning with cultural expectations. The single-method limitations of self-reports present another critical weakness, as they cannot distinguish between authentic change and perceptions of growth; without corroborating behavioral measures or informant reports, researchers merely document what people believe about themselves rather than objective change. A high self-reported score on "improved relations with others" on the PTGI would ideally be corroborated by, for example, informant reports from friends noting more frequent positive interactions or behavioral data showing increased engagement in social activities.

Finally, framing effects introduced by the PTGI's exclusive focus on positive change items (e.g., "I have a greater appreciation for the value of my own life") potentially create acquiescence bias, explaining why studies using balanced measures that include items assessing *both* growth and decline typically find more modest growth estimates—a pattern suggesting systematic measurement inflation in the literature. The standard PTGI's sole focus on positive changes means a respondent isn't asked if trauma led to negative changes. If asked, "As a result of my trauma, I've changed in how much compassion I have for other people," some might report a negative change, but the standard version of the PTGI only offers positively worded options.

This widespread acceptance and use of these methods runs counter to the implications of the findings from the psychologists Cathy McFarland

and Celeste Alvaro,[13] which suggest that people tend to retrospectively exaggerate their levels of growth. They designed a study to directly test whether perceived growth might stem from a distorted view of one's pre-trauma self rather than actual positive change. Participants were asked to recall personally experienced stressful events and stressful events experienced by acquaintances. After recalling each event, they rated both their current selves and how they remembered themselves from two years before the adverse event on growth-related attributes such as kindness, tolerance, and reflectiveness.

The results revealed a striking pattern that aligns with the self-enhancement perspective proposed by Taylor and Armor.[14] When rating current attributes, participants' self-assessments didn't differ significantly from how they rated their acquaintances. However, when evaluating past selves, participants systematically rated their own pre-stressor selves more negatively, compared to their acquaintances' past selves. This past self-deprecation suggests that perceived growth may often result not from actual improvement, but from devaluing one's pre-trauma self—essentially creating an illusion of progress by misremembering what one was like before the adversity occurred.

Assuming that individuals systematically misrepresent their pre-trauma functioning to create a sense of growth, many self-reported PTG claims may reflect motivated cognitive distortion rather than genuine change; specifically, participants compare their current positive state not to their actual pre-trauma state, but to an imagined worse state. This creates an illusion of growth even when none has occurred.

An Introspective Exercise: What's Wrong With the PTGI?

To understand the challenges of retrospective PTG measurement, consider how you might respond to the following PTGI item:

> As a result of my traumatic experience, I have a greater appreciation for the value of my own life.

Most readers would rate a typical PTGI item on a scale from 0 ("I did not experience this change") to 5 ("I experienced this change to a very great degree"), perceiving it as a straightforward assessment task. Yet this seemingly simple self-evaluation demands an extraordinarily complex series of metacognitive psychological operations that remain largely invisible to both respondents and researchers.[15]

The process begins with reconstructing your pre-trauma self: You must accurately recall how much you valued life *before* the traumatic event, accessing memories that may be years old and inevitably colored by subsequent experiences and current mental states. Next comes assessing your current condition, evaluating your present appreciation for life in a judgment heavily influenced by transient factors, including current mood, recent experiences, and even the immediate context in which you're completing the questionnaire. Then you must perform the cognitive calculation of mentally subtracting your reconstructed pre-trauma state from your current state to determine the magnitude of change—a complex comparative judgment vulnerable to numerous cognitive biases and estimation errors. Finally, you face perhaps the most challenging step: attributing causality by deciding whether any perceived difference was specifically caused by the trauma itself ("as a result of my traumatic experience") rather than countless other potential influences, including other life events, normal developmental processes, or random fluctuations in outlook.[16]

This multistep cognitive task—demanding accurate memory, unbiased self-assessment, precise calculation, and complex causal attribution—reveals why retrospective self-reports of growth may reflect cognitive reconstruction more than objective change. Each of these steps introduces potential sources of error or bias that have nothing to do with actual growth. Consider Maria, a hypothetical car accident survivor completing the PTGI one year after her trauma. Maria reads the item about appreciating life's value and reflects, "I definitely value life more now," selecting 5 on the scale to indicate a very great change. But beneath this seemingly straightforward response lies a complex web of psychological processes that may shape her answer independent of actual personality change. Memory distortion likely influences her assessment, as Maria may misremember her pre-accident self as taking life for granted, even if she was already quite appreciative—as noted above, research shows that people tend to exaggerate differences between past and present states to create a coherent narrative arc.[17] Through therapy sessions and countless conversations with loved ones, Maria has engaged in narrative integration, repeatedly telling her story as one of change until this account has become a central part of her identity, regardless of whether measurable change actually occurred.

Cultural expectations further shape her response, as Maria has absorbed her society's valorization of redemptive narratives and the implicit message that trauma survivors should "find the silver lining." Cognitive dissonance creates additional pressure toward reporting growth, as Maria psychologically benefits from believing her suffering served some purpose—the alternative, that her pain was meaningless, is emotionally harder to accept. Social desirability influences her as well; Maria wants to appear resilient to both herself and the researcher, making growth claims feel more acceptable than admitting continued struggle. If Maria happens to feel positive on the day she completes the questionnaire, mood-congruent recall may color her recollections, while confirmation bias leads her to selectively notice evidence supporting her self-perception as someone who has grown, while overlooking contradictory information. These multiple psychological mechanisms—all operating largely outside conscious awareness—make Maria's high growth rating more ambiguous than it initially appears, potentially reflecting cognitive and social processes rather than authentic personality change.

I want to emphasize here that these processes are not necessarily an example of conscious deception—Maria genuinely believes she has grown. Her report reflects her own subjective "truth." But from a scientific standpoint, we cannot determine whether her response indicates actual personality change, a coping strategy, a memory bias, adherence to cultural scripts, or some combination of these factors. This introspective exercise reveals why retrospective PTG measures, while capturing something potentially real and meaningful, cannot help us distinguish between actual growth and perceived growth. If Maria also completed personality measures before her accident, or if we had behavioral observations from both time points, or if close others could verify changes in her daily habits, we would have stronger evidence for or against her claimed growth. Without such corroborating data, her high PTGI score remains ambiguous. Similarly, recall our divorce example from a few pages back: The person in a new relationship who now sees their past marriage as "entirely miserable from day one." The PTGI would capture this perception as "growth," but without pre-divorce assessments, we cannot know if this represents actual change or protective reframing.

The purpose of highlighting these limitations is not to dismiss subjective experience, but to recognize its complexity and the challenges in assessing and interpreting it. Maria's perception that she has grown may provide comfort and meaning, regardless of whether researchers can verify objective change. Indeed, this example reminds me of conversations I had with Tamil Sri Lankan war survivors who would assert growth when asked directly ("Yes, things are better now"), yet whose subsequent discussion of their daily lives revealed ongoing struggles that seemed inconsistent with their reported change (with multiple examples of displacement, abuse, and other war trauma). However, for PTG to stand as a valid construct rather than simply a phenomenological one, we need methods that can differentiate between various sources of growth reports.

We recently ran a study[18] seeking to clarify the nature of these growth reports by evaluating the following question: When people complete the PTGI, do they engage in the cognitive processes that would produce valid responses? According to the clinical psychologist Julian Ford and his colleagues,[19] respondents should follow at least four distinct cognitive steps to accurately report growth: evaluate their current functioning, recall their pre-trauma functioning, compare these two states to calculate change, and then make a determination as to how much of that change resulted specifically from the traumatic event. These steps require complex metacognitive judgments that may be challenging to perform accurately.

To investigate this question, we conducted cognitive interviews with twenty-one adults who had experienced a major life event in the previous twelve months. Using a "think-aloud" methodology, participants verbalized their thought processes while responding to PTGI items, allowing researchers to observe whether the theoretically required steps were being performed. The results were revealing. Across all twenty-one interviews, not a single participant completed all four cognitive steps for every item. Most commonly, participants evaluated their current functioning (completed approximately 65 percent of the time) but rarely considered how much change was specifically attributable to the traumatic event (completed only 1 percent of the time). These findings suggest that participants are not engaging in the response processes necessary to provide valid responses on the PTGI.

We next conducted a thematic analysis to understand what cognitive processes participants were using. Three main themes emerged. First, many participants emphasized thematic coherence—describing consistency rather than change in their lives. One participant claimed they had "always been spiritual," yet reported high scores on spiritual growth items. This suggests that the PTGI may inadvertently measure awareness of existing qualities rather than genuine change.

Second, participants frequently described reappraisal coping—focusing on positive aspects of their current circumstances as a way of maintaining resilience. While this is an adaptive response to adversity, it is conceptually distinct from actual growth. We noted that many participants reported positive change in PTG-relevant characteristics while their interview responses revealed either no change or even negative experiences, suggesting a conflation between coping strategies and genuine change.

Third, participants often drew on redemptive narratives—cultural scripts suggesting that growth naturally follows trauma. This raises the possibility that PTGI scores reflect adherence to societal expectations rather than genuine psychological changes. As one participant explained when asked about spiritual growth following their mother's death: "I don't know that my spirituality changed due to my mom's death. . . . I just, you know, believe what I believe." Despite acknowledging no change, this participant still reported growth on the corresponding item. Perhaps most concerning was the observation that participants frequently equated resilience with growth. The mere act of surviving or enduring a traumatic event was sometimes interpreted as evidence of growth, even when no actual positive change had occurred. This fundamental misalignment between what the PTGI aims to measure and how participants interpret its items casts doubt on the validity of findings derived from this instrument.

If participants aren't engaging in the cognitive processes necessary to accurately report growth, what exactly are these measures capturing? The evidence suggests that the PTGI may be measuring a combination of cultural scripts about adversity, coping strategies, attempts to maintain narrative coherence, and resilience misinterpreted as growth. This study adds to a growing body of evidence questioning the construct validity of retrospective PTG measures.

Retrospective Self-Reports vs. Measured Change: The Empirical Evidence

Following the Evidence: Can We Trust the Numbers?

A central empirical question is whether self-reported growth aligns with baseline-to-post change. The evidence increasingly suggests that it does not. In a landmark study, Frazier et al.[20] directly compared perceived growth to pre-to-post change on PTG-relevant characteristics in a sample of trauma survivors. They collected baseline measures of well-being, personality, and relationships, and then tracked participants who subsequently experienced traumas. When comparing pre-post changes to PTGI scores, they found a surprising result: little to no relationship between reported growth and actual measured improvement. For instance, someone might score very highly on the PTGI domain "new possibilities," indicating they perceive many new opportunities post-trauma. However, pre- and post-trauma measures of their actual engagement in new activities, goal-setting behaviors, or vocational changes would show no meaningful difference compared to those who reported little perceived growth in "new possibilities."

Specifically, individuals who claimed the most growth on the PTGI showed no greater improvement on objective measures than those reporting little growth. Even more troubling, those with the highest PTGI scores showed *increased* distress over time, contradicting the assumption that perceived growth indicates successful coping. This finding has been replicated across multiple studies. For example, the psychologist Betina Yanez and her colleagues[21] found minimal correlation between perceived benefit and actual change in relevant characteristics indicative of PTG. The psychologists Meghan Owenz and Blaine Fowers[22] demonstrated that participants' perceptions of growth after relationship breakups were largely inaccurate when compared to measured change in PTG-relevant characteristics.

These studies collectively suggest that the PTGI and similar instruments are measuring something other than actual growth. As discussed earlier, the cognitive neuroscientist Chris Chambers would classify these issues as exemplifying at least two of his "deadly sins": *bias* in how we interpret growth claims and *hype* in how findings are presented. The field has systematically failed to clearly distinguish between perceived change (how people talk about themselves) and substantial personality change (how they actually think, feel, and behave).

As a counterpoint, however, the susceptibility to memory biases and subjective distortions notwithstanding, some recent research suggests that retrospective reports may be more accurate in some instances. For instance, the personality psychologist Ted Schwaba and his colleagues[23] provided empirical evidence that retrospective perceptions of personality change following significant life events that occurred in the last ten years can reliably correspond to objectively measured changes in personality traits assessed longitudinally. Specifically, participants retrospectively identified events they believed had the greatest impact on their personality traits, and these perceptions significantly correlated with measured personality trajectories before and after the identified events. These findings indicate that under certain conditions—such as *when* individuals are asked explicitly about highly impactful, salient events that had occurred in the past—retrospective self-reports can provide valid insights into personality development. However, future research is needed to test the specific instances in which such reports have good validity.

Cracking the Case: How Can We Do Better?

As I confronted this mounting evidence against simplistic growth narratives, my assumption that adversity reliably produces measurable growth—an assumption that had initially drawn me to this field—came apart quickly under empirical scrutiny. Yet rather than abandoning PTG research altogether, I found myself increasingly committed to understanding the reality behind the cultural scripts. Perhaps this mirrors the very process many trauma survivors undergo—replacing simplistic narratives of growth with complex, sometimes contradictory truths.

How does one capture PTG with greater methodological precision? In recent years, my lab group has proposed several approaches with demonstrated value for distinguishing genuine change from perceived growth.[24] Collecting pre-trauma baseline data represents a foundational strategy, whether for foreseeable stressors like military deployments or medical procedures, or through carefully analyzed retrospective baselines for unexpected events. This provides the crucial reference point against which to measure actual change rather than relying solely on retrospective estimation.[25] Using control or comparison groups adds another layer of methodological rigor, allowing researchers to distinguish changes unique to trauma from those reflecting normal age-related development or general life experiences. Longitudinal designs with multiple follow-up assessments are also important, as they can reveal when and how changes develop over time, rather than providing just a single post-event snapshot that may reflect temporary adaptation rather than enduring change.

Triangulating growth measures represents another approach: Combining self-reports with other ratings of their traits by close others, behavioral coding, and narrative analysis creates a comprehensive assessment where convergence across methods substantially increases confidence in growth claims; while divergence (particularly when only self-reports indicate change) warrants more cautious interpretation.[26] Further refinement comes from distinguishing between growth domains, rather than treating PTG as a unitary construct, recognizing that some aspects (like spiritual change) may be inherently more subjective and challenging to verify than others (such as new relationships or activities) that leave observable behavioral traces. Finally, accounting for personality traits that predispose individuals toward reporting growth regardless of actual change—including optimism, extraversion, and openness to experience—helps separate genuine change from trait-driven response tendencies that can inflate growth estimates independently of actual adaptation to adversity.

When effectively implemented, these methods may help clarify when perceived growth aligns with true behavioral change. Most importantly, they transform PTG research from a field dominated by potentially misleading claims to one grounded in valid assessment.

Tracking Growth in Real Time

Recent studies attempt to refine PTG measurement by shifting away from purely retrospective approaches. In one study,[27] we examined the following question: If PTG represents genuine positive personality change following adversity, shouldn't we be able to observe it in people's day-to-day lives?

Drawing from personality psychology methods, we developed a measure that captures momentary manifestations of PTG, which we then tested using experience-sampling methodology. Rather than asking "How much have you changed?" we asked "What are you experiencing right now?" This approach allowed us to capture PTG as it manifested in daily life, examining how it fluctuated from moment to moment in everyday life. We adapted items from the PTGI to create a state-oriented measure suitable for repeated daily assessments. For example, we transformed the PTGI item "I have a greater appreciation for the value of my own life" into "Today, I appreciated the value of my own life." Participants who had experienced significant adversity (alongside a control group) completed these assessments multiple times daily over nine consecutive days.

So, what did we find? First, the five familiar domains of PTG emerged in people's daily experiences: relationships, spirituality, appreciation of life, personal strength, and new possibilities. More importantly, PTG experiences changed substantially from day to day, showing significant within-person variability across time and contexts. This finding challenges the notion of PTG as a stable outcome and suggests that growth might be better understood as a dynamic process characterized by both positive and negative fluctuations across the day. In other words, our manifestation of change likely ebbs and flows depending on the situations we encounter and how we respond to them. Perhaps most striking was the discovery that high scores on trait-level PTG (measured by the PTGI) did not necessarily correspond to more frequent daily growth-related experiences and behaviors. People who believed they had grown since their trauma weren't necessarily experiencing more growth-oriented states in their daily lives. With the exception of spirituality, trait and state measures were weakly correlated.

This discrepancy raises fundamental questions about what the PTGI actually captures. Is it measuring genuine behavioral changes, or is it primarily tapping into benefit-finding to cope with adverse events? Both might be key aspects of the growth process, but they appear to be distinct rather than unified phenomena. We identified several contextual factors associated with daily fluctuations in state PTG. Social interactions involving emotional disclosure and support predicted higher state PTG on the same day. Engagement in meaning-making activities was similarly associated with elevated growth experiences. Different domains of PTG also showed distinct patterns of fluctuation, suggesting growth processes may unfold differently across these areas. From a theoretical perspective, these findings suggest that PTG might be better conceptualized as an ongoing, dynamic process rather than a stable end state or outcome. This reconceptualization aligns with theories that view growth as emerging through repeated cycles of cognitive and emotional processing following trauma.

The study had limitations, including the relatively small sample size and the nine-day assessment period, which may not capture longer-term patterns. There also could be potential reactivity effects where the daily monitoring itself may shift participants' responses. Nevertheless, by developing and validating a measure that captures change at the momentary level, we provided a new way to understand how growth unfolds in daily life. Our finding that PTG fluctuates over time and is influenced by contextual factors opens new avenues for understanding—and potentially facilitating—positive change following trauma. These findings suggest that while people may perceive themselves as having grown, their actual day-to-day behaviors may not always reflect such change.

Can Informants Detect Growth?

A parallel method is corroboration of PTG scores using informants or the other ratings provided by people close to the target participants. In other words, if someone believes they've grown following trauma, can their friends and family members corroborate these changes? In one study we ran, ninety-nine participants were recruited who had experienced significant adversity within the previous five years—events like the sudden death of loved ones, life-threatening illness, and physical assault.[28] Each participant nominated close others who had known them both before and after the traumatic event. Using the PTGI-42, which measures both positive changes (PTG) and negative changes (post-traumatic depreciation or PTD), we compared participants' self-perceptions with informants' observations. When examining overall growth scores, we found that informants could only reliably corroborate negative changes. These findings suggest that, while broad trends in post-traumatic change can be detected by others, the specific details of self-perceived growth may be more influenced by personal narratives than by observable changes in their thoughts, feelings, and behavior.

This finding does reinforce skepticism about the PTGI's validity. However, we also ran a profile analysis to examine whether informants recognized the pattern of change across different PTG domains. Here, we found significant agreement between participants and informants about which domains showed relatively higher levels of perceived growth, and which showed relatively lower levels of perceived growth in the target's profile. In other words, while informants might not agree with the absolute magnitude of perceived growth, they could accurately identify the shape of the growth profile—recognizing, for instance, that a person had grown more in relationships and spirituality than in personal strength or new possibilities. This profile agreement persisted even when controlling for stereotypical beliefs about how people typically change after trauma, suggesting that informants were tuned into the idiosyncratic ways that PTG manifested in each individual; in other words, they were able to detect distinctive changes in their personality (see Table 5.1).

Table 5.1 Selected Studies Examining Self–Other Agreement on Post-Traumatic Growth

Authors (Year)	Sample	Trauma Type	Self–Other Measurement	Key Findings	Agreement Level
Shakespeare-Finch & Enders[a]	61 emergency service workers and significant others	Occupational trauma exposure	PTGI (self) and PTGI-Observer (other)	Significant other ratings correlated with self-reports across all domains. Others rated PTG slightly higher than self-reports.	Moderate to high (r = .69)
Blackie et al.[b]	99 community members + 141 informants	Major life events	PTGI	Independent raters identified growth themes in participants' narratives that corresponded with self-reported growth.	Low (r = .16)
Park et al.[c]	160 college students who experienced stressful events and friends	Various stressful events	Stress-Related Growth Scale (SRGS) for self and observer version	Modest correlations between self-reported growth and observer ratings.	Low to moderate (r = .21)
McMillen & Cook[d]	42 individuals with spinal cord injury and nominated informants	Physical injury/disability	Perceived Benefits Scale (PBS)—self and observer version	Informants identified similar domains of growth as patients, particularly community closeness, spirituality, and material gain.	Moderate (r = .06-.47)
Helgeson[e]	180 breast cancer survivors and partners	Cancer	Benefit-Finding Scale (BFS)—self and observer version	Partner perceptions of survivor growth correlated modestly with growth.	Not significantly correlated

[a] Jane Shakespeare-Finch and Tracey Enders, "Corroborating Evidence of Posttraumatic Growth," *Journal of Traumatic Stress* 21, no. 4 (2008): 421–424.
[b] Blackie et al., "Investigating the Veracity of Self-Perceived Posttraumatic Growth."
[c] Crystal L. Park, Lawrence H. Cohen, and Renee L. Murch, "Assessment and Prediction of Stress-Related Growth," *Journal of Personality* 64, no. 1 (1996): 71–105.
[d] J. Curtis McMillen and Cynthia Loveland Cook, "The Positive By-Products of Spinal Cord Injury and Their Correlates," *Rehabilitation Psychology* 48, no. 2 (2003): 77–85.
[e] Vicki S. Helgeson, "Corroboration of Growth Following Breast Cancer: Ten Years Later," *Journal of Social and Clinical Psychology* 29, no. 5 (2010): 546–574.

Informant Corroboration in Cross-Cultural Contexts

However, we did not find similar levels of profile agreement among a sample of war-affected Tamil Sri Lankans.[29] Specifically, we investigated whether self-reported PTG among Sri Lankan Tamil civil war survivors could be corroborated by close others. We also used the PTGI-42 to measure both PTG and PTD across five domains: relationships, new possibilities, personal strength, spiritual matters, and appreciation of life. We assessed agreement between self-reports and informant ratings at different and complementary levels: overall trait level, specific domains, overall profile patterns, and distinctive profile patterns.

Participants showed modest levels of agreement on overall levels of both PTG and PTD (correlations around .2). Domain-specific agreement was mixed, with significant correlations for some domains but not others. While there was significant agreement on overall profile patterns, there was no significant agreement on distinctive profile patterns. The lack of distinctive profile agreement suggests that informants were not sensitive to survivors' idiosyncratic patterns of change but instead relied on shared cultural narratives about how people typically change after trauma. One likely implication of this study is that the PTGI-42 may inadequately capture post-traumatic change in this cultural context.

It should be noted that PTG may look different following collective trauma (e.g., ethnopolitical violence) in collectivistic cultures compared to individually-experienced trauma in individualistic cultures. One focus for future research could be the development of a culturally sensitive measurement of post-traumatic change (both positive and negative change), emphasizing the importance of using other more appropriate methods, including prospective longitudinal designs that allow researchers to track changes in participants across time from before to after the experience of different, collectively experienced adverse events.

The "Self-Fulfilling" Hypothesis: Can Believing You've Grown Spark Real Change?

One possible response to critiques of the validity of perceived growth measures may be to say that perceiving growth might be beneficial, even if that perception doesn't perfectly align with reality.[30] Perhaps believing you've become stronger, more appreciative, or spiritually deeper might function as a self-fulfilling prophecy, gradually transforming perception into reality—in other words, a "fake it until you make it" scenario.

We tested this "self-fulfilling" hypothesis in a sample of 864 adults who had experienced significant adverse events within the past year—events like the death of loved ones, serious illness, physical assault, and financial disaster. We asked a series of questions of these individuals three times over six months, employing three distinct methods to assess growth. First, participants completed the PTGI. Second, we assessed current standing on PTG domains using a modified version of the PTGI that captured present levels rather than perceived change (e.g., "I appreciate the value of my own life"). Third—and most innovatively—participants engaged in experience sampling, reporting their momentary PTG-relevant experiences twice daily for three weeks at each wave, generating over 32,000 assessments of growth as it manifested in daily life. This approach allowed us to examine whether believing you've grown predicts actual observable changes in both self-reported current standing and day-to-day experiences. If perceived growth functions as a catalyst for actual positive change, we should see PTGI scores at one time point predicting increases in current standing and momentary PTG at subsequent time points.

Using sophisticated statistical models,[31] we found no evidence that perceived growth predicted subsequent positive change. This null finding held whether we examined overall PTG or specific domains like relationships, personal strength, or appreciation of life. Among the many possible cross-lagged paths tested, only one showed significance—and it ran in the opposite direction, with state spiritual change predicting later perceived spiritual change.

In other words, not only do measures such as the PTGI correlate weakly with pre- to post-trauma changes (as previous research has shown), but they also fail to predict future changes in PTG-relevant domains. Whatever is being captured by the PTGI, it does not appear to function as a catalyst for genuine personality change—at least not within a six-month time frame. This challenges theoretical models like the Janus Face model of PTG,[32] which proposes that even "illusory" PTG might eventually become functional by prompting genuine positive change. These findings align with our earlier work showing that PTG fluctuates substantially from day to day, manifesting differently across situations and contexts.

Together, these studies suggest that if we want to understand genuine positive change following adversity, we need to move beyond asking people how much they think they've changed. Instead, we should focus on tracking

Table 5.2 Indicators of Perceived vs. Authentic Change

Indicator	Illusory Growth	Authentic Growth
Measurement method	Retrospective self-report only	Multimethod (self-report, informant-report, behavioral coding)
Timing	One-off survey post-event	Repeated measures over time
Content	Broad, positively framed statements	Specific, anchored to specific thoughts, feelings, and behaviors
Corroboration	None	Consistent across different informants (e.g., partner, family, friends, work colleagues)
Example	"I'm a better person now"	Sustained changes in helping others pre- to post-event

thoughts, feelings, and behaviors as they unfold in daily life, using methods that minimize the biases inherent in retrospection. Only then can we begin to untangle the complex relationship between adversity and growth, between perception and reality, and between what we believe about our change and the change itself. This challenges the assumption that self-perceived growth necessarily translates into long-term behavioral or personality change. Indeed, it is very important that we distinguish clearly between these two types of data. Table 5.2 provides a helpful summary of these differences, and in particular highlights what type of data counts as evidence of authentic growth.

Confronting the "Sin" of Confirmation Bias in PTG Research

The critique by the neuroscientist Chris Chambers that we discussed earlier provides a compelling framework for understanding systemic problems in psychological science, but it becomes even more persuasive when examined through the lens of specific empirical work in PTG research. My own research program has documented many of these "sins" in action, revealing how they collectively distort our understanding of growth after adversity.

Consider our cognitive interview study with PTG respondents.[33] As participants verbalized their thought processes while completing the PTGI, we discovered that virtually none followed the cognitive steps required for valid responses. Most evaluated their current functioning, but rarely considered how much change was attributable to the traumatic event (completed only 1 percent of the time). The lack of research examining the validity of the PTGI exemplifies Chambers's "bean counting" sin—a large and ever-growing literature that used a measure that indexes growth as a numerical score without adequate attention to what those numbers in fact represent.

Similarly, our year-long study tracking changes in state-level PTG following adverse events[34] revealed the consequences of the "hidden flexibility" Chambers identifies. Unlike standard cross-sectional designs that allow researchers to selectively report favorable outcomes, our intensive longitudinal approach showed that mean levels of both state PTG and trait eudaimonic well-being remained relatively stable across the year, despite participants' experiences of negative life events. These findings contradict the narrative of "reliable" growth that emerges from other, less methodologically sound research designs.

However, the "sin" of confirmation bias is perhaps most pervasive in the PTG literature. This becomes evident when comparing our findings on perceived versus actual growth.[35] We found no evidence that perceived growth predicted subsequent positive change, contradicting theoretical models like Maercker and Zoellner's Janus Face model, which proposes that even "illusory" PTG might eventually become functional (i.e., "fake it till you make it"). Yet arguments about the ubiquity of growth continue to generate headlines suggesting that adversity reliably transforms people for the better. Relatedly, the limited self–other agreement on PTG in our cross-cultural work with Tamil survivors of Sri Lanka's civil war[36] suggests that Western-developed measures may inadequately capture growth as experienced in collectivistic contexts. These findings underscore how culturally biased assumptions can be embedded in seemingly objective research tools, potentially marginalizing non-Western experiences of recovery and adaptation.

Our research on the response processes behind PTG measures[37] further illustrated this bias. The thematic analysis revealed that participants frequently drew on redemptive narratives—cultural scripts suggesting that growth naturally follows trauma—even when their actual experiences contradicted these narratives. This inclination highlights how the academic incentive structure rewards findings that confirm culturally appealing stories about adversity, despite the messier, more complex reality our detailed investigation uncovered. Chambers's framework helps explain why, despite mounting evidence from our lab and others questioning the validity of standard PTG measures, the field has been slow to adopt more rigorous methods. The "unreliability" sin is perpetuated when researchers continue using problematic measures without adequate replication or methodological triangulation. Our multimethod studies[38] represent an attempt to break this cycle by examining PTG through experience sampling, informant reports, and longitudinal tracking rather than relying solely on retrospective self-assessment.

These empirical findings from my research program don't merely corroborate Chambers's critique; they provide concrete evidence of how confirmation bias systematically distorts our understanding of PTG. More importantly, they demonstrate that alternative methodological approaches are needed to yield a more accurate, if less culturally satisfying, picture of how people actually respond to adversity.

The Need for a Stronger Conceptual Foundation

The philosophical framework discussed in Chapter 2 that the philosopher Michael Brady and I developed provides more than abstract conceptual clarity. It offers a lens for understanding why current PTG measurement approaches consistently fall short. Specifically, our six conceptual constraints map directly onto the methodological problems identified in this chapter and provide a framework for more robust empirical work. Table 5.3 provides a summary of this mapping.

Consider the first constraint: that PTG must refer to actual change, not merely perceived change. This philosophical position directly explains why retrospective self-reports like the PTGI are fundamentally inadequate measurement tools. When participants report feeling "stronger" after trauma without demonstrable behavior change, they may be engaging in meaning-making but not experiencing what we would recognize as genuine change. Our cognitive interview findings[39] illustrate this challenge—participants completing the PTGI weren't comparing their pre- and post-trauma selves but were instead offering present-moment evaluations shaped by cultural redemption scripts. The conceptual distinction between "story" and "reality" demands methodological approaches that can distinguish between the two.

Table 5.3 Growth Credibility Checklist

Criterion	Description	Example
1. Actual change	Is there observable change in thoughts, feelings, or behavior, not just words?	Reports of greater patience matched by friends noting calmer responses.
2. Beyond recovery	Does the change go beyond simply returning to baseline?	Not just regaining old social life, but forming deeper, more reciprocal friendships.
3. Enduring	Has the change lasted months/years, not just weeks?	Sustained volunteering two years after the event.
4. Unambiguously positive	Would most people see this as beneficial in context?	Increased compassion rather than increased mistrust.
5. Causally linked	Is the adversity a plausible cause, not just a coincidence?	Loss leading to career change aligned with newfound values.
6. Corroborated	Is the change confirmed by other methods or people?	Narratives, behavioral data, and peers agree on the shift.

The second constraint—that growth must be (at least somewhat) enduring rather than temporary—exposes another limitation in current research. Cross-sectional studies using the PTGI capture momentary self-perceptions that likely reflect transient coping responses rather than lasting change. This explains why longitudinal studies consistently do not find strong relationships between initial PTGI scores and sustained positive outcomes over time. What appears as "growth" in a single assessment may instead reflect a temporary narrative construction that helps manage immediate distress.

Similarly, that third constraint—that growth must be conceptually distinct from coping mechanisms—illuminates why studies finding high correlations between PTG self-reports and ongoing distress[40] reveal a core measurement problem. If PTG represents genuine positive change rather than a coping strategy, then we would expect it to correlate with improved well-being.[41] The persistence of these contradictory findings suggests that standard PTG measures may be capturing coping rather than authentic growth.[42] In other words, when someone endorses "I discovered that I'm stronger than I thought I was," they might be articulating a coping mantra that helps them persevere rather than reporting "actual" change.

The fourth constraint demands that growth be significant and meaningful. The McFarland and Alvaro[43] findings about systematic depreciation of one's past self directly illustrate this violation. Without pre-trauma baselines, participants unconsciously construct degraded versions of their former selves, making current functioning appear improved by comparison. In the absence of proper comparison standards, it may not be wise to take self-reported growth at face value.

The fifth constraint—that growth should represent clear positive change—reveals how the PTGI's exclusive focus on positive items creates systematic bias. By preventing detection of negative changes, these measures may compel participants into reporting positive change that may not reflect the complex reality of post-trauma adaptation.

Perhaps most significantly, the sixth constraint—that growth must result non-accidentally from trauma—explains why longitudinal designs with pre-trauma baselines are not merely methodologically superior but conceptually vital. Without establishing a causal connection between adversity and subsequent changes, we cannot determine whether observed differences represent genuine PTG or simply normal developmental processes that would have occurred regardless of trauma. Our lab's finding that participants almost never considered whether changes resulted specifically from their trauma (completing this attribution only 1 percent of the time)[44] reveals that the PTGI fails to capture even attempted causal reasoning. The philosophical requirement for non-accidental connection demands specific methodological approaches that current cross-sectional assessments simply cannot provide.

These six limitations aren't merely independent methodological flaws; they represent a systematic failure to operationalize and study PTG credibly. The PTGI and similar measures assume that perceived change represent reality, capture snapshots instead of enduring change, conflate coping with growth, force positive narratives while ignoring complexity, lack proper baselines for judging change, and fail to establish the causal link between adversity and the reported change. Thus, each of the philosophical constraints presented in Chapter 2 highlights not just a measurement limitation in current research, but clear conceptual confusion about what growth after adversity entails.

By recognizing how philosophical constraints necessitate specific empirical methods, we can see that the methodological reforms proposed in this chapter are not merely technical improvements but conceptual necessities for studying PTG in a valid and credible manner. Prospective designs, multimethod assessments, and behavioral measures aren't just "better" methods—they're key approaches for capturing the presence of change.[45] The integration of better conceptual and methodological perspectives can offer a more coherent and rigorous foundation for future research—one that combines both conceptual clarity and empirical validity.

Moving Toward a More Credible PTG Framework

The methodological "reality check" on PTG research demands fundamental reconsideration of how we study, measure, and conceptualize growth after trauma. The uncritical acceptance of PTG scales has persisted not through scientific merit, but through the convergence of several social and professional forces: the cultural appeal of redemptive narratives, academic incentives favoring positive findings, the intuitive plausibility of growth, and the methodological convenience of questionnaires. Breaking free of these constraints requires addressing several critical challenges.

First, retrospective self-reports alone are insufficient to capture true growth. The field must prioritize longitudinal designs, experience-sampling methods, and multimethod assessment. The value of these approaches lies in their ability to establish temporal precedence, reduce recall bias, and provide convergent validity evidence. Without such methodological triangulation, we cannot build a credible science of PTG.

Second, the dominant narrative suggests that PTG is common, even normative. The empirical evidence contradicts this: Different individuals navigate adversity in wildly different ways, and genuine growth appears much rarer than previously assumed. Statistical approaches like latent class analysis and growth mixture modeling can identify distinct trajectories, avoiding the oversimplification inherent in mean-level analyses (and typically showing little evidence of a group who experienced positive change following adversity).[46]

Third, the field suffers from what psychologists call the "jingle-jangle" problem—using different terms for what may be the same construct, or the same term for different constructs. Consider the proliferation of PTG-adjacent concepts: perceived growth, narrative change, benefit-finding, personality development, and adaptive functioning. Are these distinct phenomena or merely different labels for the same underlying process? Without clear differentiation, we cannot determine whether each has unique antecedents and consequences. For instance, "benefit-finding" (actively searching for silver linings)[47] is likely a coping strategy rather than a reflection of genuine change. Current research frequently treats these constructs as interchangeable, but clear definitions and measurement specificity are essential to advancing our understanding of PTG.

Fourth, while subjective perceptions do matter for well-being, they need to be interpreted carefully. A truly comprehensive assessment would include informant ratings, behavioral measures, physiological indicators, and performance tasks alongside self-reports. Such multilevel assessment can distinguish between what people believe about themselves and how they function in daily life.

The systematic critique of psychology that Chambers provides[48] applies with force to PTG research, which exemplifies many of his described academic "sins." The field has been characterized by confirmation bias favoring growth narratives, significant methodological shortcomings, publication bias toward positive outcomes, and hype in reporting findings. Breaking this cycle requires not just methodological tinkering but a complete paradigm shift in how we approach the study of post-trauma adaptation. Indeed, I have argued elsewhere that researchers should reconsider using the label "post-traumatic growth" in psychological research.[49] This is in part because philosophers argue that growth is a thick, normatively positive concept implying character improvement, which would require a principled way to weigh positive and negative change. As I discussed in Chapter 2, this is a standard we currently lack.[50]

Why has the field been so resistant to such critical evaluation? The "culturally fluent" narrative of redemptive suffering runs deep, particularly in Western societies where adversity is expected to yield personal growth.[51] Researchers themselves often have ideological commitments to the idea that suffering can be transformative. The popularity of concepts like resilience and PTG makes them attractive research topics likely to receive funding and attention. And perhaps most importantly, the comforting narrative that "trauma changes people for the better" can offer hope both to survivors and to those who work with them (although as I discussed earlier, such narratives can harm our ability to successfully be present with our suffering loved ones in a compassionate and helpful manner). These forces create powerful incentives to maintain the status quo, despite the mounting evidence of methodological flaws.

This also connects back to our earlier philosophical discussions in Chapter 2, where we examined questions of authenticity and change. The philosophical question of what constitutes "authentic" change takes on empirical dimensions when we ask how such growth should be identified and measured (see the growth credibility checklist in Table 5.3). The obvious goal should be to disentangle the actual life changes that people undertake as a result of trauma from both the cognitive manipulations they conduct to relieve distress[52] and benefit-finding in order to cope with trauma. Current PTG measures conflate these constructs, meaning that we can't be sure what they are measuring in a given context. For example, a person who reports high scores on the PTGI might engage in benefit-finding as a coping strategy without making any concrete changes in their thoughts, feelings, and behaviors, or alternatively might make such changes without engaging in positive reappraisal. Only by clearly distinguishing these constructs can researchers begin to understand when and how genuine positive change occurs versus when people are simply managing distress through cognitive strategies.[53]

The present discussion also complicates Chapter 3's exploration of religious frameworks, which often embrace the idea that suffering can lead to a strengthening of character. This claim seemingly lacks robust empirical support, at least in its frequency and universality. Finally, it expands upon Chapter 4's narrative analysis by highlighting how cultural scripts shape the stories trauma survivors tell about their own growth, often in ways that may reflect coping or self-enhancement rather than changes in people's thoughts, feelings, and behavior.

Looking forward, a methodologically rigorous approach to PTG can help us distinguish between genuine and perceived change. This distinction matters not just for scientific accuracy but also for practical applications. Interventions based on inflated expectations of growth may inadvertently harm survivors who do not experience such positive change. A more balanced understanding—one that acknowledges the rarity of genuine growth while respecting the psychological value of meaning-making—can lead to more effective, ethical ways to support trauma recovery.

Research should embrace longitudinal designs, multimethod assessments (e.g., experience sampling, informant corroboration), and ipsative approaches (that compare an individual's trait level against their own past trait level rather than to group averages) to accurately differentiate perceived change from authentic change. Addressing these methodological issues is essential for moving toward a credible, empirically sound understanding of PTG.

Next, I consider how our critique of current research on PTG can provide empirical insights that could inform a more credible line of research, offering reliable pathways to change without overstating the reality of "growth" or pathologizing those who do not report it. I argue that the path forward lies neither in uncritical acceptance of growth claims nor in cynical dismissal of any possibility of positive change, but in methodologically sound research that tracks different responses to adversity. By examining different types of personality change and the conditions under which genuine positive change appears most likely, and by providing theoretical frameworks for understanding such change, we can construct a more compelling, empirically grounded understanding of how adversity can—though not inevitably—foster meaningful growth.

6

Distilling the "Real Benefits" of Adversity

As mentioned in the introduction, I have a strong aversion to simplistic accounts of redemption in the wake of adversity. Despite this skepticism, however, I also have deep admiration for the heroism of those Sri Lankans of my childhood who risked their lives—sometimes paying the ultimate price—to fight for justice. For example, the journalist Richard de Zoysa was assassinated after challenging state power, as were the academic and human rights campaigner Rajani Thiranagama[1,2] and newspaper editor and press freedom champion Lasantha Wickrematunge.[3] All three were somewhat protected by the educated social class they belonged to, yet it was also true that they refused to back down in the face of increasing threats to their lives. Growing up aware of their courage helped model my understanding of what it meant to possess moral strength in the face of adversity. While many of us are likely not capable of such courage, their example leads us to the question: Is it possible to identify and describe the real positive changes that the experience of adversity can foster?

Chapter 5 showed how four persistent weaknesses—(1) retrospective self-report instruments, such as the PTGI, that confound memory with change, (2) one-shot or cross-sectional snapshots that blur temporal ordering, (3) single-method reliance on participants' own narratives, and (4) culturally narrow, often Western, samples that miss other cultural conceptions of facing up to adversity—together inflate the appearance of "growth." Here, I'll discuss more credible evidence for positive changes in the wake of adversity. First, longitudinal studies that track people over time, including Seery and colleagues' work on the curvilinear relationship between cumulative lifetime adversity and well-being, provide somewhat stronger evidence for the possibility of positive change following adversity. Second, multimethod research programs, such as the work of psychologists Daniel Lim and David DeSteno linking adversity with compassion, combine self-report with behavioral donations and laboratory helping tasks, breaking the single-method limitation of past research and showing when suffering predicts authentic prosocial action. Third, research on "altruism born of suffering" focuses on community and disaster-affected populations, expanding the cultural lens beyond Western contexts *and* linking adversity to outward-facing moral engagement. By highlighting these examples of more credible research, I hope to identify the conditions under which adversity can yield demonstrable benefits.

I've Got the "Abattoir Blues"

When I was in graduate school in Philadelphia in the late 2000s, one of my favorite albums was Nick Cave & the Bad Seeds's *Abattoir Blues/The Lyre of Orpheus*. I happily recall evenings spent listening to this album in our communal student house on Osage Street in West Philly. On the surface, it was his artistry—the dark, foreboding quality of "Abattoir Blues,"[4] the forlorn, hymn-like feel of "O Children"—that drew me in. But at a deeper level, it was Cave's ability to meld existential anguish and spiritual yearning into something searching and strangely, simultaneously redemptive and unresolved, a pattern particularly noticeable in his more recent work. The album felt like a dense tapestry of despair, devotion, and hope, a blend of darkness and grace. In those days, I hadn't yet identified my broader academic interest in adversity's relationship to personal growth (this would only happen a couple of years later when I moved to North Carolina), but looking back, I see that *Abattoir Blues/The Lyre of Orpheus* was, for me, a sonic mirror reflecting the dynamic we must all manage between pessimism and endurance.

More recently, Cave revisited the subject of grief and faith in his book-length conversation with the British journalist Sean O'Hagan, *Faith, Hope, and Carnage*.[5] In it, Cave explores the aftermath of his son Arthur's death—his heartbreak, restlessness, and eventual cultivation of a different kind of faith. Cave does not argue that personal tragedy automatically yields spiritual or moral gains; in fact, in contrast to the bravado of Nietzsche, which I discussed in Chapter 2, he is clear that grief cuts deeper and lingers far longer than simplistic accounts of redemption would imply. Yet in his words, it is possible to glimpse the *potential* for adversity to catalyze new forms of empathy, communal solidarity, and compassion. This tension between intense sorrow on the one hand, and a degree of hope or meaning on the other, echoes the central dilemma I have tried to unravel throughout my research and in this chapter: Why do some people channel their suffering into deeper purpose while others withdraw? And even for those who do harness adversity constructively, is the change truly genuine or partly shaped by cultural scripts about the value of overcoming?

Moreover, before we even ask this question, we should confront a more fundamental fact: In many—perhaps most—cases, the suffering caused by adversity far outweighs any potential benefits. For example, the violence I witnessed in Sri Lanka likely did not make most people stronger; it left them traumatized, displaced, and grieving. No amount of "growth" could compensate for the loss of loved ones, the destruction of communities, or the years of fear and displacement they experienced.

In earlier chapters, I questioned the universal myth that "what doesn't kill you makes you stronger." We have seen how many societies encourage redemption arcs—especially in the West, where adversity is often treated as a stepping stone toward personal growth. In this chapter, I propose that genuine growth *can* emerge from hardship, but that it arises less from the bare fact of suffering than from how individuals and communities respond to it. If we listen carefully to Cave's reflections in *Faith, Hope, and Carnage*, we can see how certain preconditions, such as deliberate meaning-making, robust social support, and a willingness to remain open and vulnerable, may help transmute pain into moral clarity or empathy. For example, when discussing the mysterious muse for the songs on his album *Ghosteen*, Cave discusses how he made meaning in the wake of experiencing trauma:

> You go to a very dark place and experience the extremities of your own pain—you are taken to the very limit of suffering. As far as I can see, there is a transformative aspect to this suffering. We are essentially altered or remade by it. Now, this process is terrifying, but in time you return to the world with some kind of knowledge that has something to do with the vulnerability as participants in this human drama. Everything seems so fragile and precious and heightened, and the world and the people in it seem so endangered, and yet so beautiful.[6]

Notably, the clinical psychologists Stephen Joseph and Alex Linley[7] argue that post-traumatic growth (PTG) aligns more with eudaimonic flourishing (enhanced meaning and purpose) than hedonic well-being (happiness or pleasure). For instance, someone grieving the loss of a loved one may continue to feel sadness while simultaneously developing a deeper sense of life's significance. PTG, then, is less about feeling "happy" per se and more about meaningful change. Growth doesn't necessarily eliminate negative emotions; rather, it integrates them into a more complex understanding of human experience. As Cave's writings illustrate, his grief remains profound *even as* he discovers new dimensions of faith and connection in his writings and songs. This coexistence of growth alongside suffering arguably represents a more realistic outcome from adversity than a more "superhero"-adjacent outcome.[8]

Personal accounts such as Cave's reveal that growth after loss often unfolds alongside ongoing vulnerability, challenging the idea of a neat, linear process of growth. This is in part because adversity can disrupt our core assumptions, shaking the foundation of who we believe we are. Cave reflects in his interviews on how his loss forced him to confront the limits of his own control, his notion of a benevolent universe, and even the creative impetus behind his songwriting. Rather than endorsing a simple trajectory of change, he lingers on the complexity of living with grief. This zigzagging path of mourning illustrates the complexities masked by simplistic claims about growth following adversity.

One distinctive feature of Cave's example—which echoes Pema Chödrön's insights on suffering from a Buddhist perspective in Chapter 3—is his reflective search for meaning and his decision to be open and vulnerable in the wake of adversity. Indeed, many individuals who may grow from suffering highlight the role of purposeful reflection, whether in therapy, personal journaling, or, as in Cave's case, through art and communal engagement.[9] Such reflective practices can support growth by aiding the reorganization of one's identity around newly clarified values. Cave's own engagement with fans online, such as his Q&A sessions, his openness about faith and doubt in *Faith, Hope, and Carnage*, and his online forum the *Red Hand Files*, suggest that such reflection, done collectively, can deepen empathy and reaffirm the shared human struggle. Notably, and in line with Pagels's invocation of the apocryphal Gospel of Thomas discussed in Chapter 3, Cave sees growth from adversity as only a possibility, and a choice we must make:

> [I] have found that embedded within these challenges there is almost always the opportunity for renewal or change. That is the plain but uncomfortable truth. I say this with a much conflicted heart, but it seems clear to me that the heartbreaks that routinely befall us—personally, societally or universally—are, in fact, the necessary gifts of change. These painful upheavals always provide us with the option for self-destruction or for transcendence. Heartbreak can be the engine of obliteration or growth. The choice is ours.[10]

Cave's music and personal testimony together illustrate that confronting adversity and being spurred to change by it is messy, often incomplete, and not completely positive. As we will see, there is some evidence that other people can be similarly transformed by adversity to become more sensitive and compassionate toward the suffering of others.

Post-Traumatic Growth as Personality Change

Theories of PTG posit that adversity can lead to meaningful changes in beliefs, behaviors, or worldviews. However, as already discussed, until recently, researchers relied mainly on self-reported positive changes rather than objective indicators of personality shifts. Critics argue that if PTG represents genuine change, it should be observable in stable patterns of thought, emotion, and behavior—core elements of personality.[11] Such scrutiny addresses whether adversity truly reshapes who a person *is*, rather than just how they report *feeling* in the wake of trauma. As I explored in Chapter 5, there's a critical distinction between perceived growth and actual change. The retrospective methods commonly used to assess PTG are susceptible to memory biases, social desirability effects, and cultural scripting. These methodological concerns have led researchers to ask more fundamental questions: Does suffering alter personality in measurable ways? And if so, what types of changes can we reliably observe, and under what conditions do they emerge?

What Is Personality?

Modern personality psychology defines personality as relatively stable patterns that influence how an individual thinks, feels, and acts across diverse situations.[12] Stability does not imply rigidity; traits such as conscientiousness or extraversion can shift across the life span and potentially in the wake of major life events. Adversity might catalyze such shifts by prompting new goals, altered behaviors, and changed self-perceptions. In this sense, PTG becomes a question of whether these challenging experiences facilitate enduring personality development rather than transient coping responses.

This distinction between temporary adaptation and lasting change is crucial. Many people report feeling different after trauma, but the key question is whether these self-perceived changes manifest in observable, persistent patterns of behavior, thoughts, and emotions. By examining PTG through the lens of personality science, we can distinguish between beliefs about change and dispositional changes in how people consistently engage with their environment.

In contemporary personality science, Dan McAdams (whose work I discussed in depth in Chapter 4)[13] has proposed a three-tier model that offers a useful framework for understanding how growth might manifest at different levels of psychological functioning. This model suggests that personality characteristics can be defined at multiple, distinct levels. At the most basic level are traits—broad, stable dispositions such as extraversion and agreeableness that form the foundation of temperament and typically show considerable consistency across situations and time. The middle tier consists of characteristic adaptations—more malleable, context-dependent elements, including personal goals, coping strategies, and relationship patterns that reflect how individuals adapt their traits to specific life circumstances. At the highest level is narrative identity—the integrative life stories that define who we are and how we interpret experiences, providing meaning and coherence to our lives.

This framework helps explain why adversity might affect individuals differently. A traumatic event may only lead to modest changes in a person's trait levels, but could be more impactful in its effects on characteristic adaptations or even dramatic revisions to their life narrative, creating a complex mapping of potential personality change following adversity.[14] This model illuminates why adversity might affect different people in different ways. Imagine Shashi, who has always been easygoing and cooperative. A serious car accident doesn't alter this underlying agreeableness, but it does spark new adaptations: She starts practicing daily mindfulness to manage anxiety and becomes more protective of family relationships, insisting on regular check-ins. The event also reshapes her life narrative—she now sees herself as a survivor whose close brush with death gave her a clearer sense of purpose. An individual may reinterpret prior suffering as an impetus for moral or psychological change, forging a "redemption narrative." However, I think that such narratives, to constitute real growth, must be a reflection of lasting changes in values or dispositions (e.g., virtues).[15]

Traits are broad, relatively stable dimensions of personality, such as extraversion, neuroticism, or openness (often summarized by the Big Five model).[16] As we'll discuss later in this chapter, research suggests that large trait change in adults is rare, but not impossible. Trauma might act as a key life event that alters one's typical level of traits like agreeableness or conscientiousness, but findings are mixed. Multiple longitudinal studies have found limited major trait shifts for most people after trauma (see Table 6.1), challenging the idea of broad personality change.

While personality traits are typically seen as relatively stable, recent theories suggest that traits also possess substantial flexibility—as highlighted in contemporary personality accounts such as Whole Trait Theory[17]—which I discuss in more detail later. This perspective highlights that personality states vary within individuals across different contexts. Consequently, intentional behavior-based interventions—such as encouraging individuals to act in ways aligned with desired traits (e.g., behaving more compassionately)—could potentially foster long-term personality change linked with PTG.

An intriguing yet underexplored hypothesis is that individuals might experience growth predominantly in domains consistent with their pre-trauma personality traits.[18] For example, those naturally extraverted may be more likely to identify social or relational growth post-trauma, whereas individuals high in openness might report growth in spirituality or life philosophy. This possibility underscores the importance of considering personality differences when evaluating and facilitating post-traumatic growth, suggesting that tailored interventions could be more effective than one-size-fits-all approaches.

Characteristic adaptations include one's goals, values, coping strategies, beliefs, and roles, which are contextualized to time and place. These adaptations reflect how we modify our traits to life's demands. Adversity may affect this level substantially. For instance, surviving a serious illness might change someone's goals (they decide to spend more time on relationships and less on work), their values (they come to cherish health and kindness more), and their coping style (perhaps they become more spiritually inclined, or start journaling to process emotions). These sets of changes align with the five domains of PTG commonly assessed:[19] improved relationships, new life possibilities, greater appreciation of life, spiritual development, and personal strength.

As we've already discussed in Chapter 4, narrative identity reflects the internalized life story that each person constructs to make sense of themselves and their place in the world. This narrative includes key episodes, turning points, and themes that give one's life a sense of unity and purpose. Adversity frequently becomes one of those pivotal chapters in the life story.[20] In fact, revising one's narrative is a primary way people experience and solidify PTG. A survivor might narrate their trauma as "the moment I realized what is truly important in life" or "the challenge that made me who I am today." Research by McAdams[21] and others has found that people who report a "redemptive narrative" often have better mental health. I've discussed the challenges of narrative approaches in Chapter 4, but for now, the philosophical accounts of growth we've discussed align more with changes in *individual* personality characteristics.

Growth Can Manifest at Different Levels of Personality

The crucial insight from this three-tier perspective is that growth may not be an all-or-nothing phenomenon (See Figure 6.1 for a depiction of how PTG would occur at each level).[22] An individual might show substantial narrative-level change (a revised life story that incorporates growth themes) with moderate characteristic adaptations (new coping skills or values) but minimal trait-level shifts. Is this still "real" growth? The answer depends partly on how we conceptualize personality itself and whether people's everyday thoughts, feelings, and behaviors are dynamically related to their subjective sense of identity.[23]

Empirical evidence for consistent changes in Big Five traits (e.g., becoming more conscientious) is sparse; many studies find increased neuroticism post-trauma instead. Rarely, a small subset shows higher openness. In past work, I have noted that trait-level changes would represent the most robust evidence for PTG, since such change would be a clear indicator of shifts in one's patterns of thoughts, feelings, and behavior. Yet such changes are the least commonly observed in longitudinal studies.[24] When trait changes do occur, they are often specific rather than global—for example, the increase in prosocial facets of agreeableness observed in bereaved caregivers rather than across-the-board trait shifts.

At the second level, adversity can modify mid-level constructs like values, goals, or moral strengths—manifesting as increased empathy or prosociality (e.g., "altruism born of suffering"). These adaptations represent the "how" of personality functioning—specific skills, coping strategies, and motivational patterns that guide behavior in context. Research shows more consistent evidence for changes at this level, with trauma survivors frequently reporting

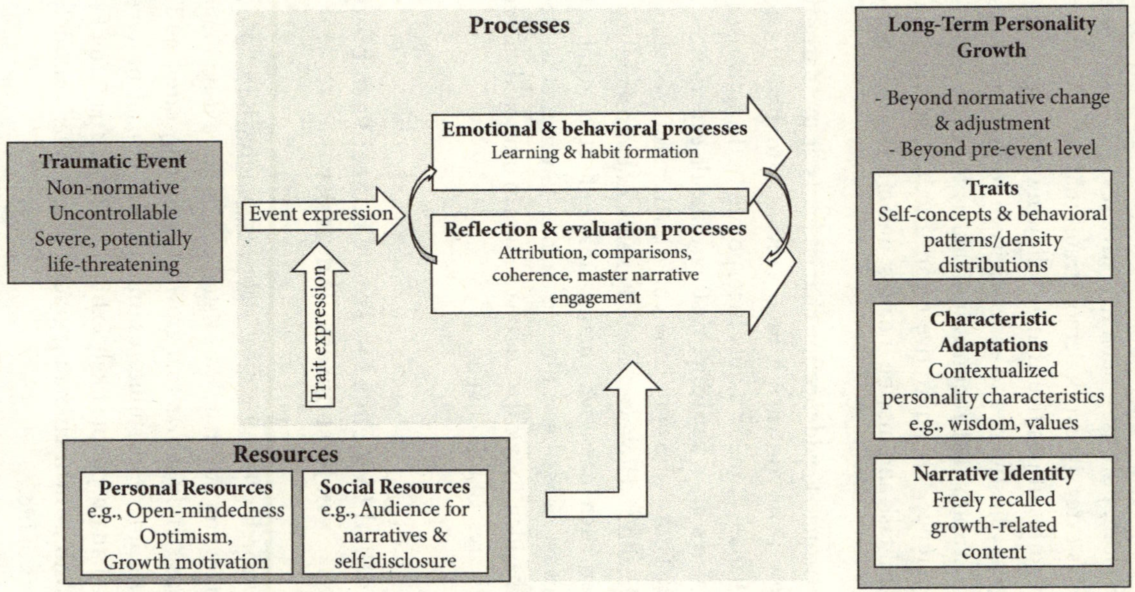

Figure 6.1 Three-tier process framework for PTG as personality change (Weststrate et al., 2022)

Reproduced with permission.

altered priorities, new goals, or enhanced relational focus. A key question is whether these adaptations eventually consolidate into more stable dispositions, as posited by current theories of personality development.[25]

At the third level, people often rewrite their life stories to highlight growth themes (e.g., wisdom, purpose). Such narrative revisions can predict well-being: McAdams's extensive work demonstrates that constructing redemptive narratives (stories of positive change following hardship) is associated with psychological adjustment and generativity in adulthood. Trauma often functions as a disruptor that requires individuals to revise their life story to maintain coherence. This narrative reconstruction represents a significant psychological task and may be the most universal form of post-trauma change.

Notably, the strongest evidence for change exists at the narrative level, where trauma survivors consistently report revisions to their life stories. As discussed in Chapter 4, many adults incorporate "redemptive sequences" into their narratives after hardship, casting difficult experiences as catalysts for growth. Those who craft coherent growth narratives tend to show better mental health.[26] However, these benefits notwithstanding, and as discussed earlier, such narrative changes may reflect cultural scripts or coping mechanisms, as well as authentic change. Given that we've already explored narrative identity, we'll focus on changes in traits and characteristic adaptations in the rest of this chapter.

Longitudinal Evidence for Trait Change: Variability in Responses to Adversity

Longitudinal research offers the most rigorous window into how personality changes following adversity. Most studies that have used longitudinal designs have consistently shown that growth is generally rare (see Table 6.1 for a selective summary of studies examining the impact of adverse life events).[27] Instead, many people likely exhibit a complex pattern of setbacks and advances, with growth emerging gradually and often unevenly across different domains of life.

The methodological strengths of longitudinal approaches are substantial: they can distinguish between temporary coping responses and enduring change, control for normative development that would have occurred regardless of trauma, identify nonlinear trajectories that cross-sectional

Table 6.1 Studies Examining Changes in Psychological Constructs Following Adversity

Authors	Sample	Adversity Type	Follow-Up Period	Psychological Constructs	Key Findings
Affleck et al.[a]	287 heart attack survivors	Medical crisis	8 years	Perceived benefits, subsequent morbidity	Early benefit-finding predicted lower morbidity at eight-year follow-up. Causal attributions influenced health outcomes.
Bonanno et al.[b]	205 bereaved spouses	Bereavement	6, 18 months	Resilience, depression, grief	Identified distinct trajectories: resilience (45.9%), common grief that captured 90.2% of the sample (10.7%), depressed-improved (10.2%), chronic grief (15.6%), chronic depression (7.8%).
Bonanno et al.[c]	2,752 New York area residents	9/11 terrorist attack	7, 18 months	PTSD symptoms, depression, resilience	Resilience was observed in 65.1% of participants.
Bonanno et al.[d]	997 individuals	SARS epidemic	6, 12, 18 months	Psychological functioning, resilience	Four trajectories: resilience (35%), recovered (10%), chronic dysfunction (42%), delayed dysfunction (13%).
Carnelley et al.[e]	768 bereaved individuals	Bereavement	<1-64 years post-loss	Grief symptoms, relationship representations	Grief decreased over time but remained periodically activated decades later. Positive representations increased.
Denson et al.[f]	333 trauma survivors	Community violence	5 days, 3, 12 months	PTSD symptoms	Initial symptom severity was the only significant predictor of later PTSD severity.
Frazier et al.[g]	122 trauma survivors	Various traumas	8 weeks	Perceived growth, actual growth (measured changes)	Perceived growth was not related to actual measured changes in psychological well-being over time.

continued

Table 6.1 *continued*

Authors	Sample	Adversity Type	Follow-Up Period	Psychological Constructs	Key Findings
Frazier et al.[h]	1,528 undergraduates (n = 122 trauma survivors)	Various stressors	8 weeks	Well-being, prosocial behavior	Lifetime trauma exposure predicted increased prosocial behavior. Engaging in prosocial behavior was linked to greater well-being for recent survivors.
Fredrickson et al.[i]	47 college students	9/11 terrorist attack	Before, after attacks	Positive emotions, resilience, psychological resources	Positive emotions buffered resilient people against depression and mediated growth in psychological resources.
Galatzer-Levy et al.[j]	178 active-duty police officers	Occupational stress	6, 12, 18, 24, and 36 months	PTSD symptoms, resilience	Three trajectories: resilience (88.1%), distress-improving (10.1%), distress worsening (1.7%).
Hobfoll et al.[k]	709 civilians	Terrorist attacks	12 months	PTSD, depression, psychosocial resource loss	Resource loss predicted increased PTSD and depression. Four distinct trajectories of distress were identified: resistance (22.1%), Resilience (13.5%), Chronic Distress (54%), and Delayed Distress (10.3%).
Holgersen et al.[l]	75 disaster survivors	Natural disaster	1, 5, 27 years	PTSD symptoms, PTG	PTG was associated with poorer general mental health, an effect mediated by concurrent post-traumatic stress.
Kraemer et al.[m]	139 breast cancer patients and their partners	Cancer	10 and 20 months post-diagnosis	General growth, perceived benefits	Patients's adaptive coping predicted improved vitality and mood; partners's adaptive coping predicted greater perceived benefits.
Lam et al.[n]	285 breast cancer patients	Cancer	5 days, 1, 4, and 8 months post-surgery	Distress, satisfaction, and physical symptom distress	Four distinct trajectories of distress were identified: resilience (66%), Chronic Distress (15%), Recovered (12%), and Delayed-Recovery (7%).

Mancini et al.[o]	464 bereaved spouses	Bereavement	4 years pre-event, year of event, 4 years post-event	Subjective well-being	Trajectories of well-being included: resilience (58.7%), Acute Recovery (21.3%), Chronic Low (14.6%), and Improved (5.4%)
McMillen et al.[p]	195 traumatic event survivors	Various disasters	4-6 weeks, 3 years	Perceived benefits, PTSD	Early benefit-finding predicted lower PTSD symptoms at 3 years. Perceived benefit increased over time.
Nolen-Hoeksema & Morrow[q]	137 students	Earthquake	2 weeks pre-disaster, 10 days and 7 weeks post-earthquake	Depression, rumination, coping	Pre-disaster rumination predicted post-disaster depression. Rumination mediated stress-depression relationship.
Norris et al.[r]	561 disaster survivors; 1,267 NYC residents of 9/11	Natural disasters and terrorism	6, 18, and 24-30 months post-event	PTSD symptoms, depression	Researchers identified four common post-trauma trajectories: resistance, resilience, recovery, and chronic dysfunction. Delayed dysfunction appeared only in the 9/11 sample; relapsing/remitting was not supported in either.
Park et al.[s]	256 undergraduates	Various stressful events	6 months	Stress-related growth, coping, social support	Growth increased over time. Positive reinterpretation coping and intrinsic religiousness predicted growth.
Sears et al.[t]	92 breast cancer patients	Cancer	3, 12 months post-treatment	Benefit-finding, positive reappraisal, PTG	Positive reappraisal coping predicted better mood, health, and PTG over time, while benefit-finding did not predict outcomes.
Seery et al.[u]	2,398 nationally-representative adults	Cumulative lifetime adversity	3 years	Mental health, well-being	Moderate lifetime adversity predicted better mental health and well-being outcomes than no adversity or high adversity.

continued

Table 6.1 *continued*

Authors	Sample	Adversity Type	Follow-Up Period	Psychological Constructs	Key Findings
Specht et al.[v]	14,718 Germans	Various life events	Annually for 25 years	Big Five personality traits	Personality predicted the occurrence of several major life events; life events predicted personality change, with different traits showing distinct trajectories based on age, event type, and valence (e.g., the trait of conscientiousness increased more strongly in individuals who started their first job and decreased more strongly in individuals who retired).
Spiro et al.[w]	1,210 veterans	Combat exposure	45 years	PTSD, psychological well-being	Combat exposure had lasting effects on mental health. PTSD symptoms remained elevated decades after service.
Updegraff et al.[x]	931 US adults	9/11 terrorist attack	2 months and 2 years post-9/11	Post-traumatic stress, finding meaning	Finding meaning early on was associated with reduced long-term post-traumatic stress symptoms, whereas searching for meaning predicted worse outcomes.
Yanez et al.[y]	162 undergraduate students	Various adversity	6 weeks	Perceived PTG, measured PTG	Measured growth predicted better adjustment, while perceived growth was linked to both greater positive mood (through approach coping) and greater distress (partly through denial coping)

[a] Glenn Affleck, Howard Tennen, Sydney Croog, and Sol Levine, "Causal Attribution, Perceived Benefits, and Morbidity After a Heart Attack: An 8-Year Study," *Journal of Consulting and Clinical Psychology* 55, no. 1 (1987): 29–35.
[b] George A. Bonanno, Camille B. Wortman, Darrin R. Lehman, Roger G. Tweed, Michelle Haring, John Sonnega, Deborah Carr, and Randolph M. Nesse, "Resilience to Loss and Chronic Grief: A Prospective Study from Preloss to 18-Months Postloss," *Journal of Personality and Social Psychology* 83, no. 5 (2002): 1150–1164.
[c] George A. Bonanno, Sandro Galea, Angela Bucciarelli, and David Vlahov, "Psychological Resilience after Disaster: New York City in the Aftermath of the September 11th Terrorist Attack," *Psychological Science* 17, no. 3 (2006): 181–186.
[d] George A. Bonanno, Samuel M. Y. Ho, Jane C. K. Chan, Rosalie S. Y. Kwong, Celia K. Y. Cheung, Claudia P. Y. Wong, and Vivian C. W. Wong, "Psychological Resilience and Dysfunction Among Hospitalized Survivors of the SARS Epidemic in Hong Kong: A Latent Class Approach," *Health Psychology* 27, no. 5 (2008): 659–667.

[e] Katherine B. Carnelley, Camille B. Wortman, Niall Bolger, and Christopher T. Burke, "The Time Course of Grief Reactions to Spousal Loss: Evidence from a National Probability Sample," *Journal of Personality and Social Psychology* 91, no. 3 (2006): 476–492.

[f] Thomas F. Denson, Grant N. Marshall, Terry L. Schell, and Lisa H. Jaycox, "Predictors of Posttraumatic Distress 1 Year after Exposure to Community Violence: The Importance of Acute Symptom Severity," *Journal of Consulting and Clinical Psychology* 75, no. 5 (2007): 683–692.

[g] Patricia Frazier, Howard Tennen, Margaret Gavian, Crystal Park, Patricia Tomich, and Ty Tashiro, "Does Self-Reported Posttraumatic Growth Reflect Genuine Positive Change?," *Psychological Science* 20, no. 7 (2009): 912–919.

[h] Patricia Frazier, Christiaan Greer, Susanne Gabrielsen, Howard Tennen, Crystal Park, and Patricia Tomich, "The Relation Between Trauma Exposure and Prosocial Behavior," *Psychological Trauma: Theory, Research, Practice, and Policy* 5, no. 3 (2013): 286–294.

[i] Barbara L. Fredrickson, Michele M. Tugade, Christian E. Waugh, and Gregory R. Larkin, "What Good Are Positive Emotions in Crisis? A Prospective Study of Resilience and Emotions Following the Terrorist Attacks on the United States on September 11th, 2001," *Journal of Personality and Social Psychology* 84, no. 2 (2003): 365–376.

[j] Isaac R. Galatzer-Levy, Anita Madan, Thomas C. Neylan, Clare Henn-Haase, and Charles R. Marmar, "Peritraumatic and Trait Dissociation Differentiate Police Officers with Resilient Versus Symptomatic Trajectories of Posttraumatic Stress Symptoms," *Journal of Traumatic Stress* 24, no. 5 (2011): 557–565.

[k] Stevan E. Hobfoll, Patrick A. Palmieri, Robert J. Johnson, Daphna Canetti-Nisim, Brian J. Hall, and Sandro Galea, "Trajectories of Resilience, Resistance, and Distress During Ongoing Terrorism: The Case of Jews and Arabs in Israel," *Journal of Consulting and Clinical Psychology* 77, no. 1 (2009): 138–148.

[l] Katrine Høyer Holgersen, Hans Jakob Boe, and Are Holen, "Long-Term Perspectives on Posttraumatic Growth in Disaster Survivors," *Journal of Traumatic Stress* 23, no. 3 (2010): 413–416.

[m] Lia M. Kraemer, Annette L. Stanton, Beth E. Meyerowitz, Julia H. Rowland, and Patricia A. Ganz, "A Longitudinal Examination of Couples' Coping Strategies as Predictors of Adjustment to Breast Cancer," *Journal of Family Psychology* 25, no. 6 (2011): 963–972.

[n] Wendy W. T. Lam, George A. Bonanno, Anthony D. Mancini, Samuel Ho, Miranda Chan, Wai Ka Hung, Amy Or, and Richard Fielding, "Trajectories of Psychological Distress Among Chinese Women Diagnosed with Breast Cancer," *Psycho-Oncology* 19, no. 10 (2010): 1044–1051.

[o] Anthony D. Mancini, George A. Bonanno, and Andrew E. Clark, "Stepping Off the Hedonic Treadmill," *Journal of Individual Differences* 32, no. 3 (2011): 144–152.

[p] J. Curtis McMillen, Elizabeth M. Smith, and Rachel H. Fisher, "Perceived Benefit and Mental Health After Three Types of Disaster," *Journal of Consulting and Clinical Psychology* 65, no. 5 (1997): 733–739.

[q] Susan Nolen-Hoeksema and Jannay Morrow, "A Prospective Study of Depression and Posttraumatic Stress Symptoms After a Natural Disaster: The 1989 Loma Prieta Earthquake," *Journal of Personality and Social Psychology* 61, no. 1 (1991): 115–121.

[r] Fran H. Norris, Melissa Tracy, and Sandro Galea, "Looking for Resilience: Understanding the Longitudinal Trajectories of Responses to Stress," *Social Science & Medicine* 68, no. 12 (2009): 2190–2198.

[s] Park, Cohen, and Murch, "Assessment and Prediction of Stress-Related Growth."

[t] Sharon R. Sears, Annette L. Stanton, and Sharon Danoff-Burg, "The Yellow Brick Road and the Emerald City: Benefit-Finding, Positive Reappraisal Coping and Posttraumatic Growth in Women with Early-Stage Breast Cancer," *Health Psychology* 22, no. 5 (2003): 487–497.

[u] Mark D. Seery, E. Alison Holman, and Roxane Cohen Silver, "Whatever Does Not Kill Us: Cumulative Lifetime Adversity, Vulnerability, and Resilience," *Journal of Personality and Social Psychology* 99, no. 6 (2010): 1025–1041.

[v] Jule Specht, Boris Egloff, and Stefan C. Schmukle, "Stability and Change of Personality Across the Life Course: The Impact of Age and Major Life Events on Mean-Level and Rank-Order Stability of the Big Five," *Journal of Personality and Social Psychology* 101, no. 4 (2011): 862–882.

[w] Avron Spiro, Paula P. Schnurr, and Carolyn M. Aldwin, "Combat-Related Posttraumatic Stress Disorder Symptoms in Older Men," *Psychology and Aging* 9, no. 1 (1994): 17–26.

[x] John A. Updegraff, Roxane Cohen Silver, and E. Alison Holman, "Searching for and Finding Meaning in Collective Trauma: Results from a National Longitudinal Study of the 9/11 Terrorist Attacks," *Journal of Personality and Social Psychology* 95, no. 3 (2008): 709–722.

[y] Yanez et al., "Understanding Perceptions of Benefit Following Adversity."

studies would miss, and allow researchers to examine the processes and mechanisms that facilitate growth over time. These advantages make longitudinal research essential for validating the concept of PTG as more than just retrospective beliefs. When combined with multiple measurement approaches (self-report, informant ratings, behavioral observations), such studies provide the most compelling evidence for when and how adversity can catalyze genuine personality development.

Examples from Intensive Longitudinal Studies

In one study, we employed a year-long study design to investigate whether experiencing major negative life events leads to changes in daily manifestations of thoughts, feelings, and behaviors related to PTG and whether these changes predict longer-term shifts in overall well-being (eudaimonic well-being). The study's theoretical framework draws from contemporary personality research, suggesting that life events may impact well-being by changing daily manifestations of thoughts, feelings, and behaviors, which can eventually lead to more enduring changes.[28]

We recruited more than 1,200 adults (with an average age of forty-four) through an online crowdsourcing platform for this study. Participants completed an intake survey measuring mental health, well-being, personality, and lifetime trauma history. They next provided weekly reports over the course of one year (forty-four assessments), including whether they had experienced any negative life events that week and their current standing on five PTG domains: appreciation of life, spiritual growth, personal relationships, new possibilities, and personal strength. Additional comprehensive assessments of well-being were administered at the beginning of the study, at week forty-five, and at week fifty-two. The design enabled us to track whether negative life events predicted changes in manifestations of PTG, whether changes in PTG predicted changes in domains of well-being such as meaning and purpose, and the immediate impact of negative life events on state PTG.

During the study, 48 percent of participants reported experiencing at least one negative life event, with the most common being illness of a close relative/family member (21 percent), death of a close relative (17 percent), death of a close friend (15 percent), and personal injury/illness (14 percent). The analysis revealed that despite the yearly trajectory showing growth, we found no significant immediate increases in overall state PTG following negative life events. In fact, participants reported decreased feelings of personal strength/mastery after negative events, while also showing some increase in feelings of connection and new possibilities. Mean levels of both state PTG and well-being also remained relatively stable across the year, indicating that while individual patterns varied, the overall group demonstrated high levels of resilience.

These mixed findings highlight important challenges in understanding PTG. While negative events didn't spark immediate increases in overall PTG, the cumulative effect over time was positive for many participants. The observed decrease in personal strength suggests that resources may initially be devoted to managing the negative event rather than enabling growth, meaning that the initial aftermath of adversity may focus more on coping and stabilization. The process of growth, it seems, is more gradual than immediate.

This study demonstrates how methodological choices can lead to different conclusions about PTG. The longitudinal approach revealed a more complex picture than what retrospective self-reports might capture. Individual differences likely play an important role. While average patterns showed stability, individual trajectories varied considerably, suggesting moderating factors (e.g., social support) that warrant further research. Additionally, future studies would benefit from examining specific characteristics of life events, potential moderators of growth, and extending the time frame to capture longer-term developments. Overall, the study supports a view of PTG as a complex process that unfolds over time, rather than an immediate transformative response to adversity. This perspective aligns with contemporary theoretical frameworks of personality development that emphasize the dynamic interplay between situational experiences and traits.[29] Additionally, Infurna and Luthar's[30] groundbreaking work further challenges overly optimistic views of post-trauma trajectories. Using statistical modeling that accounted for pre-trauma functioning, they found that resilience (i.e., maintaining stable functioning) was less common than previously thought and that genuine growth trajectories (exceeding pre-trauma levels) were relatively rare.[31]

Biopsychosocial Perspectives on Post-Traumatic Growth

Emerging research has begun to examine the biopsychosocial underpinnings of personality change following adversity. Neuroscientific studies have identified changes in brain function and structure associated with traumatic experiences—some maladaptive (e.g., heightened amygdala reactivity), but others potentially growth-promoting (e.g., enhanced connectivity in networks that support meaning-making and empathy).[32]

For example, psycho-neuroimmunological research has examined how responses to trauma affect biological stress systems. In some cases, initial physiological dysregulation gives way to enhanced resilience—a biological form of "stress inoculation" that parallels psychological growth.[33] However, an unsettling possibility is that in some cases psychological growth may come at a hidden physiological cost. In one study, the health psychologist Gene Brody and his colleagues[34] studied African American youth in the rural South and found that those who showed high psychosocial competence despite socioeconomic disadvantages—the youth rated by their teachers as thriving—had elevated allostatic load by age nineteen. As allostatic load is a measure of cumulative wear and tear on the body's systems, this study suggests that these resilient young people were paying a biological price for their psychological adaptation.

This finding complicates our understanding of PTG. When we assess growth after adversity, we typically rely on psychological measures—questionnaires about meaning-making, personal strength, or life satisfaction. Yet Brody's work suggests that what appears as successful adaptation may involve trade-offs that many PTG researchers typically do not measure. In considering PTG as both a psychological and physiological phenomenon, future research should account for these potential hidden costs, as long-term health implications of maintaining psychological resilience under chronic stress remain poorly understood in PTG research.[35]

The Adversity Sweet Spot: Does *Some* Hardship Build Resilience?

As I just noted, traditional PTG research often centers on discrete traumas (e.g., accidents, disasters), but many people face cumulative adversity—chronic poverty, systemic oppression, or displacement from war. This calls for broader research that examines long-term compounding stressors rather than one-time events and investigates cross-cultural perspectives where growth may be framed in relational or spiritual (rather than individualistic) terms.

In particular, the focus of most past research on single traumas has limited our understanding of how people adapt to chronic hardship. In many communities worldwide, adversity isn't an exceptional event but an ongoing condition. As discussed in Chapter 4, growth may take different forms in those contexts than in Western individualistic frameworks, often emphasizing collective resilience, spiritual meaning, and interconnection rather than personal strength or self-discovery.[36]

One exception to this, however, is research by the social psychologist Mark Seery and his colleagues[37] that identified a curvilinear, inverse "U-shaped" relationship between the cumulative experience of multiple adverse events and psychological functioning. Their findings revealed that participants who reported zero lifetime adverse events tended to have less resilience and more difficulty coping when something negative ultimately happened. Those with an extensive history of negative events also fared poorly, as their repeated or severe hardships led to heightened vulnerability over time. In contrast, individuals who had dealt with a moderate (but non-zero) amount of adversity in their lives reported higher levels of well-being, suggesting that overcoming moderate difficulties may foster coping skills and psychological "toughening"—often referred to as *stress inoculation*. To illustrate this further, consider responses to a major economic recession. Carol, with no prior experience of significant financial hardship, might feel overwhelmed and struggle to adapt (low adversity leading to struggle). Padma, who previously navigated a period of unemployment successfully, might draw on learned coping skills and a sense of self-efficacy to proactively seek new opportunities (moderate adversity leading to resilience). Peter, who has faced relentless poverty and multiple severe economic shocks, might experience compounded stress and diminished hope, finding it harder to mobilize resources (high adversity leading to struggle).

This nonlinear pattern challenges both the "what doesn't kill you makes you stronger" maxim *and* its opposite. It suggests that some exposure to adversity, when not overwhelming, can build psychological resources that facilitate growth when future challenges arise. This might explain why some individuals with prior coping experience are better positioned to derive meaningful growth from new hardships; they've developed the adaptive capacity to transform challenge into opportunity.

However, some work I recently conducted with my former graduate student Stephanie Bossert and the developmental and quantitative psychologist Veronica Cole may complicate these findings. We found that the relationship between adversity and subsequent psychological functioning depended to a significant extent on how adversity is operationalized—specifically, both the type of adversity and its timing across the life span. In contrast to the general findings of Seery's research, we found that different forms of adversity uniquely affect subsequent well-being.[38] For example, interpersonal conflicts, including violence and abuse, consistently had strong negative associations with psychological flourishing and life satisfaction, accompanied by heightened depressive symptoms. Conversely, adversities related to loss or bereavement, experiences of natural disasters, or political violence showed more ambiguous effects, with no clear positive or negative influence consistently emerging.

These findings challenge the assumption that the effects of cumulative lifetime adversity follow a straightforward curvilinear pattern, suggesting instead that the specific nature and context of adverse events influence outcomes. Furthermore, this work highlights the possibility that different types of adversity may not neatly fit into a single cumulative adversity metric.[39] Rather, diverse categories or types of adversity may require separate examination to clarify their unique psychological impacts. One key implication of these findings is that future research needs to carefully reconsider the operational definitions and measurement of adversity, especially to better understand their specific roles in fostering either harm or growth. While Seery's work corresponds well to the idea of adversity being a teacher of sorts, more work on how cumulative lifetime adversity leads to these outcomes is needed (particularly on how psychological change is linked to physiological measures of health).

Can Suffering Build Compassion?

While some exposure to adversity may build general resilience, recent research shows that it can also cultivate specific virtues—most notably, compassion. Indeed, consistent with insights from Nick Cave (this chapter) and from Melissa Raphael and Pema Chödrön (Chapter 3), increasing evidence suggests that adversity can nurture compassion and helping (i.e., prosocial behavior). To provide one example, social psychologists Johanna Vollhardt and Ervin Staub[40] have provided preliminary empirical evidence that adversity can foster helping toward out-groups. This "altruism born of suffering" (ABS) perspective suggests that some individuals emerge from trauma not only with heightened empathy, but also with a drive to help those who are disadvantaged—sometimes even from entirely different social or ethnic groups. In one study, they found that individuals who had endured traumatic events were more likely to volunteer for stigmatized communities (e.g., unhoused people, disabled people). A second study showed that survivors expressed stronger empathy and practical support for out-group victims of the 2004 Indian Ocean tsunami. Heightened empathy broadened their moral circles, and recognition of shared vulnerability motivated inclusive altruism. However, ongoing threat or severe personal distress can undercut such altruism, emphasizing that ABS may not be a ubiquitous outcome.

These findings underscore that the "real benefits" of adversity might extend beyond personal growth, catalyzing collective prosocial change when individuals perceive shared humanity and hold benevolence beliefs about others.[41] The concept of ABS is particularly important because it moves beyond self-focused aspects of growth to consider how adversity might inspire greater concern for others. This interpersonal dimension of growth represents a significant moral development consistent with the virtue perspective presented in Chapter 2—the capacity to transform personal suffering into compassion for those unlike oneself—as well as our discussion of communal justice concerns in Chapter 3. Notably, research suggests that this kind of altruistic response is more likely when the individual has adequate social support, their own immediate distress has been addressed, they can recognize similarities between their own suffering and that of others, and cultural or community values emphasize solidarity and helping. The emergence of altruism following trauma represents one compelling form of possible "genuine" growth, particularly when it manifests in concrete behavioral change rather than merely expressed beliefs.

Related to this work, the psychologist Daniel Lim and his colleagues have conducted a series of studies examining the relationship between adverse life experiences and compassion. Their work provides empirical evidence for the idea that suffering can foster genuine prosocial tendencies (i.e., virtues).[42] In their first investigation,[43] Lim and colleagues conducted two studies examining whether the severity of past adversity predicted increased empathy-mediated compassion and helping. They found that the severity of past adverse experiences significantly predicted both perspective-taking and empathic concern. However, only empathic concern reliably predicted dispositional compassion, which in turn predicted charitable donations to the American Red Cross. This suggested that increased motivation to care about others' welfare, rather than merely one's perspective-taking ability, was the critical link between adversity and helping.

A second study replicated these findings with enhanced experimental control. Undergraduate participants encountered a confederate working with the researchers who appeared unwell but had to complete tedious tasks. The results showed that past adversity again predicted perspective-taking and empathic concern, both of which predicted trait compassion. This dispositional compassion predicted state compassion toward the confederate, which in turn predicted helping behavior (measured as time spent helping the confederate with their tasks). These initial studies showed that the severity of past adversity—rather than its frequency or recency—predicted compassion and helping, and it did so via empathy. They also demonstrated that this relationship held across different populations and contexts.

Lim and colleagues extended their investigation to examine whether adversity might protect against the "numeracy bias"—the tendency to feel less compassion for multiple victims compared to a single victim.[44] In three studies, they found that individuals who had experienced greater adversity showed more consistent compassion regardless of the number of victims. The researchers demonstrated that people who had experienced more severe adversity showed similar levels of compassion for both individual victims and groups of victims. This finding suggests adversity may foster a robust form of compassion that isn't subject to the cognitive biases that typically diminish compassion for larger groups.

Next, Lim and DeSteno[45] identified guilt as a central mechanism mediating the relationship between adversity and compassion. Across three studies, they found that people who had experienced more adversity showed greater propensity to feel guilt, which in turn predicted increased compassion and helping behavior. Notably, in the third study, they established causality by experimentally manipulating guilt. When participants were induced to feel guilty (by causing a staged accident), those with greater past adversity experienced more intense guilt and subsequently showed more compassion-driven helping behavior. To use an example, imagine someone who, in their youth, made a serious mistake that caused harm—an adverse experience involving their own actions, such as causing a major accident while driving. Years later, witnessing someone else in a similar situation, they might experience a heightened sense of guilt related to their past. This guilt, as Lim and DeSteno's work suggests, could motivate them to offer compassionate support or assistance to the person currently struggling, transforming their past failing into a capacity for deeper empathy and prosocial action.

Lim next worked with a larger team to identify a key moderator of the adversity–compassion link: beliefs about human benevolence.[46] This work represents an important extension of his research program by identifying for whom the relationship between adversity and prosociality is strongest. In Study 1, using a cross-sectional design, they found that lifetime adverse events predicted increased volunteering, empathic concern, and self-reported altruism. The relationship between adversity and altruism was significantly stronger for individuals with greater benevolence beliefs—those who view others as fundamentally good and trustworthy.

Study 2 employed a more rigorous longitudinal design with a nationally representative sample. Benevolence beliefs were assessed first, followed by measurement of adverse life events in subsequent assessments. The results showed that recent adverse experiences predicted greater volunteering and charitable involvement, but critically, only among those with high benevolence beliefs. When benevolence beliefs were low, this relationship disappeared. This introduces an important boundary condition to the adversity–compassion link: People appear most likely to respond to adversity with increased prosociality when they believe that others are fundamentally good and trustworthy. As the authors suggest, this may be because people are sensitive to the possibility that their prosocial actions will be appreciated and reciprocated. The findings also highlight that not everyone responds to adversity with increased compassion—personal worldviews, particularly beliefs about human nature, play a crucial moderating role.

The primary strength of this research program (compared to much PTG research) is its methodological diversity and rigor. These studies consistently employed multiple methods (online and laboratory studies), populations (people participating in online panels and college students), and measures (self-report and behavioral) to test their hypotheses. The use of correlational and experimental designs strengthens causal claims, particularly in the study where guilt was experimentally manipulated.[47] The research also benefits from strong theoretical development. They systematically identified and tested potential mediating mechanisms (empathy, guilt) and moderators (benevolence beliefs) that explain the adversity–compassion relationship, building a coherent theoretical model across multiple papers.

This work provides some evidence for genuine benefits of adversity rather than simply perceived growth. Unlike studies focusing on self-reported PTG, these studies demonstrate that adversity predicts behavior that benefits others. The identification of specific psychological mechanisms (empathy and guilt) and moderators (benevolence beliefs) further strengthens the claim that these are real, not illusory, benefits. Moreover, the finding that adversity protects against the numeracy bias suggests that suffering may foster a more authentic form of compassion that doesn't diminish when faced with multiple victims. The work also highlights that not all consequences of adversity are negative and that not all people respond to adversity in the same way. While acknowledging the well-documented psychological costs, this research program reveals that adversity can simultaneously foster prosocial tendencies that benefit both individuals (through increased social connection) and communities (through enhanced cooperation)—particularly among those who maintain positive beliefs about human nature. Indeed, their findings are illustrated in Cave's post-loss work on the *Red Hand Files*, where he responds to strangers' questions about grief, meaning, and suffering with empathy and compassion.

More broadly, this research program provides empirically sound evidence that adversity *can* foster meaningful change while simultaneously clarifying the domain of change (compassion, which is not an outcome typically assessed in PTG research) and demonstrating the specific conditions and mechanisms required for such change. It also provides evidence for the validity of the virtue perspective of PTG.[48] Rather than supporting either simplistic "what doesn't kill you makes you stronger" narratives or wholesale skepticism about growth, this work recognizes both the potential for genuine benefits from adversity and the contingent nature of such benefits.

How Growth Becomes Habit: When Temporary Changes Turn Permanent

The three-level framework (traits, characteristic adaptations, and narrative identity) of personality supports the idea that personality encompasses both internal dispositions and evolving life stories. If narrative changes both result from and can shape long-term goals and behaviors, such changes can lead to positive personality development. For example, someone who engages in more helping after adversity may adopt a narrative of themselves as "more compassionate after suffering" and subsequently seek new opportunities to express that compassion, gradually developing habits and skills that solidify this new self-conception. Such a perspective is consistent with a contemporary model of personality that I have worked on for the last ten years with the personality psychologist Will Fleeson: Whole Trait Theory (WTT).[49]

In plain terms, WTT says each personality trait has two sides. One is the "what you do" side—the overall pattern of your behavior over time (denoted by Trait_DES at the bottom of Figure 6.2). WTT describes this as a "density distribution" of states, which simply means how often you act in ways that express a trait, like being sociable or organized. The other side is the "why you do it" side—the goals, beliefs, values, expectations, and self-views or identity that cause or generate those behaviors (Trait_EXP at the top of Figure 6.2, as well as the processes highlighted in Figure 6.1 earlier as they apply to traits).[50] People can be generally consistent (e.g., Isabel is usually more outgoing than Peter) and still shift in particular moments and contexts (e.g., Peter might be more outgoing than Isabel in gym class). When an individual experiences an adverse life event, both components of their personality traits may undergo significant pressure for reorganization and potential change (as shown in Figure 6.2).

Specifically, after a major stressor, both sides can be pushed to reorganize. Behavior can change first in the short term. A typically outgoing person might withdraw for a while. Deeper, more durable change happens when the "whys" shift—when beliefs, goals, and interpretations are revised. A cancer survivor, for example, may come to prioritize close relationships and read daily hassles in a new light; those changes in priorities and meaning then nudge behavior toward more gratitude, patience, or compassion. Similarly, returning to our divorce example from the previous chapter, growth would mean not just telling a different story about the past relationship (e.g., it was "miserable from day one"), but consistently demonstrating new relationship skills—better communication, healthier boundaries, increased empathy—that are observable in daily life.

One possible learning pathway as stipulated by WTT would go as follows: First, adversity disrupts old beliefs and goals. Next, people experiment with new behaviors that fit the changed reality. Useful or positive behaviors are reinforced by good outcomes. Over time, the useful behaviors—and the motivations that support them—accumulate into a new, steadier pattern. The process follows realistic limits and natural connections: biological, social, cultural, and logical. For instance, a stronger appreciation for others

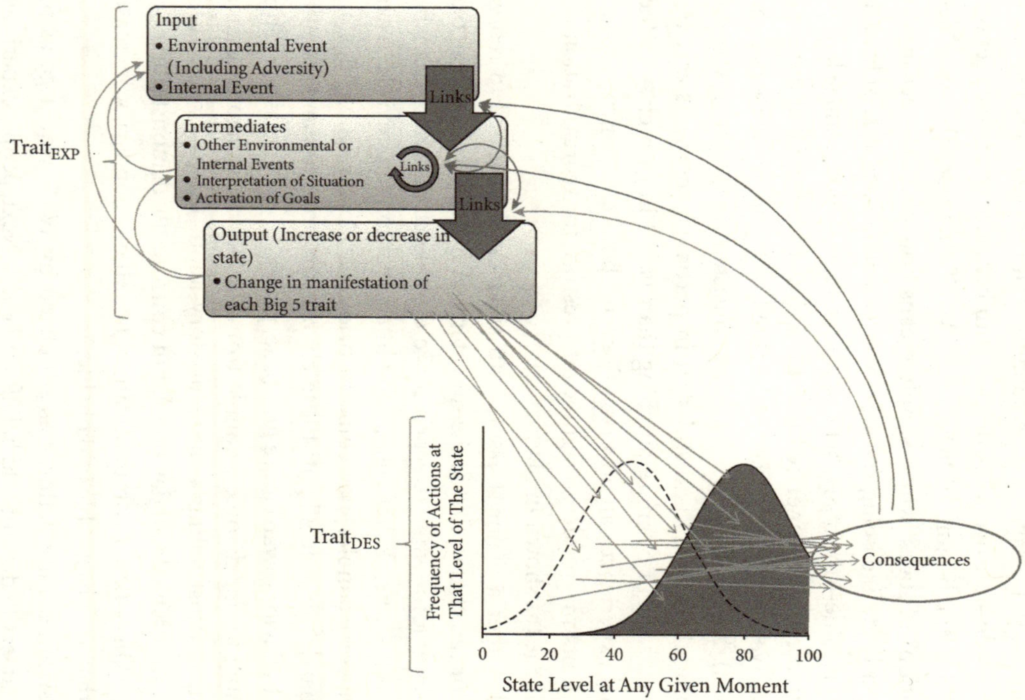

Figure 6.2 Whole Trait Theory[a]

[a]Pieces of this figure appeared in a figure published in final edited form in William Fleeson and Eranda Jayawickreme, "Whole Trait Theory," *Journal of Research in Personality* 56 (2015): 82–92.

often pairs with greater compassion because the two dynamically connect well together.

However, lasting positive change is hard because several components of the goals, beliefs, values, expectations, and self-views that work together to cause traits need to move together. Indeed, change may falter when new goals clash with old beliefs, when family or workplaces reward pre-trauma patterns, when people notice tensions between new aspirations and earlier priorities, or when new behaviors bring unanticipated costs. Any of these can pull a person back toward earlier habits.

On this view, change is more likely to endure when multiple mechanisms line up in the same direction, when communities reinforce the new behaviors, when helpful behaviors repeatedly produce good outcomes, and when the person's life story absorbs the change—"this is who I am now." For example, consider a shy neighbor who survives a natural disaster in a cooperative community. If their beliefs about mutual support shift, they may start initiating conversations, joining groups, and offering help. If these actions are encouraged and pay off (that is, they experience positive consequences from their behavior change; see the bottom right corner of Figure 6.2), their overall behavior pattern can shift toward more frequent outgoing moments. Growth here is both internal (beliefs and goals) and visible (behavior).

Taken together, WTT offers cautious optimism about the possibility of PTG. Lasting personality change will be difficult because it requires coordinated shifts in the underlying mechanisms that explain traits, but trauma can be a powerful catalyst precisely because it can impact several mechanisms at once. In other words, growth is possible but not easy to achieve—an outlook that fits both virtue-based perspectives on PTG[51] and the Aristotelian account of habit formation reviewed in Chapter 2.[52] That said, the shift toward prosocial action predicted by the ABS perspective is a good example of what WTT would predict: a traumatic experience leading to a reshaping of core beliefs and values (the "why"), which in turn drives new, observable patterns of behavior (the "what"). WTT helps us understand how this process unfolds.

Yet another example is Nick Cave reporting developing greater spiritual insights by reflecting on and responding to thousands of people who write in to his *Red Hand Files* forum.[53] My recent work has attempted to illustrate these dynamics. In a year-long study of major life events and daily social experiences, negative life events predicted more negative social encounters later on; feeling worse on one day also forecast more negative encounters the next and vice versa.[54] At the same time, some people reported that positive moments felt especially good after the experience of hardship—a possible route to growth. These patterns suggest that the "what" (daily behavior and experience) and the "why" (beliefs, goals, expectations) continually shape each other. Over time, that loop can shift a person's overall behavior pattern and, if enough mechanisms align, alter the underlying system that drives behavior.

This perspective also has practical implications for how we should expect PTG to show up in people's lives. For example, a survivor of trauma might *both* show striking compassion in community work *and* struggle with trust at home; both patterns of growth/depreciation are real and deserve equal attention.[55] The more helpful question, in other words, is not whether someone has "achieved" PTG but where, how, and under what conditions they are finding new ways to engage with their world.

Toward Personality-Based Models of Post-Traumatic Growth

The limitations of current PTG research, as detailed in Chapter 5, combined with the insights presented in this chapter, call for more sophisticated models of how people might genuinely grow through adversity. Traditional conceptualizations of PTG have relied too heavily on retrospective self-reports and failed to distinguish between perceived growth and measurable personality change. Moving forward, it is important to create integrative frameworks that differentiate coping from growth, integrate multiple levels of analysis, account for temporal dynamics, consider cultural and contextual influences, and identify mechanisms that foster growth. They should also capture the complex nonlinear trajectories that unfold over time, recognize how growth manifests differently across cultural contexts and types of adversity, and specify the processes—such as meaning-making, social validation, identity reconstruction, and deliberate practice—through which adversity sometimes leads to positive change. By addressing these considerations, researchers can develop more credible research on PTG that both acknowledges its complexity and more accurately captures its manifestation. In my view, the reconceptualization of PTG as positive personality change[56] represents one promising approach, grounding growth in established personality science while acknowledging the role of narrative and social factors. As I've discussed above, WTT represents one possible model that can undergird future research on the topic.

This chapter has explored how adversity can spark such changes. Key takeaways include the fact that authentic change can involve shifts in traits, adaptations, or narrative identity, but not all adversity leads to all forms of change. The evidence suggests that narrative-level changes are most common, characteristic adaptations show moderate evidence, and trait-level changes are documented least frequently. Additionally, the possibility of growth depends on personal resources, social supports, and cultural frames.

It should also be emphasized that many people do not experience long-term benefits from trauma. The longitudinal research I reviewed earlier indicates that while resilience (i.e., recovery to baseline) is common, growth beyond pre-trauma functioning is relatively rare and follows diverse trajectories. Such longitudinal and experience-sampling approaches are also crucial for distinguishing transient perceptions from lasting change.

In particular, the strongest evidence comes from studies that include pre-trauma baselines, multiple post-trauma assessments, and diverse measurement approaches. The curvilinear relationship between adversity exposure and well-being suggests that while moderate exposure to challenges may foster resilience, experiencing multiple adverse events typically undermines it. Additionally, collective adversity may foster communal rather than purely individual growth, as illustrated by research on ABS.

Hope *and* Realism

As my research program has evolved over the past decade, I've sometimes been asked (especially in media interviews) whether my findings have made me more cynical about human resilience. The question reflects a misunderstanding of what drives my work. My goal with this research program has not been to debunk growth narratives, but to understand how people manage adversity with greater clarity. My own journey from growing up in Sri Lanka to an academic career in the United States has shown me *both* the remarkable capacity for human adaptation *and* the danger of oversimplified narratives.[57] The empirical reality of positive change—complex, contextual, and often modest—in my mind reflects *reality* more closely than either romantic triumph stories or nihilistic dismissals.

Nick Cave's example from earlier in this chapter illustrates the importance of recognizing this complexity. Cave's "experience of growth" following his loss was neither immediate nor complete; it coexisted with profound grief and emerged through deliberate engagement with his loss—through artistic expression, spiritual questioning, and connection with others experiencing similar pain. His change was not simply a matter of "becoming stronger," but of developing new capacities for empathy, spiritual insight, and creative expression. These changes manifested not just in how he spoke about himself, but in concrete actions: his artistic output, his interactions with fans, and his embracing of vulnerability. It is also worth considering that the changes in his art, his increased empathy, and his deeper spiritual insights, while arising in part from the loss of his sons Arthur and Jethro, do not compensate for their deaths. In other words, while his growth emerged from unbearable loss, it is not necessarily a justification for it.

As we move toward a more complex understanding of adversity's potential benefits, we need to hold space for both hope *and* realism.[58] Growth is possible—sometimes profound and life-altering, as seen in Cave's life—but it emerges through complex interactions between individual psychology, social support, cultural frameworks, and deliberate engagement with suffering. By recognizing these complexities, we can better support those navigating adversity while avoiding the pitfalls of narratives that either romanticize suffering or dismiss the possibility of genuine change.

7

Fostering Growth After Adversity

Interventions and Considerations

Understanding when and how genuine growth might emerge from adversity naturally leads to practical questions: Can this process be facilitated? Should it be? What approaches might support those who wish to find meaning or change after trauma, without imposing redemptive expectations on those who don't? In this chapter, I aim to translate these theoretical insights and empirical findings into practical considerations for researchers, clinicians, and communities. By examining specific intervention approaches—including programs I've helped develop and have studied—we'll explore how both conceptual clarity and methodological rigor can inform more ethical, culturally attuned practices. These interventions represent not just practical tools but also embodiments of this book's core argument: that recovery and possible growth after adversity are only possible within supportive contexts that honor both individual agency and diverse cultural frameworks.

Should We Attempt to Cultivate Growth Following Adversity?

In July 2012, I led a training workshop for counselors working at the Family Rehabilitation Centre in Anuradhapura, Sri Lanka. Our goal was to introduce counselors, many of whom were helping survivors of Sri Lanka's civil war, to principles from positive psychology and post-traumatic growth (PTG). I vividly recall their enthusiasm as we discussed ways to help clients find meaning, identify silver linings, and uncover potential lessons in their adversity. To these counselors, a growth-oriented approach offered something distinctly hopeful, beyond standard trauma-focused therapy, which often felt insufficient given the chronic and ongoing nature of their clients' traumatic experiences. Many clients had endured multiple traumas and would likely encounter further adversity in the future; thus, the counselors saw immense value in shifting their therapeutic approach toward cultivating resilience and growth, rather than merely revisiting and reprocessing painful events.

Yet, despite the genuine enthusiasm these counselors expressed, this experience left me with questions about the assumptions underlying their interest. Is a growth-oriented approach truly beneficial for everyone, especially in contexts of prolonged trauma and systemic injustice? Could emphasizing resilience and silver linings minimize the importance of addressing the harsh realities survivors continue to face? How might culturally sensitive interventions help survivors authentically process trauma without imposing a redemption arc?

Here I shift from debates about the nature and measurement of PTG to practical questions about facilitating growth in real-world contexts. Building on the ethical, cultural, and methodological discussions of previous chapters, I examine interventions, community-based strategies, and the ethical concerns involved in attempting to foster growth. Throughout, I emphasize that growth is never guaranteed, and that individuals must have the freedom to define—or decline—the possibilities for growth within their own lived experience.[1]

Principles of Intervention

Reflective Practices and Structured Therapies

A core assumption behind many PTG-focused programs is that reflective, meaning-making activities—such as journaling,[2] narrative writing,[3] and guided self-reflection[4]—can help individuals process trauma in ways that open the door to new perspectives and possibly growth. Cognitive-behavioral therapies such as prolonged exposure (PE),[5] cognitive processing therapy (CPT),[6] and acceptance and commitment therapy (ACT),[7] as well as narrative-focused approaches, have been evaluated for their potential to spotlight lessons or strengths that may emerge from adversity.[8]

Narrative-Focused Approaches: Writing about traumatic experiences in a structured format[9] can promote emotional processing and reconstruction of personal stories.[10] Individuals are encouraged to explore how the event impacts their values, relationships, and future goals, not just to recount what happened. These narrative approaches help survivors develop coherent accounts of their experiences that integrate the trauma into their broader life story,[11] potentially facilitating a shift from feeling defined by trauma to seeing it as one chapter in a continuing narrative. So, a refugee might write about their forced displacement through guided journaling not just as a story of loss, but also as a testament to their resilience, focusing on the skills they developed and the new perspectives gained, and ultimately framing their journey as one of survival and adaptation that could inform their future contributions to a new community.

Cognitive-Behavioral Approaches: Trauma-focused psychotherapeutic interventions for trauma survivors (e.g., CPT, PE)[12,13] can facilitate growth by helping individuals identify and challenge maladaptive beliefs about themselves, others, and the world. By examining "stuck points" in thinking (e.g., "I am permanently damaged," or "The world is completely dangerous"), survivors using CPT can develop more nuanced perspectives that acknowledge both the reality of suffering and the possibility of rebuilding. This cognitive restructuring creates space for new meanings to emerge and can help translate insights into concrete behavioral changes. In PE, patients allow themselves to feel the emotions associated with the trauma. Once they do this, they have the cognitive space to reflect on their experience and change some of the beliefs they have about the trauma, themselves, their ability to cope, and the world. ACT[14] offers a particularly promising framework for genuine growth by focusing on psychological flexibility—the capacity to contact the present moment fully while persisting in or changing behavior in service of chosen values. Rather than eliminating distress, ACT helps survivors clarify what matters most to them and take committed action in those directions, even amid ongoing pain.[15] This values-based approach can foster authentic growth by encouraging survivors to engage with life in meaningful ways, rather than merely trying to feel better. For example, a person with chronic pain (adversity) using ACT might clarify that their core value is being an engaged family member. While pain might persist, they commit to actions aligned with this value, like attending a grandchild's school event for a short period, even if it's uncomfortable. The growth is the values-driven action despite pain, leading to a richer life.

Mindfulness-Based Interventions: Practices that cultivate nonjudgmental awareness of present-moment experience[16] can help trauma survivors develop a new relationship with difficult thoughts and emotions. Rather than being overwhelmed by trauma-related reactions or attempting to suppress them, mindfulness allows survivors to observe these experiences with self-compassion.[17] This stance of "witnessing" creates psychological space that may allow for new insights and perspectives to emerge organically rather than through forced positive thinking. Someone experiencing anxiety after a job loss might use mindfulness to observe their anxious thoughts ("I'll never find another job") without judgment. This creates space to realize that these are just thoughts, not facts, allowing them to engage more calmly and effectively in their job search, perhaps discovering a new capacity for managing uncertainty and fear.

Positive Reappraisal: Some interventions employ strategies to help participants reframe or reinterpret adversity in meaningful ways, rather than focusing solely on loss.[18] As earlier chapters caution, however, not every negative event yields beneficial reinterpretations—and people should not be pressured into doing such work. When introduced with sensitivity and timing, however, reappraisal techniques can help survivors recognize aspects of their experience that may contain seeds of growth, such as moments of unexpected kindness from others or discoveries of personal strength previously unrecognized.

Each of these therapeutic approaches offers distinct pathways to potential growth, but all share certain key elements: They create a safe environment for exploring painful experiences, validate suffering without defining survivors by it, offer tools for meaning-making without prescribing specific meanings, and balance acceptance of reality with the possibility for change. The most effective interventions may integrate elements from multiple approaches that are tailored to individual needs and cultural contexts.[19]

Role Modeling and Exemplars

Stories of exemplars—individuals who have navigated trauma successfully—can inspire hope and highlight diverse pathways to well-being. Yet if interventions rely too heavily on "success stories," participants may feel pressured to emulate them. Helpful programs may balance inspirational examples with open-ended exploration, inviting participants to discover their own modes of resilience without feeling obligated to produce a redemptive narrative. This balance is delicate. When we present stories of resilience, we risk implicitly suggesting that there is a "right way" to recover or respond. The most ethical approaches acknowledge multiple valid paths through adversity, some involving clear growth, others emphasizing gradual acceptance or simply finding stability in a changed life.

Two PTG-Focused Programs: SecondStory and COMPASS

My own work with PTG interventions (led by the clinical psychologist Ann Marie Roepke) has centered on SecondStory[20] and COMPASS[21]—two programs rooted in the idea that reflective meaning-making practices can help individuals cope and possibly grow after adversity. From the start, we endeavored to avoid interventions that imposed a singular redemption narrative. Instead, both initiatives encouraged diverse pathways to well-being, acknowledging that some participants may not resonate with growth language. Indeed, the original SecondStory intervention materials did not even include the term *post-traumatic growth* out of an abundance of caution, in hopes of ensuring that participants did not feel pressure to conform to a specific positive narrative. Given the methodological challenges outlined earlier, our interventions also deliberately incorporated rigorous methods to ensure we assess authentic growth.

SecondStory: Early Lessons from a Group-Based Intervention

SecondStory was our first attempt to apply PTG theory in a structured, group-based format. Initially designed by Roepke, SecondStory was intended to be helpful to adults who had experienced a range of traumatic or painful events, although for pragmatic and clinical reasons the initial randomized controlled trial focused on recruiting individuals who had experienced bereavement. SecondStory combined multiple core techniques—including guided individual reflection, group discussion, and future-oriented goal setting—drawn from well-being science, narrative therapy research, and positive psychology. The core idea was that reframing one's life story (both past and future) could help foster recovery and growth. The program consisted of a one-day intervention with a follow-up booster. The modules covered included the following:[22]

Session 1: Getting Started Together. Participants begin by helping everyone feel comfortable. They introduce themselves through an icebreaker activity, learn what the program involves, and play a card game that shows how we all create stories about our lives. This sets the stage for thinking about how they can reshape their own stories after difficult experiences.

Session 2: Discovering Your Strengths. Participants explore personal strengths they may not have recognized. Using a deck of cards showing different character strengths (like courage, kindness, or creativity), they watch a video of people displaying these strengths and then share stories about times they showed strength during their own struggles. The group offers supportive feedback, helping each person see capabilities they might have overlooked.

Session 3: Seeing Things Differently. Through optical illusion videos that change depending on your viewing angle, participants explore how perspective shapes experience. They discuss how their beliefs and priorities may have shifted after their loss or trauma—what once seemed important might now feel trivial, while things they overlooked before might now hold deep meaning.

Session 4: Understanding Changed Relationships. Participants create diagrams showing how their social circles changed after their adversity—who moved closer, who drifted away, who unexpectedly appeared. They discuss how trauma can deepen some relationships while straining others and explore how their own suffering might have made them more compassionate toward others facing difficulties.

Session 5: Imagining New Directions. Through drawing and writing exercises, participants explore possibilities for their future that they might not have considered before their adversity. They discuss how their values may have shifted and what new paths might now feel meaningful or important.

Session 6: Making Concrete Plans. Moving from possibility to action, participants create specific, achievable goals (i.e., SMART goals [Specific, Meaningful, Adaptive, Realistic, and Time-framed])[23] for the coming months. They learn a practical framework for goal setting and work with peers to refine their plans, identifying potential obstacles and strategies to overcome them.[24] Each person makes a public commitment to their goal, creating accountability.

Session 7: Wrapping Up. The group reflects on what they've learned and expresses appreciation for one another's courage in sharing their stories. Participants write letters of encouragement to future program participants and receive similar letters from past participants—creating a chain of support across time.

Follow-Up Booster Session: Checking Progress. Several weeks later, the group reconvenes to share progress on their goals and any new insights. Through an exercise where they imagine looking back from a successful future,[25] participants refine their plans and recommit to their chosen paths forward.

Our randomized controlled trial (RCT) with 112 bereaved adults yielded mixed results. SecondStory participants showed significant improvements in depression scores compared to participants in an active control condition (in this case, expressive writing) at both post-intervention and six-month follow-up, suggesting that the activities included in this program can ease distress. However, SecondStory was not necessarily more effective than the active control for facilitating PTG: Both SecondStory participants and expressive writing participants showed increases in scores on the Post-Traumatic Growth Inventory (PTGI) after completing their respective activities. When PTG was measured in another way (the Current Standing PTGI), there was a modest effect size suggesting that SecondStory participants experienced gains whereas expressive writing participants did not; however, this effect size was not statistically significant. Of note, this RCT tested SecondStory against an intervention already documented to facilitate PTG (i.e., expressive writing), and as such, is a more rigorous initial test; many initial RCTs compare a novel intervention to a waiting list.

COMPASS: Expanded Scope, Additional Values-Based Exercises, and Technological Innovations

COMPASS evolved from SecondStory, retaining its reflective and narrative underpinnings but with significant changes to its content and its format. First, we broadened the participant base: The study was open to anyone experiencing traumatic or adverse events, not just bereavement. This expanded scope enabled us to test whether similar meaning-making approaches could be beneficial across different types of adversity. We also extended the intervention from one day to six weeks, which allowed more time for processing, and included more explicit values clarification exercises, self-compassion techniques, and role-model examples. Participants identified personal values using structured exercises and reflected on how these values could guide them even amid suffering. In addition, self-compassion practices helped participants acknowledge their pain without judgment, creating psychological space for exploration without pressure to "move on" prematurely. Also, embedded exemplar stories featured diverse individuals who had navigated similar challenges, highlighting various paths to recovery without presenting a single "right way" to heal. The intervention was delivered online, rather than in person, in order to increase access—particularly in the context of the COVID-19 pandemic. We also included weekly text-based reminders to support participants in integrating the program content into their daily lives (as outlined below).

The COMPASS program structure included six separate group-based sessions instead of one long session, allowing more time for processing, integration, action, and skill-building:

Session 1: Values and Goals. The session opens with a concise orientation that previews the program's scope, transitions into participant introductions enlivened by a lighthearted icebreaker, and then pivots to a discussion of values—their definition, their influence on everyday choices, and the ways exemplary figures embody them. Similar to session 1 of SecondStory, participants next engage in a card-sorting exercise, ranking values by personal importance to clarify individual priorities. The session concludes with a brief tutorial on implementation intentions ("If... then..." plans) that translates identified values into concrete, actionable goals.

Session 2: Activating Your Strengths. Similar to session 2 of SecondStory, the session begins with a guided exploration of character strengths, followed by a short video that showcases specific strengths. After a facilitated discussion that unpacks the exemplar's key strengths, participants pair up or form small groups to share key moments from their own life stories and receive supportive, strengths-based feedback from peers. The meeting concludes with a group discussion on how consciously mobilizing one's signature strengths can improve coping in the face of adversity.

Session 3: Self-Compassion. The session starts with a focused exploration of self-compassion, anchored by curated video clips that contrast moments of its presence with instances where these qualities are absent. Guided discussion then invites participants to examine how self-judgment and self-compassion surface in their own lives, setting the stage for the introduction of a practical, evidence-based self-compassion tool. The meeting ends with a reflective prewriting exercise followed by a guided loving-kindness meditation.

Session 4: Deeper Relationships. The session begins with a set of talking points on connection and support, followed by a brief video/narrative that traces how relationships evolve in the aftermath of adversity. Participants next map their own networks in three snapshots—before the challenging event, as they exist today, and as they would like them to look in the future—creating a visual trajectory of change and aspiration. A facilitated discussion next unpacks patterns that emerge from these models, leading to a collaborative exercise in which attendees outline concrete steps to strengthen ties: identifying whom to approach for connection, where to seek help, and how to offer assistance to others.

Session 5: New Possibilities and Goals. This session centers on cultivating hope and envisioning new possibilities. Concise talking points are discussed that link goal setting with mental contrasting and implementation intentions, popularly framed as the WOOP method (Wish, Outcome, Obstacle, Plan). A brief video narrative is used that illustrates these principles in action, after which participants pair up to coach one another through the process of articulating clear goals and drafting WOOP-based action plans. The workshop ends with a "backward-imaging" exercise that invites each person to visualize their desired future state and mentally trace the concrete steps required to reach it, reinforcing both motivation and strategic planning.

Session 6: Closing and Contributing. The program concludes with a reflective wrap-up session in which participants articulate their key takeaways and distill the insights they most want to carry forward. A guided dialogue then invites them to formulate advice they would offer others facing adversity, crystallizing group insights. To translate reflection into tangible support, attendees receive an open invitation to craft a personalized self-help artifact—whether a letter, song, or another creative medium—designed to share strategies and encouragement for navigating future challenges.

The integration of ACT principles was particularly important. By focusing on values clarification, COMPASS helped participants identify what mattered to them beyond the trauma, creating a bridge between their pre-trauma identity and their emerging post-trauma self. This values-based approach avoided prescribing a specific form of growth, instead asking: What matters to you now, and how might you move toward it, even amid pain?

Our COMPASS mixed-methods trial ran between February and July 2022 with thirty-nine adults who had experienced significant adversity yielded more encouraging findings. COMPASS participants showed significantly larger reductions in depressive symptoms than a wait-list control across the twelve-week assessment window, indicating that the program's activities can meaningfully ease distress. They also demonstrated greater gains in PTG when measured with the Current Standing PTGI, whereas controls showed little change. Session ratings were uniformly high, facilitator fidelity was judged good to excellent, and daily-diary completion exceeded

65 percent, underscoring the feasibility of conducting such assessments. Although these results emerge from a relatively small sample and against a wait list rather than an active comparator, they nevertheless position COMPASS as a more promising, scalable intervention that warrants a larger trial to confirm efficacy and benchmark it against established programs.

Online Access

COMPASS was delivered via online platforms in a group-based format, as an acknowledgment of the *social* nature of resilience. Specifically, given that the intervention was tested in the context of the COVID-19 pandemic, it was likely that participants felt comfortable finding connection with others given the common anxiety about the pandemic—even online—and additionally found the reliable structure of the meeting schedule helpful. In addition, we added a text-based system called MobileCoach that sent weekly reminders and encouragement, helping sustain participants' momentum between sessions. The MobileCoach platform delivered brief daily or biweekly prompts that reinforced session content. Our approach also recognized cultural adaptation: This intervention can be adjusted to respect local beliefs and norms, whether spiritual or secular. For example, when implementing COMPASS with more religious populations, it would be possible to incorporate faith-based language and examples when discussing values and meaning.

The digital component of COMPASS addressed a practical challenge: encouraging participants to enact the skills learned in the sessions in their daily lives outside of formal therapeutic/intervention settings. By extending support into participants' daily lives, we created more opportunities for the integration of insights and practice of new skills. The online and text-based system also reached those who might otherwise have limited access to support, particularly in remote or underserved communities.

Ethical Lessons and Methodological Refinements

Both SecondStory and COMPASS highlighted valuable lessons about how to ethically and effectively support people after adversity. Both programs confirmed that some participants prioritize stability or acceptance over change. Neither approach forced a "redemptive" interpretation. We learned more about concrete ways to validate multiple outcomes, framing growth as one possibility among many legitimate responses to adversity. Additionally, instead of relying solely on retrospective PTG scales, COMPASS used a "current-standing" PTG assessment (i.e., we asked participants to report their current level on a PTG-relevant domain, rather than estimate how much they had grown in the domain) and experience-sampling methods that sampled daily thoughts, feelings, and behaviors to capture incremental, real-time changes in well-being. This methodological shift helped us detect changes that might not be captured by standard PTG measures.

Also, by encouraging participants to share culturally specific narratives (e.g., exemplars they admire), the interventions supported multiple frameworks for understanding responses to adversity. We introduced multiple themes relevant to PTG and invited participants to engage—or not engage—with these themes in the ways that felt right to them. This included discussion of both individual transformation and more relational dimensions of recovery and growth.

The methodological refinements in measurement deserve particular attention, given our discussions in Chapter 5 about the limitations of current PTG assessments. By using current-standing measures and real-time assessments, COMPASS attempted to capture actual changes in functioning rather than just perceptions of growth. These approaches aligned with our understanding that authentic growth should manifest in observable patterns of thought, emotion, and behavior—not just in how people tell their story.

Our experience-sampling method involved brief daily assessments through the MobileCoach platform, where participants reported on current mood and stress levels, as well as growth-relevant behaviors. This approach provided a richer picture of participants' daily experiences than traditional pre-post measures, revealing patterns and fluctuations that helped us understand the nonlinear nature of recovery and growth. SecondStory and COMPASS demonstrate that while structured reflection can foster emotional healing, PTG is not guaranteed. Allowing multiple valid outcomes—be it growth, acceptance, or coping—supports a more humane approach aligned with the ethical imperative to honor individual trajectories of recovery and change.

SecondStory and COMPASS represent significant advances in developing interventions specifically designed to facilitate PTG. Their shared theoretical foundations in positive psychology, future-directed thinking, meaning-making, narrative approaches, and ACT provide a coherent framework for understanding how to intentionally foster growth after adversity. The evolution from SecondStory to COMPASS demonstrates how intervention development can be refined through empirical testing, theoretical expansion, and listening to participants with lived experience. While both interventions showed promise for enhancing self-perceived PTG and reducing depression symptoms, the more significant benefits for depression highlight how PTG-focused interventions may support overall psychological adjustment rather than exclusively targeting growth outcomes.

Additionally, the contrast between self-perceived growth (which showed clear improvements) and current-standing growth measures (which showed more modest, non-statistically significant changes in the SecondStory trial, but stronger changes in the COMPASS trial) underscores the complexity of the PTG construct and the challenges in measuring and facilitating actual change in PTG domains. Nevertheless, these interventions offer novel approaches for supporting individuals after adversity, particularly those who may not want to seek out standard mental health treatment. They suggest that focusing on meaning, strengths, relationships, and future possibilities—rather than directly targeting symptoms and distress—may be a valuable complement to existing clinical approaches. As research on PTG interventions continues to evolve, these pioneering PTG-focused interventions provide a foundation for understanding how to help individuals not only recover from adversity but also potentially grow through it.

Shifting from Retrospective Change to Observed Change

As I explored in Chapter 6, the most convincing evidence for authentic growth appears when beliefs about growth translate into consistent patterns of thoughts, feelings, and behaviors. Thus, effective interventions should not stop at helping people reframe their experience but should facilitate the enactment of new values and insights in everyday life. For example, a survivor who identifies increased compassion as a potential growth area might be encouraged to engage in small acts of kindness, gradually building a new pattern of behavior that reinforces this emerging value.

As discussed above, a key ingredient of many interventions involves encouraging clients to reflect on and reframe their experiences. While this is an important strategy for successfully managing the impact of trauma, it remains unclear whether these strategies produce long-term positive change, an issue discussed in Chapter 6. Indeed, in line with Whole Trait Theory, personality-based intervention approaches that target daily behavior and life goals may be more likely to yield genuine, observable shifts. Programs like COMPASS illustrate how reflective exercises, when combined with values clarification and a focus on daily behavior and life goals, can encourage participants to act in line with new insights. By repeatedly engaging in values-aligned actions, survivors may eventually internalize these changes as part of their personality.

From the Individual to the Collective: Community-Based Approaches

Group Therapy and Mutual Support Networks

A number of psychological interventions move beyond one-on-one counseling, emphasizing social contexts where survivors share experiences: validation of common struggles, collective meaning-making, vicarious learning, and opportunities for contribution. Realizing that others confront similar emotional or practical hurdles can diminish stigma, with group settings allowing participants to recognize that they are not alone in their responses, as well as normalizing a wide range of reactions to trauma. Rather than focusing solely on personal growth, survivors may collectively redefine adversity and form supportive networks that reduce isolation, often generating shared language and metaphors for understanding trauma.

Witnessing others' progress can provide hope and practical strategies without the pressure of direct instruction, with this modeling effect demonstrating that growth is a gradual, nonlinear process rather than an immediate change. Groups also offer members chances to help others, which can reinforce emerging altruistic tendencies and provide a sense of purpose, creating a pathway to growth through service even for those who struggle to find meaning in their own trauma.

The power of collective meaning-making is important here. In group settings survivors often discover that their experiences, while unique, contain universal elements that others can recognize and validate. This shared understanding can be profoundly healing, reducing the isolation that often accompanies trauma. Moreover, witnessing others' growth can provide hope and concrete examples of resilience without imposing a prescriptive narrative.

Several specific group-based approaches have shown promise. Structured interventions like Seeking Safety (for post-traumatic stress disorder and substance use)[26] or the Trauma Recovery and Empowerment Model (TREM)[27] provide both therapeutic content and peer support, creating multiple pathways to healing. Peer-facilitated groups for specific traumas (e.g., bereavement, sexual assault, combat) often incorporate growth-oriented elements alongside emotional support. The leadership role of fellow survivors can be particularly empowering, demonstrating that trauma does not define one's future. Programs where survivors share their stories with supportive listeners can facilitate meaning-making while creating community connections. These approaches, such as testimony therapy[28] or the Public Conversations Project,[29] emphasize the healing power of having one's experience heard and validated.

Trauma-Informed Community Initiatives

In communities affected by collective hardship, such as war, natural disasters, and systemic oppression, healing often depends on local social structures. Community-based interventions may include locally organized groups blending psychosocial education, cultural rituals (e.g., storytelling), and resource sharing. These informal networks often emerge spontaneously after community traumas and can be strengthened through thoughtful facilitation. Additionally, survivors confronting structural injustices (e.g., poverty, discrimination) can find renewed agency through activism, discovering forms of growth in communal solidarity. By working to prevent similar traumas for others, individuals may transform their suffering into purposeful action. One example of such a program is Macro MI,[30] an adaptation of the technique of motivational interviewing—a collaborative counseling approach that elicits people's own reasons for change—that weaves structural analysis of oppression into client-centered engagement. The program guides practitioners to link personal distress to socially engineered trauma (i.e., trauma occurring in the context of oppressive macro structures such as poverty or long-standing discrimination) and to motivate both individual behavior changes and collective action.

In addition, collaborative creative endeavors—murals, theater productions, memorial installations—can provide avenues for collective expression and meaning-making. These projects often involve both trauma survivors and the broader community, bridging individual healing with social change. Culturally relevant ceremonies acknowledging collective traumas can also help communities process grief and reaffirm shared values. Whether religious or secular, these rituals provide structured opportunities to honor losses while articulating hopes for the future.

Of special relevance to contexts such as Sri Lanka, programs that address practical needs alongside emotional healing recognize that trauma recovery requires material security. Microenterprise projects, job training, or cooperative businesses can help survivors rebuild not just psychologically but also economically, creating sustainable foundations for growth. One example comes from Rwanda, where post-genocide community interventions blend traditional practices with contemporary psychosocial approaches. Programs like Sociotherapy Rwanda organize village-based healing groups that combine emotional processing with practical problem-solving.[31] Participants meet weekly to discuss both trauma-related challenges and everyday concerns, developing solutions together. These groups have shown reductions in mental health symptoms along with improvements in social cohesion—a collective form of growth following unimaginable tragedy.

Similarly, in disaster-affected communities, initiatives like the Community Resilience Model[32] train local residents to become "resilience champions" who teach stress-regulation skills to neighbors. This cascade approach builds local capacity while honoring community knowledge, strengthening the social fabric that may have been damaged by the disaster. These approaches recognize that trauma does not occur in isolation; it often reflects broader social conditions and inequities. By addressing these systemic factors, community initiatives can create environments where growth becomes more possible. This perspective aligns with my earlier point about the importance of context in shaping both the experience of adversity and the potential for positive adaptation.

Relatedly, the francophone studies scholar Caroline Williamson's[33] research on collective PTG in post-genocide Rwanda, discussed in Chapter 3, offers some insights for designing more culturally responsive and potentially more effective interventions. Recall that Williamson identified four distinct response patterns among Rwandan genocide survivors based on their pursuit of agency (autonomy from governmental authority) and communion (meaningful reconciliation across ethnic lines). The fourth pattern—simultaneously seeking both agency and communion—represented what she termed "genuine" collective PTG. This framework suggests that interventions targeting growth after collective trauma should address both vertical relationships (between survivors and authorities) and horizontal relationships (between different groups affected by the trauma).

This more collective lens provides some interesting implications for developing PTG interventions. Rather than focusing solely on individual meaning-making and personal strengths, programs addressing collective trauma can explicitly incorporate modules that help participants recognize and question dominant narratives about their trauma—particularly those imposed by authorities or powerful institutions. In COMPASS, for instance, values clarification exercises could be expanded to include critical examination of whose values are being promoted and why. Participants might explore questions like: Whose story about our collective trauma is being told? Who benefits from this narrative? What alternative stories remain unheard?

Additionally, Williamson's research revealed that genuine collective growth requires meaningful engagement across group boundaries. Carefully facilitated intergroup dialogues that bring different communities together could help participants develop the communion dimension of collective PTG. Communal PTG interventions could also create what Williamson has termed "counter-ideological spaces"[34]—environments where survivors can safely develop narratives that challenge official accounts without fear of reprisal. For example, the Jaffna People's Forum for Coexistence in northern Sri Lanka (founded by a group of activists including the academics Ahilan Kadirgamar and Mahendran Thiruvarangan) has sought to bring Hindu Tamil, Catholic Tamil, and Muslim community members in Jaffna into collaborative activities with the goal of practicing critical self-reflection and building empathy across differences.[35] Such activities might involve partnering with community organizations that can provide protection and advocacy or developing anonymous platforms for sharing alternative perspectives.

While SecondStory emphasized individual narrative change, a group-oriented intervention could facilitate communal story-building. Drawing from our findings in Rwanda[36] that emphasized communal resources over individual characteristics, such interventions might focus on collective assets: What strengths does our community possess? How can we rebuild our social institutions? What shared values will guide our collective recovery? Interventions should also track both individual well-being and collective indicators—such as community cohesion, intergroup trust, and progress toward structural change. Success of these interventions would be measured not just by improved mental health but also by enhanced collective efficacy and communal outcomes.

Importantly, this collective approach doesn't replace individual healing but complements it by recognizing that, in contexts of collective trauma, individual and collective growth are linked. Such an integration also addresses an important ethical concern raised throughout this book: the danger of making systemic problems the sole responsibility of the individual to solve. By explicitly incorporating collective dimensions, PTG interventions can avoid the trap of making individuals responsible for their own healing while ignoring the structural conditions that created and maintain their suffering. Instead, these interventions become tools not just for individual growth but for social change.

Ethical Concerns

Before discussing any intervention aimed at fostering growth, I should be clear: Most adversity should ideally be prevented rather than seen primarily as an opportunity for growth. Our primary ethical obligation is to reduce suffering when possible, and growth-focused interventions should not distract from or replace efforts to prevent adversity in the first place.[37]

That said, what are the ethical challenges that practitioners should be aware of when working with trauma survivors? One is the risk of framing survivors as obliged to find silver linings.[38] This "growth imperative" can invalidate ongoing distress or complicated grief. Clinicians and interventionists must balance empowerment with a measure of realism and encourage participants to explore potential strengths without labeling them as "failures" if they don't. In addition, in the early stages, many individuals are better served by basic coping strategies or stabilizing resources rather than deep existential reflection.

The issue of timing deserves particular emphasis. Research suggests that growth-oriented interventions may be most appropriate after acute distress has stabilized. Prematurely focusing on potential benefits can feel unempathetic, or even harmful, to someone still struggling with intense grief or fear. Instead, interventions should create a foundation of safety and basic coping before gently opening space for reflection on meaning or potential positive changes.

Some survivors also face chronic stressors (e.g., domestic violence, poverty, racism) that impede any straightforward resolution. Growth-oriented programs that emphasize only "positive thinking" risk overlooking essential material or legal supports. Ethical interventions must integrate broader social advocacy to address systemic barriers, recognizing that personal resilience alone is not enough.

This consideration connects directly to our discussions in earlier chapters about the cultural and socioeconomic factors that shape vulnerability and recovery. When working with marginalized populations or those facing ongoing adversity, interventions must address immediate safety and basic needs alongside any focus on growth. Moreover, recognizing systemic factors shifts the burden of adaptation away from individual survivors alone, acknowledging the societal responsibilities for creating conditions where healing is possible.

Empirical Insights: Measuring Real Change

Longitudinal and Experience-Sampling Designs

As emphasized before, detecting authentic growth—not just self-reported or culturally scripted improvements—calls for robust methodologies. Following my own work, gathering data before, during, and after interventions helps identify real shifts in thoughts, feelings, and behavior. Methods such as experience sampling (ESM) can be utilized to track participants' day-to-day experiences in close to real-time, illuminating changes in coping, interpersonal engagement, and emotional regulation.

These methodological approaches align with our critique in Chapter 5 of retrospective self-reports. By measuring change in the moment, rather than relying on memory, we can more confidently identify genuine growth. For example, an ESM approach over an extended period can track daily instances of gratitude, social connection, or value-aligned actions, providing a more detailed picture of how trauma survivors are functioning in their everyday lives.[39]

Cross-Cultural Adaptation

Effective interventions must adapt to cultural norms and collective values. Such adaptations may involve sensitivities to communal or individualistic orientations. As discussed in our overview of narratives in Chapter 4, some societies may emphasize societal outcomes, while others may highlight personal engagement and introspection. In addition, faith-based approaches can resonate in strongly religious contexts, while existential or humanistic perspectives may be more appropriate in secular settings.[40]

This cultural sensitivity extends beyond just translating interventions; it requires rethinking fundamental assumptions about what constitutes healing or growth. Growth is inextricably linked to the topic of values, which are culturally informed. As I explored in Chapter 6, collectivist cultures may emphasize relational harmony or community contribution over individual self-discovery. Effective programs honor these cultural frameworks, working within local understandings rather than defaulting to Western individualistic models.

Acknowledging Non-Growth Outcomes

Valuing Stability or Acceptance

Not everyone desires "growth" or even sees it as feasible; developing virtue in the face of adversity may not be an option for many.[41] Often, merely stabilizing mental health or reclaiming daily functioning can be profoundly meaningful. Interventions should respect the possibility that acceptance may be a desirable outcome, and this quest for peace or equilibrium may not entail a dramatic worldview shift. Additionally, as noted in Chapter 2, growth in one domain (e.g., empathy) may coexist with persistent struggles in another (e.g., anxiety).

For example, for an elderly individual who has recently lost their spouse of fifty years, the goal of an intervention might not be to foster "new possibilities" or "personal strength" in the typical PTG sense. Instead, success might be defined as helping them adapt to living alone, maintain essential social connections, find moments of peace in their daily routine, and accept their grief as a natural part of life. This stability and acceptance, rather than dramatic change, can be a deeply meaningful and valid outcome.

Having respect for diverse outcomes reflects a more complex understanding of post-trauma recovery than simplistic mainstream accounts of PTG suggest. Rather than viewing growth as the ideal of positive adaptation, we can appreciate the many ways people can rebuild meaningful lives after adversity. Some ways may involve dramatic change of the form described by the philosopher L. A. Paul (see Chapter 2), while others may involve more subtle shifts in perspective or priorities.[42]

Tying It All Together

A focus on growth need not overshadow other ways of regaining well-being. An intervention that validates multiple endpoints (e.g., acceptance, improved coping) reflects a complex and multifaceted view of treatment, and one that also avoids pressuring survivors into redemption narratives. When designing or evaluating interventions, we should consider success in terms of whether participants find personally meaningful ways forward, rather than whether they achieve a predefined notion of growth. This approach honors the agency of survivors, positioning them as the ultimate authorities on their own recovery journey.

Key Considerations

When evaluating interventions to foster growth after adversity, several critical considerations arise. Timing and readiness are paramount; interventions should not begin during acute distress phases or while ongoing trauma continues, as other needs such as basic stability and safety must be established before meaningful growth-focused work can proceed. Also, accurately assessing the facets of positive change requires innovative methodological approaches beyond traditional self-reports. Researchers advocate incorporating informant corroboration, diary methods, and even physiological indicators, such as stress biomarkers, to verify tangible behavioral shifts and genuine stress reduction. As discussed in Chapters 5 and 6, multimethod approaches are important for distinguishing between genuine personality change and coping, as high self-reports of growth may sometimes mask ongoing distress rather than reflect authentic change.

Another key challenge lies in reconciling and honoring cultural differences regarding adversity and resilience. Effective interventions should thus be thoughtfully adapted to local contexts, considering culturally specific spiritual practices, communal values, and norms around storytelling or group healing. Individualistic frameworks emphasizing personal strength may be inappropriate for collectivistic cultures that may prioritize values such as communal healing and relational harmony, requiring practitioners to develop culturally sensitive interventions that go beyond simple translation of techniques. Finally, it's crucial to acknowledge that individual-focused interventions cannot adequately address systemic causes of adversity.[43] While practical considerations may mean that such interventions are used as a front-line option, focusing solely on individual resilience may neglect structural inequalities that perpetuate future trauma.

A holistic approach, therefore, integrates psychological support with initiatives aimed at addressing resource deficits and advocating for policy changes. By explicitly linking personal coping strategies with broader systemic support, such as policy advocacy or improved resource provision, interventions can facilitate comprehensive, sustained recovery that respects diverse definitions of growth and resilience. Practitioners should also monitor for "redemption pressure"—the subtle expectation that clients *should* find silver linings in their suffering—and maintain flexibility for nonlinear processes where growth may emerge slowly, deteriorate over time, or never occur despite effective intervention. These questions encourage continued reflection on both the potential and limitations of growth-oriented interventions. They remind us that, while we can create conditions that facilitate growth, it is important to remain humble about the possible outcomes of this work and careful not to override individual agency or cultural beliefs about the impact of adversity.

This returns us to a central theme that has run throughout this book: The tension between suffering and change is complex, culturally embedded, and deeply personal. While the scientific evidence suggests that genuine growth is possible, it emerges not from the trauma itself but from how individuals engage with it—through reflection, connection, and purposeful action. Our role as researchers, clinicians, and community members is not to prescribe growth but to create spaces where it might naturally unfold at the individual and communal level, always honoring the diverse ways people make meaning of their most difficult experiences.

The intervention approaches explored in this chapter represent attempts to translate critical scholarship into constructive practice, and to create spaces where growth may emerge naturally without imposing redemptive expectations. They embody the central tension that has animated this book:

how to acknowledge the possibility of change through adversity without romanticizing suffering or prescribing universal paths. As we conclude our journey through philosophical foundations, religious perspectives, narrative influences, methodological challenges, empirical evidence, and practical applications, we return to the fundamental question posed at the outset: Is there always value to adversity?

8

Conclusion

Revisiting the Myth—and the Future of PTG Research

In June 2025, my wife and I took our six-year-old son to Sri Lanka for the first time. While he was flying kites on Galle Face Green (a prominent ocean-front urban park and promenade in central Colombo) on our last evening in the country, I stood gazing at the Indian Ocean, thinking that just a few years earlier this very space had been the epicenter of the *aragalaya*, the mass protests that forced President Gotabaya Rajapaksa to flee after the 2022 economic collapse (which I briefly noted in Chapter 2). Indeed, the postwar years have witnessed a cascade of new challenges for Sri Lanka: communal violence against Muslims in 2014 and 2018; the 2019 Easter Sunday bombings that claimed more than 250 lives—among them worshippers at St. Anthony's Shrine in Kochchikade, featured on this book's cover; and the recent financial meltdown that left citizens (including my parents) queuing for fuel and food. In late 2024, voters responded to these challenges by electing a government led by the Janatha Vimukthi Peramuna (JVP), a party that had itself led a violent insurrection against the then–Sri Lankan government during my childhood but now promised radical change through democratic means.

As I stood at Galle Face Green, I was struck by the absurdity of asking whether Sri Lankans had "grown" from decades of violence. The disappeared persons, the war crimes, the economic collapse—these represent losses that no amount of growth could likely balance. The question isn't whether adversity made people stronger, but how we can prevent such suffering from recurring. As I complete this book in the fall of 2025, Sri Lanka stands at another crossroads, its people once again hoping that economic relief, justice, and possibly a better future will follow decades of challenges.[1]

To take a step back, throughout this book I've used memories of my childhood experiences in Sri Lanka during the turbulent 1980s and 1990s to illustrate the complexity of adversity and challenge narratives of growth following adversity. Yet, as much as I've reflected on these formative years,

I'm still grappling with the precise ways my childhood experiences shaped me. For example, when I was interviewed by the journalist Shankar Vedantam for National Public Radio's *Hidden Brain* program, I spoke about my response to the mosque attacks in Christchurch, New Zealand, in 2019. Staying awake through the night with my one-month-old son to follow the unfolding tragedy, I felt an unexpected, oddly visceral fear: not only sympathy for the victims, but also the unsettling, likely unreasonable sense that I could possibly be the target of such violence in the future. This reaction marked a shift from my earlier, more distanced reactions to similar events, such as the September 11 attacks that occurred less than a month after my arrival to the United States as a first-year undergraduate student at Franklin & Marshall College, an event that I had viewed largely from an emotional distance. The Christchurch massacre confronted me, perhaps for the first time since leaving Sri Lanka, with the personal vulnerability inherent in random, politically driven violence—a reality I had learned to normalize and detach from as a bi-ethnic child growing up amid Sri Lanka's civil conflicts.[2]

Reflecting on this moment highlighted a fundamental complexity underlying the entire discussion of adversity and post-traumatic growth (PTG): How do we balance the adaptive need for psychological detachment with the ethical imperative of facing injustice squarely? My evolving responses to trauma—from a detached normalization of ongoing violence during childhood to a sense of visceral vulnerability decades later—underscore that personal growth from adversity is not straightforward. My understanding of myself and my relationship to adversity evolved over time, influenced significantly by changing contexts and my shifting social and cultural locations. This personal insight underscores the core message of this book: Growth after adversity is possible but likely rare, contextual, and implicitly mandated by our culture. In this chapter, I revisit the book's central themes, integrating personal reflection with empirical and theoretical insights, and offer measured recommendations for how we might more realistically and compassionately approach adversity in both research and everyday life.

Throughout this book, I have traced how PTG is conceived, measured, and debated. While some individuals emerge from hardship with new strengths or deeper perspectives, many do not. The journey is rarely as linear or redemptive as cultural narratives such as "what doesn't kill you makes you stronger" imply. Instead, the reality of navigating trauma and stress is shaped by an interplay of personal attributes, communal ties, cultural scripts, and structural factors that can foster, obstruct, or reshape recovery and growth.

At the heart of these debates lies an existential question: Does suffering build character, or do we simply want to believe it does? Is it just one of the many narratives people around the world tell themselves to explain the suffering that exists in our world? Indeed, adversity can catalyze positive changes for some, but it can also leave others wounded, unchanged, or striving for stability rather than change. By critically interrogating current PTG research, I have tried to provide a more honest and humane understanding of what it means to grow from hardship—acknowledging multiple possible outcomes instead of a single redemptive truth.

A key motivation for this book is that I believe that current PTG research is guilty of what the philosopher Mara van der Lugt terms "the overburdening of the will."[3] She invokes the psychologist David Smail's concept of magical volunteerism: "The belief that it is within every individual's power to make themselves what they want to be."[4] Of course, possessing such agency in the wake of adversity is important and frequently beneficial. The danger is when belief exclusively in these positive benefits becomes the norm.

Revisiting Core Tensions: What Doesn't Kill You. . .?

This book's journey through philosophical and religious work, empirical evidence, and possible intervention strategies has revealed several persistent tensions in how we should understand PTG. Let me try to summarize them here.

Growth Is Not a Given

Longitudinal evidence shows that adversity does not inherently strengthen individuals. While a few people exhibit measurable personality changes, most report only perceived growth, which may be an adaptive but not necessarily transformative coping mechanism. In some studies, those who claim the highest PTG also report high distress, calling into question whether these reports reflect genuine change or a form of coping.

The complex relationship between adversity and growth was particularly evident in our examination of longitudinal research in Chapter 6. Studies tracking survivors over time revealed that while many report feeling transformed by trauma, observable changes in personality traits are less common and less dramatic than subjective accounts would suggest. Moreover, as we saw in Chapter 6, some evidence suggests that the relationship between adversity exposure and well-being appears curvilinear—moderate adversity may foster resilience, but severe or chronic trauma typically undermines it. This complex picture challenges simplistic cultural narratives claiming that suffering inherently builds character. In thinking about the nature of growth, the journalist Anya Kamenetz's musing that "post-traumatic growth is rarer, not automatic. It's like certain tree species with seeds that are released only by the heat of the wildfire"[5] nicely captures the notion that specific capacities or virtues may develop in the wake of adversity (without the promise of positive overall change).

Acknowledging Diverse Forms of "Growth"

PTG is not just about individual change. Social support, communal rituals, or relational healing can also define meaningful adaptation. As I've discussed throughout this book, different cultures emphasize collective change rather than a solitary journey.[6] Whether through "altruism born of suffering" (Chapter 6) or communal activism (Chapter 7), adversity sometimes unites people around shared values and virtues, highlighting that growth can be social as much as personal (echoing our discussion of virtue in Chapter 2).[7]

Our exploration of cross-cultural perspectives in Chapters 3 and 6 highlighted how growth may manifest differently across contexts. Western conceptualizations typically emphasize individual change—personal strength, autonomy, self-actualization—while collectivist cultures often prioritize relational harmony, community contributions, or fulfillment of social roles. These variations remind us that PTG is not a uniform construct but takes shape in line with cultural values and social contexts. As researchers and practitioners, we must remain sensitive to these differences, avoiding the imposition of Western individualistic frameworks on diverse populations.

Confronting Redemption Pressure

Telling survivors that they "should" find meaning in their suffering can create a redemption imperative, invalidating genuine pain. Ethical PTG research and practice must allow for non-growth outcomes (e.g., acceptance, recovery, stability, or ongoing struggle) without implying these are "failures." Interventions like SecondStory and COMPASS (Chapter 7) revealed that structured self-reflection can help some participants reduce distress or reframe adversity, but others simply needed support or found solace in less-dramatic changes.

The ethical dimensions of PTG discourse emerged as a crucial concern throughout this book. As we discussed in Chapters 4 and 5, the cultural valorization of redemptive narratives can help people cope with adversity but can also place undue pressure on trauma survivors to find meaning in their suffering. This "redemption pressure" may compound distress by suggesting that those who fail to grow are somehow lacking in character or resilience. Moreover, an overemphasis on individual growth risks overlooking the systemic factors—poverty, discrimination, violence—that shape trauma exposure and recovery. An ethical approach to promoting PTG must acknowledge these structural dimensions and avoid placing the burden of adapting to trauma *solely* on individuals.

Identifying Genuine Growth

A central challenge in PTG research is separating genuine change from narratives that arise from memory bias, social desirability, or coping. Retrospective self-reports like the Post-Traumatic Growth Inventory (PTGI) often confound perceived change with demonstrable personality shifts. Moreover, longitudinal and experience-sampling designs show that many who say they have grown do not exhibit trait-level or behavioral changes, indicating that at times PTG reflects coping more than substantive change. The implication here is that future studies must pursue multimethod approaches, incorporating informant reports, behavioral observations, repeated measures, and cross-lagged panel models to ensure that we distinguish illusion from authentic development.

The methodological critiques presented in Chapter 5 highlighted how measurement issues have compromised our understanding of PTG. Most PTG research relies on retrospective self-reports, which are vulnerable to memory biases, social desirability, and the influence of cultural scripts. As a result, reported growth often exceeds objectively measured changes, raising questions about whether PTG sometimes represents a coping strategy rather than genuine change. To address these limitations, we need more sophisticated research designs—prospective studies with pre-trauma baselines, experience-sampling methods that capture real-time functioning, and multi-informant approaches that go beyond self-perception.

That said, future research should also explore the conditions under which retrospective self-reports can reflect valid insights into personality changes after adversity. The work by Schwaba and colleagues[8] discussed in Chapter 5 provides an important recent example of such work, demonstrating that when individuals identified events retrospectively as particularly meaningful or transformative, their perceptions aligned with measured personality changes. Moving forward, studies could further examine which specific characteristics of events, individual differences, or time frames enhance retrospective accuracy, helping researchers better harness retrospective reports to understand the processes underlying PTG.

One additional argument I have tried to make in this book is the importance of merging insights from personality psychology, philosophy, and religious studies to better understand how adversity is framed across societies. Greater collaboration can help us develop pluralistic models of growth.[9] Throughout this book, I have emphasized the multidimensional nature of PTG. Understanding this complex phenomenon requires collaboration across disciplines—from personality psychology and neuroscience to philosophy, anthropology, and cultural studies. By bringing together diverse perspectives, researchers can develop more comprehensive models that account for the biological, psychological, social, and cultural dimensions of adversity and adaptation. Moreover, cross-cultural collaboration is essential for moving beyond Western-centric frameworks and developing truly pluralistic approaches to PTG.

Avoiding a One-Size-Fits-All Model

Most PTG research originates in Western, individualistic contexts. Yet other cultures interpret adversity as a communal or spiritual phenomenon,[10] which notably aligns with work on *altruism born of suffering* discussed in Chapter 6, highlighting the prosocial or collective dimension of post-adversity growth. A single, universal PTG narrative risks ignoring these diverse frameworks. Our exploration of cultural variations in Chapters 3, 4, and 6 underscored the importance of exhibiting cultural humility in PTG research and practice. The dominant Western model of PTG emphasizes individual change and autonomous meaning-making, but many other cultures understand adversity and resilience in more collective or spiritual terms. Imposing a universal framework on diverse populations not only misrepresents their experiences but also risks invalidating culturally meaningful forms of adaptation and healing. As the field evolves, researchers must work collaboratively with diverse communities to develop culturally sensitive measures and interventions.

In addition, rather than viewing PTG only as an individual-level phenomenon, future research should also focus on communal resilience and interpersonal changes. This aligns with the altruism born of suffering concept, highlighting the prosocial or collective dimension of post-adversity growth. Our examination of collectivist cultural perspectives in Chapters 3 and 4 highlighted the importance of measuring growth at both individual and communal levels. When adversity affects entire communities—as in natural disasters, political conflicts, or pandemic conditions—collective resilience may be as important as individual adaptation. Future research should develop metrics that capture these relational aspects of growth, such as community cohesion, collective efficacy, and shared meaning-making processes.

In this regard, the personality psychologists Jonathan Adler and Ted Schwaba[11] recently provided a thoughtful, radical critique of current PTG research (which includes a critique of some of my own thinking on this question). They highlight limitations inherent in the traditional conceptualization of PTG, questioning each element: "post," "traumatic," and "growth." Particularly compelling is their argument against the assumed temporal discreteness of trauma, suggesting instead the need to consider extended temporal or spatial metaphors that reflect the experience of individuals for whom adversity is not a single, discrete experience, but complex, ongoing, or intergenerational. Moreover, Adler and Schwaba critique the dominant centrality of the term *trauma*, noting that—similar to the redemption narrative—it can impose a reductive narrative on diverse forms of suffering and resilience. They also critique individual-level predictive models for understanding PTG, advocating instead for idiographic, narrative-based methods. Such qualitative and mixed-method approaches allow individuals to articulate their own retrospective sense-making processes, potentially offering richer and more authentic insights into how adversity shapes personal and collective identity over time.

In embracing these new directions, interdisciplinary collaborations that integrate psychology with humanities and the social sciences could significantly enrich PTG research. While I think that some of these approaches (e.g., more idiographic methods) run the risk of identifying exemplars of growth that we subsequently use as a standard to hold others to,[12] I agree that the future of PTG research lies in this type of innovative, interdisciplinary thinking and research.

Addressing Systemic Factors

Many hardships (e.g., poverty, discrimination, political conflict) are rooted in structural injustice. Focusing solely on individual growth can obscure the need for material, legal, or policy interventions that enable a fair chance at recovery and adaptation. Throughout this book, and particularly in Chapters 4 and 5, I have emphasized that trauma is often embedded in broader social, economic, and political conditions. When adversity stems from systemic injustice, focusing exclusively on individual adaptation may inadvertently perpetuate harmful conditions by suggesting that resilience is merely a matter of personal character. In line with Adler and Schwaba's recommendations,[13] future approaches to PTG must acknowledge these structural dimensions and advocate for changes that address the root causes of trauma, not just its psychological aftermath.

Additionally, much PTG research has focused on isolated traumas. Yet many endure cumulative adversity—chronic illness, oppression, repeated setbacks. Understanding growth (or its absence) over a lifetime of challenges demands more holistic, integrative study designs. As discussed in Chapters 5 and 6, traditional PTG research has often focused on discrete traumatic events—accidents, natural disasters, acute illnesses. However, many people experience adversity not as isolated incidents but as ongoing conditions or repeated challenges. Future research must expand beyond the single-trauma framework to examine how individuals navigate cumulative adversity over time. This expanded scope would better capture the reality of marginalized populations who face chronic stressors related to poverty, discrimination, or political instability.[14]

In my view, research on PTG should also confront the possibility that championing "growth through adversity" inadvertently romanticizes suffering. For many survivors, real healing does not arise from "silver linings," but from improved social conditions, supportive networks, or professional care.[15] This tension between acknowledging potential benefits of adversity and avoiding romanticization of suffering emerged repeatedly in our exploration. While research suggests that some individuals do experience meaningful growth after trauma, overemphasizing these positive outcomes risks trivializing genuine pain or implying that suffering is somehow beneficial or necessary for development. As discussed in Chapters 3 and 7, ethical approaches to PTG must maintain balance—recognizing the possibility of growth while never suggesting that trauma is desirable or that those who do not grow have somehow failed.

When It Occurs, Growth Happens in a Context

Throughout this book, I have critically examined the idea that adversity inevitably leads to personal growth. While PTG is a compelling concept, the empirical evidence suggests a more complex reality: Growth is possible but not typical, and the process is likely neither linear nor guaranteed. The popular belief that "what doesn't kill you makes you stronger" may offer comfort, but it risks oversimplifying the diverse ways in which people respond to hardship.

Rather than assuming that suffering is inherently transformative, we must ask: Under what conditions does real change occur? The findings presented in earlier chapters emphasize that meaningful growth (when it happens) depends on a confluence of psychological, social, and cultural factors. It is not merely about individual resilience but also about the environments, relationships, and resources that shape recovery and adaptation.

As we saw in Chapter 6, several factors appear to facilitate positive change: moderate (but not overwhelming) adversity that challenges (but does not shatter) one's capacity to cope, social support and community connections that provide validation and practical assistance, cultural frameworks that offer meaningful ways to interpret suffering, opportunities for reflection and meaning-making without pressure to find redemption, agency and control in at least some aspects of the recovery process, and material resources that allow for basic security and stability. When these conditions are present, individuals may indeed experience growth that manifests meaningfully in their personality. However, when these supporting factors are absent, the likelihood of such growth diminishes significantly.

Refining Interventions

Programs like SecondStory and COMPASS (Chapter 7) demonstrate that structured reflection can reduce distress and offer new perspectives, but they must remain flexible, culturally sensitive, and respectful of those who do not seek change. Ethical practice entails providing multiple pathways—one participant might find relief in acceptance, another in activism, and still another in redemptive meaning-making.

The other interventions discussed in Chapter 7 illustrated both the potential and limitations of growth-oriented approaches. While structured reflection and meaning-making can benefit some individuals, these interventions must avoid imposing expectations of change. Future programs should be designed with flexibility in mind, offering participants multiple pathways to healing and explicitly validating diverse outcomes, including specific virtues, but also stability and acceptance. Moreover, interventions should be adapted for different cultural contexts, recognizing that the means and meaning of growth vary across societies.

A Hopeful Perspective

Rather than endorsing a universal narrative of triumph over adversity, this book has proposed an evidence-based view. Growth after trauma *can* happen, yet it is not guaranteed. Many people emerge from suffering feeling no sense of redemption, or they discover smaller shifts—like enhanced empathy or communal solidarity—that do not register as sweeping personality change or major shifts in character.

If we step back from the comforting maxim that "suffering builds character," does this undercut our sense of meaning or hope? Not necessarily. While some individuals do convert pain into deeper wisdom or virtue, others simply persevere or seek relief. Acknowledging this reality affirms that human worth does not hinge on whether one's struggles yield redemptive lessons. Indeed, life's value can lie in relationships, communal ties, or quietly enduring adversity without forced narratives of heroic change. Consider a parent who dedicates years to caring for a child with a severe, life-limiting disability. They may not report "personal growth" in terms of new life possibilities or spiritual awakenings; their daily life may indeed be characterized by exhaustion and sorrow. Affirming that their worth, and the meaning found in their dedication and love, does not depend on a redemptive "growth" narrative is crucial. The value lies in the steadfast care itself, even if the outcome is struggle and eventual loss. As the counseling researcher Mary Beth Werdel[16] notes, "In my many years as a counselor, educator and clinician, I have seen how a belief in the *possibility* of growth is an essential part of trauma work and how the *expectation* of growth leads to working with people who are suffering in less than helpful ways" (italics added).[17,18]

Such a view is consistent with philosopher Kieran Setiya's[19] defense of a realistic form of hope that acknowledges the reality of enduring suffering:

> The question, then, is not whether to hope but what we should hope for. . . [T]he answer's not an ideal life. What we need is acknowledgement and close reading of the lives we have. I can hope to see my mother again, to hold her hand and walk with her along the foreshore where the estuary gathers the tides and the great bridge sweeps across the river mouth, curving with the Earth. But I know she won't recover.[20]

From a scientific perspective, this realism encourages us to refine PTG studies with longitudinal and multimethod designs, to remain culturally inclusive of different conceptualizations of adaptive responses to adversity, and to integrate structural considerations that can promote or hinder change. From an ethical standpoint, it also reminds us to honor those who do not experience change, and to avoid romanticizing adversity at the expense of providing support to those who struggle. In truth, the question is less about whether "what doesn't kill us makes us stronger" than how we can create personal, communal, and systemic conditions that nurture healing in its many forms.

Embracing this critical yet hopeful stance allows us to see that while adversity does not guarantee growth, there are meaningful ways to help survivors manage in the aftermath of adversity. By recognizing the importance of scientific rigor, cultural awareness, and ethical sensitivity, it is possible to design better quality research that clarifies the prevalence of positive change, as well as to develop flexible interventions that respect the different ways people rebuild their lives.

To be clear, I'm not claiming that all experiences of PTG are illusory. My main claim here is that its promise is too compelling to accept without clearer evidence. Suffering may indeed propel some people toward deeper compassion, clearer life goals, or greater spiritual insight—yet testing these possibilities should involve the same empirical rigor that we would demand of the best science. By challenging inflated claims, highlighting our bias toward discerning and celebrating growth, refining our assessments of change, and situating our conception of growth within different cultural and structural contexts, my hope is to safeguard it as a viable topic of scientific study. A credible science of adversity that can withstand empirical scrutiny is the one most likely to yield practical applications and interventions that meaningfully help individuals and communities to flourish.

Finally, what do the arguments in this book mean for our lives? Supporting ourselves and others without automatically imposing growth narratives begins with giving ourselves permission not to turn every hardship into a mandate for growth. With others, it looks like what the psychotherapist Lori Gottlieb has termed "compassionate witnessing": listening, witnessing, and accompanying without pressuring them to change.[21] Such an intentional approach honors all paths from adversity—whether they lead to growth, recovery, acceptance, or even ongoing struggle—affirming that human worth does not hinge on a story of growth. It demands a thoughtful awareness of the difference between a story and reality, appreciating that narrative can be a powerful coping tool without confusing it for authentic change. Crucially, we also must look beyond the individual to acknowledge the systemic injustices that so often cause and perpetuate trauma, recognizing that personal resilience, while undeniably important, cannot be the sole answer to structural problems. Finally, we need to exhibit patience with ourselves and others, respecting that genuine change, if it occurs at all, is often a slow, uneven, and nonlinear process, not a sudden or guaranteed transformation.

So, my hope is that this journey through the philosophical, religious, empirical, and practical dimensions of PTG has revealed both the potential and limitations of this challenging concept. The evidence suggests that while growth is possible, it is neither assured, nor universal, nor in some cases even feasible. This more balanced understanding honors the complexity of the human response to suffering, without minimizing pain, imposing unwarranted expectations, or losing sight of the wider structural contexts that shape our capacity to heal. The path forward lies in maintaining this balance: being open to the possibility of change while acknowledging the negative and sometimes terrible impact of adversity and trauma, and respecting the diversity of human responses to adversity that will in many cases fall short of growth; pursuing rigorous science while remaining attuned to our own biases; recognizing individual agency while addressing structural factors; and offering hope to others without denying the reality of suffering. By navigating these tensions, we can develop approaches to understanding the possible benefits of adversity that are both helpful to and respectful of the experiences of those who have experienced it, in all their humanity, complexity, and dignity.

Acknowledgments

This book represents the culmination of more than fifteen years of thinking and research on the nature of growth following adversity. It would not have been possible without the generous support, collaboration, and encouragement of many individuals and institutions.

My broader interest in this project was stimulated by the pioneering work critiquing research on PTG by Howard Tennen at the University of Connecticut School of Medicine and by Pat Frazier at the University of Minnesota. I'm very much in their debt and am grateful for the opportunity to have worked with them. Laura Blackie, who worked with me on the first research grant I received to study this topic, also deserves special recognition. She is an exceptional scholar who contributed significantly to much of the work presented here.

I am also deeply grateful to the other scholars who have shaped my thinking and contributed to this work. Marie Forgeard and Annie Roepke, graduate school colleagues and friends who joined me on that initial grant, as well as Will Fleeson, my former mentor and current colleague at Wake Forest, played pivotal roles in developing these ideas. Marty Seligman also provided valuable support in the early years of this work. Michael Brady has played an invaluable role in sharpening my understanding of PTG as a philosophical concept. Adriel Boals and Crystal Park have done excellent work critiquing the PTG literature, and I'm grateful for their collaborative spirit and collegiality. I'm also grateful to my identical twin brother Nuwan Jayawickreme for being both a supportive sibling and valued collaborator throughout this journey.

I have also had the opportunity to work on multiple grants related to this research with Michael Brady, Laura Blackie, Stephen Grimm, Frank Infurna, Will Fleeson, Michael Lamb, and Sarah Schnitker—many thanks to all of you. My gratitude also extends to numerous other collaborators who have enriched this research over the years, including Santushi Amarasuriya, Stephanie Bossert, Veronica Cole, Meghan Gangel, Sydney Glickson, Amaris Grant, Igor Grossmann, Erik Helzer, Nuwan Jayawickreme, Rowan Kemmerly, Jamieson Nathan, Zand O'Neill, Caleb Reynolds, Eli Tsukayama, Nic Weststrate, Lindsey Wilson, Cornelia Wrzus, and Linn Zapffe. My old friend Michelle Goonasekera played a key role in establishing my research program in Sri Lanka. I'm also grateful to the Family Rehabilitation Centre in Sri Lanka, and especially Amalka Edirisinghe, Niranjala Somasundaram, and Lahiru Perera, for their support of my work there.

I am profoundly grateful to the Templeton philanthropies for supporting much of this work since 2011. The writing of this book was directly supported by the Pathways to Character grant that Frank Infurna and I received from the John Templeton Foundation (grant ID #60699), with additional research funded by multiple grants from the John Templeton Foundation, the Templeton World Charity Foundation, and the Templeton Religion Trust. Special thanks to Kimon Sargeant and Michael Murray for their early support of my work, and to Sarah Clement and Rich Bollinger for their thoughtful guidance.

Additional funding for my work came from the Tribble Professorship fund, the Provost's Office, and the Psychology Department at Wake Forest University, as well as from the United States Agency for International Development, the Asia Foundation, and the European Association for Personality Psychology. Funding from the Center of Theological Inquiry facilitated a series of very helpful conversations with Michelle Panchuk, which informed the discussion in Chapter 3. The Humanities Institute at Wake Forest University, with the support of a National Endowment for the Humanities challenge grant, provided the opportunity for me to discuss some of the ideas in Chapter 2 with Emily Austin, Saylor Breckenridge, and John Oksanish. I'm grateful for both this support and my colleagues' thoughtful feedback.

I've presented multiple talks on the topics discussed here over the last few years, and I'm grateful for the many productive discussions I've had at the University of Toronto, University of Colombo, University of Peradeniya, University of Oxford, High Point University, Cornell University, University of Mainz, Franklin & Marshall College, University of Nottingham, University of North Carolina–Greensboro, University of North Carolina–Chapel Hill, Duke University, Colby College, Biola University, McGill University, University College London, Tufts University, Davidson College, University of Chicago, Technical University of Munich, and the University of Birmingham (UK). I'm also thankful for discussions at multiple conferences, including those organized by the Society for the Study of Human Development, the Society for Personality and Social Psychology, the Association for Psychological Science, the Association for Research on Personality (my favorite academic community), the Society for Philosophy and Psychology, the International Society for the Science of Existential Psychology, and the European Association for Personality Psychology.

Several individuals provided invaluable feedback on this manuscript. Nuwan Jayawickreme offered thoughtful comments on two early drafts *and* the final manuscript. Marion Johnson provided detailed copyediting suggestions on an early draft. Michael Brady and Annie Roepke provided very helpful feedback on specific chapters, and Lisa Blee significantly improved the final version of the manuscript with her edits and comments. I'm also very grateful to three excellent Wake Forest psychology graduate students: Sophia Dixon read the manuscript carefully twice and provided very helpful and constructive feedback, Jamieson Nathan helped with developing the tables presented here, and Tsion Eshetu did a great job with formatting the references. In addition, Leanna Bernish carefully reviewed the final proofs and made many helpful suggestions. I also made use of large language models to clarify some examples, stress-test specific arguments, and edit sections of the text (particularly the discussion of specific research studies) to make it more accessible to nonspecialist readers.

Wake Forest University has been the ideal academic home for developing this work. I have already mentioned Will Fleeson, and I'm particularly grateful for my ongoing collaboration with him. Mike Furr has taught me a great deal about personality assessment over the years. Christian Miller's commentary on one of my early articles on PTG sparked my interest in philosophical explorations of this topic. Further, his gentle encouragement in the fall of 2024 that I complete this book helped motivate me to finish it. I am also grateful for the opportunity I had to co-lead a grant with Michael Lamb, a stellar political scientist and leader of the Program for Leadership and Character at Wake Forest, which led to the development of much of the intervention research discussed in this book. Thanks also to all my colleagues in the Psychology Department—especially Dale Dagenbach, Eric Stone, and Christy Buchanan, who have served as department chairs during my time at Wake Forest, as well as Christian Waugh, Shannon Brady, Heath Greene, and Wayne Pratt, for both helpful conversations and for creating a dynamic and supportive intellectual environment. I'm also grateful for all that Michele Gillespie has done to support my career as dean of the college and as provost of the university.

The specific structure and content of this book are very much based on my lecture notes for an interdisciplinary first-year seminar on PTG that I taught at Wake Forest in the spring of 2024. I am grateful to Joshua Bowling, Courtney Campbell, Brennan Carlin, Angelica Dileo, Scarlett Knapp, Ava LeBeau, Davis Munn, Aidan Oliss, Caroline Prince, Hanna Shakarov, and Nur Turner, whose deep engagement with the material helped clarify many of the core arguments presented here. I'm also thankful to the undergraduate and graduate students at Wake Forest who have engaged with my research as students and researchers, as well as Norah Burke, Brian Davis, Vicki Lawson, Ashley Hawkins Parham, and Kathleen Stimely for their administrative help over the years.

Sarah Harrington at Oxford University Press did an excellent job with the edited volume on PTG that I worked on with Frank Infurna, and I'm grateful for her support of (and patience with!) this project. Thanks to Phoebe Aldridge-Turner, Lacey Harvey, Alexcee Bechthold, and Swetha Kodimari at Oxford University Press for their assistance, and to Keith Cline for his careful copyediting. I thank the anonymous reviewers who provided careful comments on both the book proposal and full manuscript, with particular gratitude to Robert Wicks, who signed his review and offered encouraging feedback. I'm also grateful for a series of conversations I had with Margo Beth Fleming at the beginning of 2023, which helped me see the value of making this book more accessible to a broader audience. Thanks also to Paul Bloom for suggesting over a dinner with Joanne Chung in Toronto that I discuss my life and work in Sri Lanka as part of this book.

I'm also grateful to Shankar Vedantam, Brigid McCarthy, Annie Paul, and Tara Boyle at Hidden Brain Media for giving me the chance to think about my research as the outcome of my experiences and narrative identity. Thanks also to David Robson, Moya Sarner, Anya Kamenetz, Kate Woodsome, and Laura Newberry for their thoughtful media coverage of my work. (David's award-winning piece on PTG for the BBC is particularly worth reading.) Thanks to Valerie Tiberius and Dan Haybron for giving me the courage to submit the first draft of this manuscript for review while on a beach walk in Pine Knoll Shores. Special appreciation goes to Layne Amerikaner, Laura Blackie, Monique O'Connell, Veronica Cole, and Nisha Ramachandran; and to my parents Bandula and Dawn. In particular, Amma has helped us keep our home fires burning over the last three years, enriching our family's lives in so many ways.

I also want to mention my broader family, in particular Nuwan and his wife Jenny, my elder brother Dasa and his wife Amy, and my cousins Shaihan and Nihal and their wives Maria and Ally. We came together in the wake of my aunt Darshini's death in September 2014, and our engaging and enduring WhatsApp family group chat is perhaps an example of growth in the face of adversity that this book explores and questions.

Finally, this book is dedicated to my wife Lisa Blee, and to our children Micah and Maya. I'm so grateful for their love and our shared life.

Glossary of Technical Terms

Acceptance and Commitment Therapy (ACT): A form of psychotherapy that helps people accept difficult thoughts and feelings while committing to actions aligned with personal values, rather than trying to eliminate distress.

Adversity: Significant life challenges, hardships, or difficult circumstances that people encounter, ranging from personal losses to natural disasters to systemic oppression.

Altruism Born of Suffering (ABS): The phenomenon where people who have experienced trauma become more likely to help others, including those from different social groups.

Amor Fati: A concept from Nietzsche's philosophy that means "love of one's fate." It refers to courageously facing and affirming all of life's challenges, good and bad.

Autobiographical Reasoning: The process of creating connections between past experiences and one's sense of self, often used to make meaning from life events.

Behavioral Activation: A therapeutic technique that encourages engagement in meaningful activities, especially when someone has withdrawn due to depression or trauma.

Big Five Personality Traits: The five broad dimensions psychologists use to describe personality: openness, conscientiousness, extraversion, agreeableness, and neuroticism.

Biopsychosocial Perspective: An approach that examines how biological factors (e.g., neurobiology, stress systems), psychological processes (e.g., beliefs, coping), and social factors (e.g., support, culture) interact to influence health and well-being.

Characteristic Adaptations: The middle level of personality including personal goals, values, coping strategies, and social roles that can change based on life circumstances.

Cognitive-Behavioral Therapy (CBT): A type of therapy that helps people identify and change negative thought patterns and behaviors.

Cognitive Processing Therapy (CPT): A specific type of CBT designed for trauma, helping people examine and modify unhelpful beliefs related to their traumatic experience.

Collectivistic Cultures: Societies that prioritize group harmony, interdependence, and collective well-being over individual achievement.

Confirmation Bias: The tendency to seek out or interpret information in ways that confirm what we already believe.

Contamination Sequences: Life story patterns where positive experiences are followed by negative outcomes (opposite of redemption sequences).

Cross-Sectional Study: Research that examines people at a single point in time, rather than following them over time.

Cultural Scripts: Socially shared stories or expectations about how people should think, feel, or behave in certain situations.

Current-Standing Measures: Assessments that ask about someone's present state rather than how much they've changed.

Curvilinear Relationship: A relationship between two variables that forms a curve rather than a straight line, often an inverse U shape. In the context of PTG, some research suggests that individuals with a moderate amount of lifetime adversity report better psychological outcomes than those with either no adversity or very high levels of adversity.

Demand Characteristics: Cues in a research setting that might influence participants to respond in ways they think researchers expect.

Density Distribution: In personality research, the pattern showing how often someone displays different levels of a trait in daily life.

Dukkha: A central concept in Buddhism translated as suffering, dissatisfaction, or stress. The recognition of *dukkha* is considered the starting point for seeking compassion and wisdom.

Empathic Concern: The emotional response of caring for someone who is suffering, involving feelings of warmth and compassion.

Empirical: Based on observation, experience, or experiment rather than theory alone.

Eudaimonic Well-Being: A type of well-being focused on meaning, purpose, and personal growth rather than just happiness or pleasure.

Experience Sampling Method (ESM): A research method where participants report on their thoughts, feelings, and behaviors in real time or multiple times per day in their natural environments. This avoids the biases of retrospective recall.

Factor Analysis: A statistical method used to identify underlying patterns or groupings in data.

Hedonic Well-Being: Well-being defined by pleasure, happiness, and the absence of negative emotions.

Hester Panim: A Jewish theological concept meaning "hiding of the face," where God seems to withdraw His presence from a sufferer, which is seen as necessary to allow for human freedom and moral responsibility.

Idiographic Approach: Research methods that focus on understanding individuals in their uniqueness rather than comparing them to group averages.

Illusory Growth: The perception of positive change that doesn't reflect actual change in behavior or personality.

Individualistic Cultures: Societies that emphasize personal autonomy, self-reliance, and individual achievement.

Informant Reports: A research method where the self-reports of a participant are compared with reports from close others (informants) like friends or family members to see if they agree, thus providing external validation.

Ipsative Approaches: Methods that compare a person to themselves rather than to other people.

Latent Class Analysis: A statistical method used to identify distinct underlying subgroups or "classes" of individuals within a larger population based on their patterns of responses.

Longitudinal Study: Research that follows the same people over an extended period, allowing researchers to track actual changes.

Master Narratives: Culturally dominant and shared stories, or "cultural scripts," that provide templates for how to understand life experiences like suffering and redemption. The American "redemption story" is a prominent example.

Meaning-Making: The process of creating understanding or significance from life experiences, especially difficult ones.

Meta-Analysis: A statistical technique that combines results from multiple studies to identify overall patterns.

Mindfulness: The practice of paying attention to present-moment experiences without judgment.

Multimethod Assessment: Using various measurement approaches (self-report, observation, biological markers) to get a more complete picture.

Narrative Identity: The internalized life story that people construct to make sense of their past, present, and future.

Neuroticism: A personality trait characterized by a tendency toward negative emotions like anxiety, sadness, and emotional instability.

Personality Psychology: The scientific study of the relatively enduring patterns of thoughts, emotions, motives, and behaviors that distinguish one person from another, as well as the processes that produce and shape those patterns across situations and over time.

Personality States: How someone thinks, feels, and behaves in a specific moment (as opposed to their general traits).

Personality Traits: Relatively stable patterns of thinking, feeling, and behaving that characterize individuals.

Positive Psychology: The scientific study of human strengths, well-being, and optimal functioning.

Post-Traumatic Growth (PTG): Positive psychological changes that some people report experiencing as a result of struggling with highly challenging life circumstances.

Post-Traumatic Growth Inventory (PTGI): The most widely used questionnaire for measuring self-reported growth after trauma.

Post-Traumatic Stress Disorder (PTSD): A mental health condition triggered by experiencing or witnessing a terrifying event, characterized by intrusive memories, avoidance, and heightened reactivity.

Prolonged Exposure (PE): A therapy for PTSD that involves gradually confronting trauma-related memories and situations.

Prospective Design: Research that identifies participants before an event occurs and follows them forward in time.

Psychometric Properties: The reliability and validity of a psychological measure—essentially, how well it measures what it claims to measure.

Randomized Controlled Trial (RCT): A research design where participants are randomly assigned to treatment or control groups to test intervention effectiveness.

Redemption Pressure: The social or cultural expectation that people should find positive meaning or growth in their suffering.

Redemptive Sequences: Life story patterns where negative experiences lead to positive outcomes.

Resilience: The ability to maintain relatively stable functioning despite experiencing adversity.

Retrospective Bias: Distortions in memory when people try to recall how they were in the past.

Schema: Core beliefs about oneself, others, and the world that shape how we interpret experiences.

Secondary Control Coping: Adapting to situations by changing oneself rather than trying to change the situation.

Self-Report Measures: Questionnaires where people describe their own thoughts, feelings, or behaviors.

Social Desirability Bias: The tendency to present oneself in a favorable light, especially in research settings.

State-Trait Distinction: The difference between how someone is in a particular moment (state) versus their general tendencies (trait).

Systematic Review: A comprehensive analysis of all available research on a particular topic using explicit methods.

Stoicism: A school of philosophy from ancient Greece and Rome that emphasizes virtue as the only true good. It teaches resilience through accepting what one cannot control and focusing on one's own rational choices and discipline.

Theodicy: Attempts to explain why a good and all-powerful God would allow evil and suffering to exist.

Three-Tier Model of Personality: A framework dividing personality into traits, characteristic adaptations, and narrative identity.

Trait: A relatively stable characteristic that describes consistent patterns in how people think, feel, and behave.

Transformative Experience: An experience that fundamentally changes both what you know and who you are.

Trauma: An event or series of events that overwhelm a person's ability to cope, often involving threat to life or safety.

Validity: The extent to which a measure actually assesses what it claims to measure.

Virtue Ethics: An ethical theory, most associated with Aristotle, that focuses on the development of moral character and virtues (like courage, patience, and prudence) as the key to living a good life (*eudaimonia*).

Well-Being: A broad term that in psychology encompasses life satisfaction, positive emotions, and sense of meaning or purpose.

Whole Trait Theory (WTT): A personality theory proposing that traits consist of both patterns of behavior (what people do) and the underlying mechanisms explaining those patterns (why they do it).

Notes

Chapter 1

1. Neil DeVotta, *Blowback: Linguistic Nationalism, Institutional Decay, and Ethnic Conflict in Sri Lanka* (Stanford University Press, 2004); Eranda Jayawickreme, Nuwan Jayawickreme, and Elise Miller, "Triumphalism, Fear and Humiliation: The Psychological Legacy of Sri Lanka's Civil War," *Dynamics of Asymmetric Conflict* 3, no. 3 (2010): 208–222; Ahilan Kadirgamar, "Polarization, Civil War, and Persistent Majoritarianism in Sri Lanka," in *Political Polarization in South and Southeast Asia: Old Divisions, New Dangers*, ed. Thomas Carothers and Andrew O'Donohue (Carnegie Endowment for International Peace, 2020), 53–66; Daya Somasundaram, *Scarred Communities: Psychosocial Impact of Man-Made and Natural Disasters on Sri Lankan Society* (SAGE Publications, 2014); Samanth Subramanian, *This Divided Island: Stories from the Sri Lankan War* (Atlantic Books, 2015).
2. Friedrich Nietzsche, Twilight of the Idols, trans. Duncan Large (Oxford: Oxford University Press, 1998), 5.
3. Daphna Oyserman, "Culturally Fluent Theories, Metascience, and Scientific Progress: A Case Example: Commentary on Macnamara and Burgoyne (2023) and Burnette et al. (2023)," *Psychological Bulletin* 149, no. 3–4 (2023): 220–228.
4. Alan J. Lambert, John P. Schott, and Laura Scherer, "Threat, Politics, and Attitudes: Toward a Greater Understanding of Rally-'Round-the-Flag Effects," *Current Directions in Psychological Science* 20, no. 6 (2011): 343–348.
5. Dan P. McAdams, *The Stories We Live By: Personal Myths and the Making of the Self* (Guilford Press, 1993).
6. Dan P. McAdams, *The Stories We Live By*.
7. Throughout this book, *adversity* will be used as a broad term to encompass significant life challenges, hardships, misfortunes, and difficult circumstances that people encounter. These experiences often involve *suffering*, which refers to the resultant physical, emotional, or psychological pain, distress, and hardship individuals may endure. *Trauma* can be understood as a particularly intense or overwhelming form of adversity and suffering, often involving events that threaten life or safety, significantly disrupt core beliefs, and have the potential for profound and lasting psychological impact.
8. Sebastian Junger, *Tribe: On Homecoming and Belonging* (Twelve, 2016).
9. Vedantam (2023), Robson (2022), Sarner (2021), and Newberry (2023) have all done thoughtful work incorporating my PTG research.
10. Frances Harrison, *Still Counting the Dead: Survivors of Sri Lanka's Hidden War* (Portobello Books, 2012).
11. The author Chimamanda Ngozi Adichie has made a similar (broader) argument: Chimamanda Ngozi Adichie, "The Danger of a Single Story," TED Talk, TEDGlobal 2009, July 2009, video, 18:33, https://www.youtube.com/watch?v=D9Ihs241zeg.
12. Richard G. Tedeschi and Lawrence G. Calhoun, "The Posttraumatic Growth Inventory: Measuring the Positive Legacy of Trauma," *Journal of Traumatic Stress* 9, no. 3 (1996): 455–471.
13. Xiaoli Wu, Atipatsa C. Kaminga, Wenjie Dai, Jing Deng, Zhipeng Wang, Xiongfeng Pan, and Aizhong Liu, "The Prevalence of Moderate-to-High Posttraumatic Growth: A Systematic Review and Meta-Analysis," *Journal of Affective Disorders* 243 (2019): 408–415.
14. Eranda Jayawickreme and Laura E. R. Blackie, "Post-Traumatic Growth as Positive Personality Change: Evidence, Controversies and Future Directions," *European Journal of Personality* 28, no. 4 (2014): 312–331; Howard Tennen and Glenn Affleck, "Assessing Positive Life Change: In Search of Meticulous Methods," in *Medical Illness and Positive Life Change: Can Crisis Lead to Personal Change?*, ed. Crystal L. Park, Susan C. Lechner, Michael H. Antoni, and Annette L. Stanton (American Psychological Association, 2009), 31–49.

15. Adriel Boals, "Illusory Posttraumatic Growth Is Common, but Genuine Posttraumatic Growth Is Rare: A Critical Review and Suggestions for a Path Forward," *Clinical Psychology Review* 103 (2023): 102301; Jayawickreme and Blackie, "Post-Traumatic Growth as Positive Personality Change," 318; Tennen and Affleck, "Assessing Positive Life Change."
16. Sara Etz Mendonça, Ann Marie Roepke, Eli Tsukayama, Amaris Grant, and Eranda Jayawickreme, "Randomized Controlled Trial of COMPASS, an Online Psychosocial Intervention Targeting Posttraumatic Growth: Addressing Acceptability and Feasibility," *The Journal of Positive Psychology*, 20, no. 5 (2025): 774–790.
17. Frank J. Infurna and Suniya S. Luthar, "Re-Evaluating the Notion That Resilience Is Commonplace: A Review and Distillation of Directions for Future Research, Practice, and Policy," *Clinical Psychology Review* 65 (2018): 43–56.
18. Eranda Jayawickreme, Michael Brady, and Nuwan Jayawickreme, "Multidisciplinary Recommendations for Improving the Credibility of Research on Post-Traumatic Growth" (manuscript under review, 2025); Richard A. Shweder, Nancy C. Much, Manamohan Mahapatra, and Lawrence Park, "The 'Big Three' of Morality (Autonomy, Community, Divinity) and the 'Big Three' Explanations of Suffering," in *Morality and Health*, ed. Allan M. Brandt and Paul Rozin (Routledge, 1997), 119–169.
19. Mara van der Lugt, Dark Matters: Pessimism and the Problem of Suffering (Princeton University Press, 2021).
20. Jim Rendon, *Upside: The New Science of Post-Traumatic Growth* (Simon & Schuster, 2015); Stephen Joseph. *What Doesn't Kill Us: The New Psychology of Posttraumatic Growth.* Basic Books, 2013.
21. Agnes Callard, "The Philosophy of Anger," *Boston Review* 16, no. 4 (2020). Barbara Ehrenreich, *Bright-Sided: How Positive Thinking Is Undermining America* (Metropolitan Books, 2009).
22. Barbara Ehrenreich, *Bright-Sided: How Positive Thinking Is Undermining America* (Metropolitan Books, 2009).

Chapter 2

1. Most of those people who were "disappeared" were likely executed and their bodies deposited in mass graves (Francis 2025).
2. I first wrote about this experience in 2015 for a piece in the online magazine *Slate* that was sponsored by the John Templeton Foundation.
3. Michelle Panchuk, "What Doesn't Kill Me Makes Me Stronger? Post-Traumatic Growth and the Problem of Suffering," *Religious Studies* 60, no. 3 (2024): 428–444, at 436.
4. Christian B. Miller, "A Satisfactory Definition of 'Post-Traumatic Growth' Still Remains Elusive," *European Journal of Personality* 28, no. 4 (2014): 344–346.
5. Jonathan M. Adler and Ted Schwaba, "Beyond 'Post,' 'Traumatic,' 'Growth,' and Prediction in Research on Posttraumatic Growth," *American Psychologist* 79, no. 8 (2024): 1227–1240.
6. Tennen and Affleck, "Assessing Positive Life Change."
7. Shweder et al., "The 'Big Three' of Morality."
8. Jayawickreme et al., "Multidisciplinary Recommendations."
9. Aristotle, *Nicomachean Ethics*, trans. W. D. Ross (Clarendon Press, 1925); Michael Brady and Eranda Jayawickreme, "A Philosophical Approach to Improving Empirical Research on Posttraumatic Growth," *Philosophical Psychology* 38, no. 2 (2025): 796–819.
10. Jonathan Haidt, *The Happiness Hypothesis: Finding Modern Truth in Ancient Wisdom* (Basic Books, 2006), chap. 7.
11. Michael S. Brady, *Suffering and Virtue* (Oxford University Press, 2018).
12. Jayawickreme et al., "Multidisciplinary Recommendations."
13. St. Thomas Aquinas (2014) similarly posited a logical relationship between certain kinds of adversity and virtue. It is also worth noting that the high level of prudence shown in this context may have been the result of learning from previous adversity, meaning that adversity doesn't just provide the occasion for the exercise of virtue, but can also play a key role in the development of virtue. Thanks to Michael Brady for this point.
14. William B. Irvine, *The Stoic Challenge: A Philosopher's Guide to Becoming Tougher, Calmer, and More Resilient* (W. W. Norton & Company, 2019); Nancy Sherman, *Stoic Wisdom: Ancient Lessons for Modern Resilience* (Oxford University Press, 2021).
15. Epictetus, *Discourses: Book 1–2* (Dover Publications, 2004), 46.
16. Marcus Aurelius, *Meditations*, trans. Martin Hammond (Penguin, 2015).

17. Sherman, *Stoic Wisdom*; Massimo Pigliucci and Gregory Lopez. A *H*andbook for *N*ew *S*toics: How to *T*hrive in a World *O*ut of *Y*our Control—52 *W*eek-by-*Week L*essons. The Experiment, 2019.
18. Erik G. Helzer and Eranda Jayawickreme, "Control and the 'Good Life': Primary and Secondary Control as Distinct Indicators of Well-Being," *Social Psychological and Personality Science* 6, no. 6 (2015): 653–660. Friedrich Wilhelm Nietzsche, *Beyond Good and Evil: Prelude to a Philosophy of the Future*, trans. R. J. Hollingdale (Penguin Books, 1990).
19. Irvine, *The Stoic Challenge*, 106; Aikin and Stephens, *Epictetus's Encheiridion*, 254.
20. Irvine, *The Stoic Challenge*, chap. 2.
21. Aikin and Stephens, *Epictetus's Encheiridion*, 67.
22. Martha C. Nussbaum, *Anger and Forgiveness: Resentment, Generosity, Justice* (Oxford University Press, 2016).
23. Indeed, we would likely think worse of someone who was not angered by deep injustice or significant violations of important values. Thanks to Michael Brady for this point.
24. Michael S. Brady, "Group Emotion and Group Understanding," in *The Epistemic Life of Groups: Essays in the Epistemology of Collectives*, ed. Michael S. Brady and Miranda Fricker (Oxford University Press, 2016), 95–110; Elaine H. Pagels, *Why Religion?: A Personal Story* (HarperLuxe, an imprint of HarperCollins Publishers, 2018), chap. 6; Katie Stockdale, *Hope Under Oppression* (Oxford University Press, 2021), chap. 3.
25. Nuwan Jayawickreme, Eranda Jayawickreme, Amy Z. McCaffrey, and Mahendran Thiruvarangan, "Mental Health Futures in Post-War Sri Lanka: Resilience, Relational Pluralism, and Implementation Pathways," *SSM–Mental Health* 7, no. 5 (2025): 100465.
26. Nussbaum, *Anger and Forgiveness*.
27. Callard, "The Philosophy of Anger."
28. Olúfẹ́mi O. Táíwò, *Elite Capture: How the Powerful Took Over Identity Politics (and Everything Else)* (Haymarket Books, 2022).
29. Daryl R. Van Tongeren and Sara A. Showalter Van Tongeren, *The Courage to Suffer: A New Clinical Framework for Life's Greatest Crises* (Templeton Foundation Press, 2020).
30. Edward C. Chang, "An Appraisal of Nietzsche's Philosophical Concept of *Amor Fati*: A Potentially Useful Psychological Construct in the Study of Positive Human Existence?," *The Humanistic Psychologist* 53, no. 2 (2024): 183–196; Robert Zaretsky, *A Life Worth Living* (Harvard University Press, 2013).
31. Jennifer Anna Gosetti-Ferencei, *On Being and Becoming: An Existentialist Approach to Life* (Oxford University Press, 2020).
32. Karl Jaspers, *Psychologie der Weltanschauungen* (Max Niemeyer Verlag, 1925).
33. I first cited this in Mendonça, Roepke, Tsukayama, Grant, and Jayawickreme, "Randomized Controlled Trial of COMPASS." Thanks to Ed Chang for pointing me to this quote.
34. Scott Samuelson, *Seven Ways of Looking at Pointless Suffering: What Philosophy Can Tell Us About the Hardest Mystery of All* (University of Chicago Press, 2018).
35. Thanks to Lisa Blee for pointing me to this example.
36. John Green, *Everything Is Tuberculosis: The History and Persistence of Our Deadliest Infection* (Random House, 2025); Frank M. Snowden, *Epidemics and Society: From the Black Death to the Present* (Yale University Press, 2019).
37. Emmy van Deurzen, *Existential Counselling and Psychotherapy in Practice* (SAGE, 2008).
38. van der Lugt, *Dark Matters*.
39. Joel Vos, "Meaning and Existential Givens in the Lives of Cancer Patients: A Philosophical Perspective on Psycho-Oncology," *Palliative & Supportive Care* 13, no. 4 (2015): 885–900.
40. Robin R. Wang, "Understanding of Yin Yang," *Religion Compass* 7, no. 6 (2013): 214–224.
41. Ian James Kidd, "Adversity, Wisdom, and Exemplarism," *The Journal of Value Inquiry* 52, no. 4 (2018): 379–393.
42. Sara Etz Mendonça, Michael Brady, and Eranda Jayawickreme, "Can Exemplars Promote Character Development in the Wake of Adversity?," in *The Routledge International Handbook of Multidisciplinary Perspectives on Character Development, Volume II*, ed. Michael D. Matthews and Richard M. Lerner (Routledge, 2024), 165–176.
43. Brady and Jayawickreme, "Philosophical Approach to Improving Empirical Research."
44. Melissa R. Raphael, "The Price of (Masculine) Freedom and Becoming: A Jewish Feminist Response to Eliezer Berkovits's Post-Holocaust Free Will Defence of God's Non-Intervention in Auschwitz," in *Feminist Philosophy of Religion: Critical Readings*, ed. Pamela Sue Anderson and Beverley Clack (Routledge, 2004): 136–150.

45. Miller, "A Satisfactory Definition of 'Post-Traumatic Growth.'"
46. Tedeschi and Calhoun, "The Posttraumatic Growth Inventory."
47. Stephen Joseph and P. Alex Linley, "Positive Adjustment to Threatening Events: An Organismic Valuing Theory of Growth through Adversity," *Review of General Psychology* 9, no. 3 (2005): 262–280.
48. Laura E. R. Blackie and Eranda Jayawickreme, "Promoting Change in Post-Traumatic Growth Research: Response to Commentaries," *European Journal of Personality* 28, no. 4 (2014): 351–361.
49. While the experience of adversity would provide the opportunity to develop specific virtues, I stress here that the failure to subsequently develop those virtues does not necessarily make you less virtuous as a person. Thanks to Marion Johnson for raising this concern.
50. Brady and Jayawickreme, "Philosophical Approach to Improving Empirical Research."
51. Brady, *Suffering and Virtue.*
52. Boals, "Illusory Posttraumatic Growth Is Common, but Genuine Posttraumatic Growth Is Rare."
53. L. A. Paul, *Transformative Experience* (Oxford University Press, 2014).
54. Harrison, *Still Counting the Dead*, 92–113.
55. Although it should be noted that specific personality characteristics (e.g., being more open to new experiences; Jayawickreme and Blackie, "Post-Traumatic Growth as Positive Personality Change") may increase the likelihood that one will see the experience as positive.
56. Shahar Hechtlinger, Christin Schulze, Christina Leuker, and Ralph Hertwig, "The Psychology of Life's Most Important Decisions," *American Psychologist* (2024).
57. Soliciting the viewpoints of close others about us may assist us here (e.g., Blackie et al. 2015).
58. However, for an example of such an approach, see Hechtlinger et al., "The Psychology of Life's Most Important Decisions."
59. Exceptions to this may include people who volunteer for military service in times of conflict, firefighters and other emergency staff, and those who sign up for extreme physical challenges.
60. I should acknowledge here that such norms can also help with imposing positive limits on our self-identities as well, such as being a good citizen, being fair, or considering others. Thanks to Michael Brady for this point.
61. Rebecca Chan, "Transformative Experience," in *The Stanford Encyclopedia of Philosophy* (Spring 2024 Edition), ed. Edward N. Zalta and Uri Nodelman, https://plato.stanford.edu/archives/spr2024/entries/transformative-experience/
62. Elizabeth Barnes, "Social Identities and Transformative Experience," *Res Philosophica* 92, no. 2 (2015): 171–187.
63. Brady, *Suffering and Virtue.*
64. Santushi Devini Amarasuriya, Maria Guadalupe C. Salanga, Charisse T. Llorin, Marie Rose H. Morales, Eranda Jayawickreme, and Igor Grossmann, "Deconstructing Wisdom Through a Cultural Lens: Folk Understandings of Wisdom and Its Ontology in the Philippines and Sri Lanka," *Transcultural Psychiatry* 61, no. 5 (2024): 767–782.
65. Anna Dorfman, David A. Moscovitch, William J. Chopik, and Igor Grossmann, "None the Wiser: Year-Long Longitudinal Study on Effects of Adversity on Wisdom," *European Journal of Personality* 36, no. 4 (2022): 559–575.
66. Jayawickreme et al., "Multidisciplinary Recommendations."
67. Shweder et al., "The 'Big Three' of Morality."
68. Tennen and Affleck, "Assessing Positive Life Change."
69. Shweder et al., "The 'Big Three' of Morality."
70. Brady and Jayawickreme, "A Philosophical Approach to Improving Empirical Research on Posttraumatic Growth."
71. Miller, "A Satisfactory Definition of 'Post-Traumatic Growth.'"
72. For an example of how not considering structural conditions can lead to incorrectly valorizing Stoicism in the wake of adversity in Sri Lanka, see Jeremy Laurance, "The Danger of Stoicism," *The Lancet* 376, no. 9747 (2010): 1137.

Chapter 3

1. DeVotta, *Blowback.*
2. Pagels, *Why Religion?*.
3. Elaine Pagels, *Miracles and Wonder: The Historical Mystery of Jesus* (Doubleday, 2025).
4. Pagels, *Why Religion?*, xiv.

5. Robert W. McChesney, *The Soul Also Keeps the Score: A Trauma-Informed Companion to the Spiritual Exercises of St. Ignatius* (Liturgical Press, 2025).
6. Pagels, *Why Religion?*, 23.
7. Pagels, *Why Religion?*, 103–104.
8. Pagels, *Why Religion?*, 109.
9. Eleonore Stump, *Wandering in Darkness: Narrative and the Problem of Suffering* (Oxford University Press, 2010).
10. C. S. Lewis, *A Grief Observed* (Zondervan, 2001).
11. Note, however, that Panchuk (2024a) has critiqued Stump for her uncritical embrace of the PTG literature in advancing this argument. We'll discuss this later in the chapter.
12. Michael Ignatieff, *On Consolation: Finding Solace in Dark Times* (Metropolitan Books, 2021), 22.
13. John Hick, *Evil and the God of Love*, 2nd ed. (Palgrave Macmillan, 2010).
14. Kate C. McLean, *Why Change Is Hard: The Power of Master Narratives over Self and Society* (Oxford University Press, 2024).
15. Michelle Panchuk, "Distorting Concepts, Obscured Experiences: Hermeneutical Injustice in Religious Trauma and Spiritual Violence," *Hypatia* 35, no. 4 (2020): 607–625; Panchuk, "What Doesn't Kill Me Makes Me Stronger?"; Michelle Panchuk, *Religious Trauma* (Cambridge University Press, 2024b).
16. Miranda Fricker, *Epistemic Injustice: Power and the Ethics of Knowing* (Oxford University Press, 2007).
17. I have written elsewhere that Fricker's work on epistemic injustice can arguably be applied to PTG research more broadly. (Corinne E. Zachry and Eranda Jayawickreme, "Unbelieving Wisdom: Does Critiquing Reports of Perceived Growth Following Adversity Constitute an Epistemic Injustice?," in *Post-Traumatic Growth to Psychological Well-Being: Coping Wisely with Adversity*, 31–42, ed. Melanie Munroe and Michel Ferrari (Springer International Publishing, 2022).)
18. Panchuk, "Distorting Concepts, Obscured Experiences."
19. Panchuk, *Religious Trauma.*
20. Panchuk, "Distorting Concepts, Obscured Experiences."
21. Panchuk, "Distorting Concepts, Obscured Experiences."
22. Panchuk, *Religious Trauma, 12.*
23. Panchuk, *Religious Trauma.*
24. V. F. Gunaratna, *The Significance of the Four Noble Truths* (Buddhist Publication Society, 1968).
25. Emily McRae, "Suffering and the Six Perfections: Using Adversity to Attain Wisdom in Mahāyāna Buddhist Ethics," *The Journal of Value Inquiry* 52, no. 4 (2018): 395–410.
26. Notably, this fivefold framework does share some degree of overlap with currently studied domains of PTG, which identifies increased appreciation of life, strengthened relationships, personal strength, changed priorities, and spiritual development as potential post-traumatic benefits.
27. Shweder et al., "The 'Big Three' of Morality."
28. Pema Chödrön, *When Things Fall Apart: Heart Advice for Difficult Times* (Shambhala Publications, 2000).
29. Chödrön, When Things Fall Apart, 89.
30. For an example of how this plays out in a context of a religious ritual, see Balkaya-Ince et al., "Does Ramadan Serve as a Naturalistic Intervention?"
31. Balkaya-Ince et al., "Does Ramadan Serve as a Naturalistic Intervention?"
32. Ibn Qayyim al-Ǧauzīya, *Patience and Gratitude: An Abridged Translation*, trans. Nāṣir al-Dīn al-Ḫaṭṭāb (Ta-Ha Publishers, 1997).
33. Tarek Badawia, "Islamic Practical Theology: Waqf and Zakāt as Theological Foundations," in *Exploring Islamic Social Work: Between Community and the Common Good*, ed. Hansjörg Schmid and Amir Sheikhzadegan (Springer International Publishing, 2022), 151–164.
34. Eliezer Berkovits, *Faith after the Holocaust* (Ktav Publishing House, 1973).
35. Berkovits, *Faith after the Holocaust*, 94–96.
36. Berkovits, *Faith after the Holocaust*, 61.
37. Raphael, "The Price of (Masculine) Freedom and Becoming."
38. Many thanks to Michelle Panchuk for a very helpful conversation around this article. I'm also very much indebted to her discussion of these texts in Panchuk, *Religious Trauma*, 44–45, 62–64.

39. Judith Tydor Baumel, "Women's Agency and Survival Strategies During the Holocaust," *Women's Studies International Forum* 22, no. 3 (1999): 329–347.
40. Raphael, "The Price of (Masculine) Freedom and Becoming," 140.
41. Raphael, "The Price of (Masculine) Freedom and Becoming," 138.
42. Harold S. Kushner, *When Bad Things Happen to Good People* (Vintage, 1981).
43. David Wolpe, *Making Loss Matter: Creating Meaning in Difficult Times* (Penguin, 2000).
44. Caroline Williamson, "Towards a Theory of Collective Posttraumatic Growth in Rwanda: The Pursuit of Agency and Communion," *Traumatology: An International Journal* 20, no. 2 (2014a): 91–102; Caroline Williamson, "Posttraumatic Growth and Religion in Rwanda: Individual Well-Being vs. Collective False Consciousness," *Mental Health, Religion & Culture* 17, no. 9 (2014b): 946–955.
45. Williamson now publishes under her married name of Williamson Sinalo.
46. David Bakan, *The Duality of Human Existence: An Essay on Psychology and Religion* (Rand McNally, 1966).
47. McAdams, *The Stories We Live By.*
48. John T. Jost, Brian A. Nosek, and Samuel D. Gosling, "Ideology: Its Resurgence in Social, Personality, and Political Psychology," *Perspectives on Psychological Science* 3, no. 2 (2008): 126–136.
49. Williamson, "Towards a Theory of Collective Posttraumatic Growth," 96.
50. Williamson, "Towards a Theory of Collective Posttraumatic Growth," 97.
51. Williamson, "Towards a Theory of Collective Posttraumatic Growth," 97.
52. Williamson, "Towards a Theory of Collective Posttraumatic Growth," 98.
53. Linn Zapffe, Kaitlyn Hennig, Nuwan Jayawickreme, and Eranda Jayawickreme, "What Does It Mean to Flourish, Languish, and Grow? A Qualitative Analysis of Civilian Interviews from Survivors of the 1994 Rwandan Genocide," *SSM–Mental Health* 4 (2023): 100274.
54. U.S. Agency for International Development, *Rebuilding Postwar Rwanda: The Role of the International Community (A.I.D. Evaluation Special Study Report No. 76)* (Washington, DC: U.S. Agency for International Development, 1996).
55. Williamson, "Posttraumatic Growth and Religion in Rwanda."
56. Amartya Sen, *Home in the World: A Memoir* (Liveright Publishing, 2021).
57. Panchuk, "Distorting Concepts, Obscured Experiences."
58. Laura E. R. Blackie, Eranda Jayawickreme, Nicki Hitchcott, and Stephen Joseph, "Distinguishing Post-Traumatic Growth from Psychological Adjustment among Rwandan Genocide Survivors," in *Varieties of Virtue Ethics*, ed. David Carr, James Arthur, and Kristján Kristjánsson (Palgrave Macmillan, 2016), 299–317.
59. Williamson, "Posttraumatic Growth and Religion in Rwanda," 952.
60. Also, arguably both the Stoic and Buddhist traditions make the case for people withdrawing from the world to manage their response to adversity.
61. Panchuk, "What Doesn't Kill Me Makes Me Stronger?"
62. Stump, *Wandering in Darkness.*
63. This observation mirrors the critique of both Brady and Jayawickreme, "A Philosophical Approach to Improving Empirical Research," and Miller, "A Satisfactory Definition of 'Post-Traumatic Growth.'"
64. Panchuk, "What Doesn't Kill Me Makes Me Stronger?," 441–442.
65. Kendall Cotton Bronk, Zach T. Swanson, William B. Whitney, Merve Balkaya-Ince, and Sarah Schnitker, "Exploring Conceptions of Patience Among a Sample of Muslim, Buddhist, Christian, and Nonreligious Young Adults," *Psychology of Religion and Spirituality* 17, no. 3 (2025): 270–281.
66. Thich Nhat Hanh, *Interbeing: The 14 Mindfulness Trainings of Engaged Buddhism* (Parallax Press, 2020).
67. Stump, *Wandering in Darkness*, 459.

Chapter 4

1. McAdams, *The Stories We Live By.*
2. Brian Klaas, *Fluke: Chance, Chaos, and Why Everything We Do Matters* (Simon & Schuster, 2024).

3. Minoli Salgado, *Twelve Cries from Home: In Search of Sri Lanka's Disappeared* (Repeater, 2022) provides a detailed account of narratives by civilians who were victims of war trauma and extrajudicial killings in Sri Lanka.
4. Shehan Karunatilaka, *The Seven Moons of Maali Almeida: Winner of the Booker Prize 2022* (Sort of Books, 2022).
5. I first wrote about this point in a piece for *Psychology Today* (Eranda Jayawickreme, "Is Redemption Redeeming?," *Psychology Today*, November 8, 2022, https://www.psychologytoday.com/us/blog/pathways-flourishing/202211/is-redemption-redeeming).
6. Viktor E. Frankl, *Man's Search for Meaning* (Simon & Schuster, 1985).
7. Abby Maslin, *Love You Hard: A Memoir of Marriage, Brain Injury, and Reinventing Love* (Dutton, 2019), 298–299.
8. Dan P. McAdams and Bradley D. Olson, "Personality Development: Continuity and Change over the Life Course," *Annual Review of Psychology* 61 (2010): 517–542.
9. Tilmann Habermas and Susan Bluck, "Getting a Life: The Emergence of the Life Story in Adolescence," *Psychological Bulletin* 126, no. 5 (2000): 748–769; Dan P. McAdams, "First We Invented Stories, Then They Changed Us: The Evolution of Narrative Identity," *Evolutionary Studies in Imaginative Culture* 3, no. 1 (2019): 1–18; Dan P. McAdams and Kate C. McLean, "Narrative Identity," *Current Directions in Psychological Science* 22, no. 3 (2013): 233–238.
10. Gay Becker, *Disrupted Lives: How People Create Meaning in a Chaotic World* (University of California Press, 1997); Ronnie Janoff-Bulman, *Shattered Assumptions: Towards a New Psychology of Trauma* (Free Press, 1992).
11. Dan P. McAdams, Jennifer Reynolds, Mara Lewis, A. H. Patten, and Philip J. Bowman, "When Bad Things Turn Good and Good Things Turn Bad: Sequences of Redemption and Contamination in Life Narrative and Their Relation to Psychosocial Adaptation in Midlife Adults and in Students," *Personality and Social Psychology Bulletin* 27, no. 4 (2001): 474–485.
12. McAdams et al., "When Bad Things Turn Good."
13. Dan P. McAdams and Jennifer L. Pals, "A New Big Five: Fundamental Principles for an Integrative Science of Personality," *American Psychologist* 61, no. 3 (2006): 204–217.
14. Dan P. McAdams, "The Psychology of Life Stories," *Review of General Psychology* 5, no. 2 (2001): 100–122.
15. Mark J. Landau, Aaron C. Kay, and Jennifer A. Whitson, "Compensatory Control and the Appeal of a Structured World," *Psychological Bulletin* 141, no. 3 (2015): 694–722.
16. Kate C. McLean, Jillian Fish, Leoandra Onnie Rogers, and Moin Syed, "Integrating Systems of Power and Privilege in the Study of Resilience," *American Psychologist* 79, no. 8 (2024): 999–1011.
17. William J. Clinton, "Address Accepting the Presidential Nomination at the Democratic National Convention in New York," speech, Madison Square Garden, New York, July 16, 1992.
18. As a cricket enthusiast, a good example of this for me are the cricketers Ben Stokes's and Steve Smith's returns from various controversies (a fight at a nightclub in Bristol and a ball-tampering scandal, respectively). Geoff Lemon's (2020) *The Comeback Summer* includes some excellent chapters critiquing the redemption framing of their comebacks.
19. One recent example are the allegations of embellishment against Raynor Winn, author of the 2018 memoir *The Salt Path* (*The Economist*, 2025).
20. Dan P. McAdams, Ed de St. Aubin, and Regina L. Logan, "Generativity Among Young, Midlife, and Older Adults," *Psychology and Aging* 8, no. 2 (1993): 221–230.
21. Williamson, "Towards a Theory of Collective Posttraumatic Growth."; Williamson, "Posttraumatic Growth and Religion in Rwanda."
22. Shweder et al., "The 'Big Three' of Morality."
23. Zapffe et al., "What Does It Mean to Flourish, Languish, and Grow?"
24. Raphael, "The Price of (Masculine) Freedom and Becoming."
25. Shigehiro Oishi, Ayano Yagi, Asuka Komiya, Florian Kohlbacher, Takashi Kusumi, and Keiko Ishii, "Does a Major Earthquake Change Job Preferences and Human Values?" *European Journal of Personality* 31, no. 3 (2017): 258–265.
26. Landau, Kay, and Whitson, "Compensatory Control."
27. Adler et al., "Variation in Narrative Identity."
28. William L. Dunlop and Jessica L. Tracy, "Sobering Stories: Narratives of Self-Redemption Predict Behavioral Change and Improved Health Among Recovering Alcoholics," *Journal of Personality and Social Psychology* 104, no. 3 (2013): 576–590.

29. McLean, *Why Change Is Hard.*; McLean et al., "Integrating Systems of Power and Privilege."
30. McLean, *Why Change Is Hard*, 29.
31. Kate C. McLean and Moin Syed, "Personal, Master, and Alternative Narratives: An Integrative Framework for Understanding Identity Development in Context," *Human Development* 58, no. 6 (2016): 318–349.
32. Geoff Lemon, *The Comeback Summer*. Hardie Grant Publishing, 2020.
33. Junger, *Tribe.*
34. Kate C. McLean, Brianna C. Delker, William L. Dunlop, Rowan Salton, and Moin Syed, "Redemptive Stories and Those Who Tell Them Are Preferred in the US," *Collabra: Psychology* 6, no. 1 (2020).
35. Thanks to the psychologist Simine Vazire, who discussed this challenge with me at a 2016 meeting on PTG.
36. Ehrenreich, *Bright-Sided.*
37. Ann Marie Roepke, Eli Tsukayama, Marie J. C. Forgeard, Laura E. R. Blackie, and Eranda Jayawickreme, "Randomized Controlled Trial of SecondStory, an Intervention Targeting Post-traumatic Growth, with Bereaved Adults," *Journal of Consulting and Clinical Psychology* 86, no. 6 (2018): 518–532.
38. Laura E. R. Blackie and Kate C. McLean, "Examining the Longitudinal Associations Between Repeated Narration of Recent Transgressions Within Individuals' Romantic Relationships and Character Growth in Empathy, Humility, and Compassion," *European Journal of Personality* 36, no. 4 (2022): 507–528.
39. Andreas Maercker and Tanja Zoellner, "The Janus Face of Self-Perceived Growth: Toward a Two-Component Model of Posttraumatic Growth," *Psychological Inquiry* 15, no. 1 (2004): 41–48.
40. Tennen and Affleck, "Assessing Positive Life Change."

Chapter 5

1. Valerie Tiberius, "Growth and the Multiple Dimensions of Well-Being: A Philosopher's Take on the Idea of Post-Traumatic Growth," in *Redesigning Research on Post-Traumatic Growth: Challenges, Pitfalls, and New Directions*, ed. Frank J. Infurna and Eranda Jayawickreme (Oxford University Press, 2021), 1–11; Laura E. R. Blackie, N. Somasundaram, Victoria Britt, and Eranda Jayawickreme, "Narratives of Redemption among a Sample of Tamil War-Affected Women in Eastern Sri Lanka." Manuscript in preparation, 2025.
2. Subramanian, *This Divided Island.*
3. Daphna Oyserman (2023), "Culturally Fluent Theories."
4. Chris Chambers, *The Seven Deadly Sins of Psychology: A Manifesto for Reforming the Culture of Scientific Practice* (Princeton University Press, 2017).
5. Jayawickreme and Blackie, "Post-Traumatic Growth as Positive Personality Change."
6. Adriel Boals, Eranda Jayawickreme, and Crystal L. Park, "Advantages of Distinguishing Perceived and Veridical Growth: Recommendations for Future Research on Both Constructs," *The Journal of Positive Psychology* 18, no. 5 (2023): 773–783.
7. McLean, *Why Change Is Hard.*
8. Frank J. Infurna and Eranda Jayawickreme, "Fixing the Growth Illusion: New Directions for Research in Resilience and Posttraumatic Growth," *Current Directions in Psychological Science* 28, no. 2 (2019): 152–158.
9. Boals, Jayawickreme, and Park, "Advantages of Distinguishing Perceived and Veridical Growth."
10. Julian D. Ford, Howard Tennen, and David Albert, "A Contrarian View of Growth Following Adversity," in *Trauma, Recovery, and Growth: Positive Psychological Perspectives on Posttraumatic Stress*, ed. Stephen Joseph and Alex Linley (John Wiley & Sons, 2008), 295–324.; Jayawickreme and Blackie, "Post-Traumatic Growth as Positive Personality Change"; Eranda Jayawickreme and Laura E. R. Blackie, *Exploring the Psychological Benefits of Hardship: A Critical Reassessment of Posttraumatic Growth* (Springer, 2016).
11. Landau, Kay, and Whitson, "Compensatory Control and the Appeal of a Structured World."
12. Shelley E. Taylor and David A. Armor, "Positive Illusions and Coping with Adversity," *Journal of Personality* 64, no. 4 (1996): 873–898.
13. Cathy McFarland and Celeste Alvaro, "The Impact of Motivation on Temporal Comparisons: Coping with Traumatic Events by Perceiving Personal Growth," *Journal of Personality and Social Psychology* 79, no. 3 (2000): 327–343.
14. Taylor and Armor, "Positive Illusions and Coping with Adversity."

15. Ford, Tennen, and Albert, "A Contrarian View of Growth Following Adversity."
16. This critique of the PTGI was first posited in Ford, Tennen, and Albert, "A Contrarian View of Growth Following Adversity."
17. McFarland and Alvaro, "The Impact of Motivation on Temporal Comparisons."
18. Grant, Amaris I., R. Michael Furr, and Eranda Jayawickreme. "Assessing the Response Process Validity of the Posttraumatic Growth Inventory Using Cognitive Interviews." Journal of Personality Assessment (2026): 1–12.
19. Ford, Tennen, and Albert, "A Contrarian View of Growth Following Adversity."
20. Patricia Frazier, Howard Tennen, Margaret Gavian, Crystal Park, Patricia Tomich, and Ty Tashiro, "Does Self-Reported Posttraumatic Growth Reflect Genuine Positive Change?," *Psychological Science* 20, no. 7 (2009): 912–919.
21. Betina R. Yanez, Annette L. Stanton, Michael A. Hoyt, Howard Tennen, and Suzanne Lechner, "Understanding Perceptions of Benefit Following Adversity: How Do Distinct Assessments of Growth Relate to Coping and Adjustment to Stressful Events?," *Journal of Social and Clinical Psychology* 30, no. 7 (2011): 699–721.
22. Meghan Owenz and Blaine J. Fowers, "Perceived Post-Traumatic Growth May Not Reflect Actual Positive Change: A Short-Term Prospective Study of Relationship Dissolution," *Journal of Social and Personal Relationships* 36, no. 10 (2019): 3098–3116.
23. Ted Schwaba, Jaap J. A. Denissen, Maike Luhmann, Christopher J. Hopwood, and Wiebke Bleidorn, "Subjective Experiences of Life Events Match Individual Differences in Personality Development," *Journal of Personality and Social Psychology* 125, no. 5 (2023): 1136–1156.
24. Eranda Jayawickreme, Frank J. Infurna, Kinan Alajak, Laura E. R. Blackie, William J. Chopik, Joanne M. Chung, Anna Dorfman, et al., "Post-Traumatic Growth as Positive Personality Change: Challenges, Opportunities, and Recommendations," *Journal of Personality* 89, no. 1 (2021): 145–165.
25. Infurna and Jayawickreme, "Fixing the Growth Illusion."
26. Patricia Frazier, James Coyne, and Howard Tennen, "Post-Traumatic Growth: A Call for Less, but Better, Research," *European Journal of Personality* 28, no. 4 (2014): 337–338.
27. Laura E. R. Blackie, Eranda Jayawickreme, Eli Tsukayama, Marie J. C. Forgeard, Ann Marie Roepke, and William Fleeson, "Post-Traumatic Growth as Positive Personality Change: Developing a Measure to Assess Within-Person Variability," *Journal of Research in Personality* 69 (2017): 22–32.
28. Laura E. R. Blackie, Eranda Jayawickreme, Erik G. Helzer, Marie J. C. Forgeard, and Ann Marie Roepke, "Investigating the Veracity of Self-Perceived Posttraumatic Growth: A Profile Analysis Approach to Corroboration," *Social Psychological and Personality Science* 6, no. 7 (2015): 788–796.
29. Caleb J. Reynolds, Laura E. R. Blackie, R. Michael Furr, A. Demaske, Ann Marie Roepke, Marie Forgeard, and Eranda Jayawickreme, "Investigating Corroboration of Self-Perceived Posttraumatic Growth Among Sri Lankan Tamil Survivors of Ethnopolitical Warfare through Trait, Domain, and Profile Agreement Approaches," *Psychological Assessment* 34, no. 12 (2022): 1155–1165.
30. Lawrence G. Calhoun and Richard G. Tedeschi, "The Foundations of Posttraumatic Growth: An Expanded Framework," in *Handbook of Posttraumatic Growth: Research and Practice*, ed. Lawrence G. Calhoun and Richard G. Tedeschi (Routledge, 2014), 3–23.
31. Specifically, random-intercept cross-lagged panel models that can disentangle within-person from between-person effects.
32. Maercker and Zoellner, "The Janus Face of Self-Perceived Growth."
33. Grant et al., "Assessing the Response Process Validity of the Posttraumatic Growth Inventory Using Cognitive Interviews."
34. Eranda Jayawickreme, Laura E. R. Blackie, Marie Forgeard, Ann Marie Roepke, and Eli Tsukayama, "Examining Associations between Major Negative Life Events, Changes in Weekly Reports of Post-Traumatic Growth and Global Reports of Eudaimonic Well-Being," *Social Psychological and Personality Science* 13, no. 4 (2022): 827–838.
35. Gangel et al., "Does Perceived Posttraumatic Growth Predict Observed Changes."
36. Reynolds et al., "Investigating Corroboration of Self-Perceived Posttraumatic Growth."
37. Grant et al., "Assessing the Response Process Validity of the Posttraumatic Growth Inventory Using Cognitive Interviews."
38. Blackie et al., "Post-Traumatic Growth as Positive Personality Change: Developing a Measure."

39. Grant et al., "Assessing the Response Process Validity of the Posttraumatic Growth Inventory Using Cognitive Interviews."
40. Frazier et al., "Does Self-Reported Posttraumatic Growth Reflect Genuine Positive Change."
41. That said, it is likely that growth will not be hedonically positive in many cases. Indeed, real change often involves trade-offs: enhanced empathy alongside increased anxiety, or deeper spirituality coupled with social withdrawal. I should note that current assessments struggle to capture this complexity.
42. Rowan Kemmerly, Howard Tennen, and Eranda Jayawickreme, "An Agenda for the Next Generation of Posttraumatic Growth Research," in *The Routledge International Handbook of Posttraumatic Growth*, ed. Roni Berger (Routledge, 2023), 67–80.
43. McFarland and Alvaro, "The Impact of Motivation on Temporal Comparisons."
44. Grant et al., "Assessing the Response Process Validity of the Posttraumatic Growth Inventory Using Cognitive Interviews."
45. I should acknowledge here that there are limitations with these methods as well, although in my mind they are clearly superior to much current research (see also Adler and Schwaba, "Beyond 'Post,' 'Traumatic,' 'Growth,' and Prediction.").
46. William J. Chopik, Whitney L. Kelley, Loryana L. Vie, Jeewon Oh, Douglas G. Bonett, Richard E. Lucas, and Martin E. P. Seligman, "Development of Character Strengths across the Deployment Cycle among US Army Soldiers," *Journal of Personality* 89, no. 1 (2021): 23–34.
47. Note that, as I've discussed earlier, benefit-finding coping has been associated with positive outcomes (e.g., lower morbidity among people who experienced a heart attack); Glenn Affleck, Howard Tennen, Sydney Croog, and Sol Levine, "Causal Attribution, Perceived Benefits, and Morbidity after a Heart Attack: An 8-Year Study," *Journal of Consulting and Clinical Psychology* 55, no. 1 (1987): 29–35. For a good discussion of jingle-jangle fallacies, see Tenelle Porter. "Jingle-Jangle Fallacies in Intellectual Humility Research." *The Journal of Positive Psychology* 18, no. 2 (2023): 221–223.
48. Chambers, *The Seven Deadly Sins of Psychology*.
49. Kemmerly, Tennen, and Jayawickreme, "An Agenda for the Next Generation of Posttraumatic Growth Research."
50. Brady and Jayawickreme, "A Philosophical Approach to Improving Empirical Research."; Miller, "A Satisfactory Definition of 'Post-Traumatic Growth.'"; Tiberius, "Growth and the Multiple Dimensions of Well-Being."
51. Oyserman, "Culturally Fluent Theories."
52. McFarland and Alvaro, "The Impact of Motivation on Temporal Comparisons."
53. Vicki S. Helgeson, Kerry A. Reynolds, and Patricia L. Tomich, "A Meta-Analytic Review of Benefit-Finding and Growth," *Journal of Consulting and Clinical Psychology* 74, no. 5 (2006): 797–816.

Chapter 6

1. H. Klodawsky, *No More Tears Sister: Anatomy of Hope and Betrayal* [video recording] (Montreal, QC: National Film Board of Canada, 2005); Rajan Hoole, Kopalasingam Sritharan, Daya Somasundaram, and Rajani Thiranagama, *The Broken Palmyra: The Tamil Crisis in Sri Lanka-An Inside Account* (Sri Lanka Studies Institute, 1990).
2. For fictionalized accounts of her life, see V. V. Ganeshananthan, *Brotherless Night: A Novel* (Random House, 2023); Karunatilaka, *The Seven Moons of Maali Almeida*.
3. Lasantha Wickrematunge, "And Then They Came for Me," in *The Sri Lanka Reader: History, Culture, Politics* (Duke University Press, 2011), 715–720.
4. His live performance of "Abattoir Blues" on *Later ... with Jules Holland* is worth checking out on YouTube: https://www.youtube.com/watch?v=bVjXAGXlqnA.
5. Nick Cave and Sean O'Hagan, *Faith, Hope and Carnage: Sunday Times Bestseller* (Canongate Books, 2022).
6. Cave and O'Hagan, *Faith, Hope and Carnage*, 31–32.
7. Stephen Joseph and P. Alex Linley, "Positive Adjustment to Threatening Events: An Organismic Valuing Theory of Growth through Adversity," *Review of General Psychology* 9, no. 3 (2005): 262–280.
8. Shankar Vedantam, "What We Gain from Pain," *Hidden Brain* (podcast), Hidden Brain Media, July 31, 2023.

9. Marie J. C. Forgeard, Anne C. Mecklenburg, Justin J. Lacasse, and Eranda Jayawickreme, "Bringing the Whole Universe to Order: Creativity, Healing, and Posttraumatic Growth," in *Creativity and Mental Illness*, ed. James C. Kaufman (Cambridge University Press, 2014), 321–335.
10. Nick Cave, *The Red Hand Files*, Issue 248 (2023).
11. Tennen and Affleck, *Assessing Positive Life Change: In Search of Meticulous Methods* (2009).
12. Brent W. Roberts, "Back to the Future: Personality and Assessment and Personality Development," *Journal of Research in Personality* 43, no. 2 (2009): 137–145.
13. Dan P. McAdams, "Personality, Modernity, and the Storied Self: A Contemporary Framework for Studying Persons," *Psychological Inquiry* 7, no. 4 (1996): 295–321. McAdams and Pals, "A New Big Five."
14. Nic M. Weststrate, Eranda Jayawickreme, and Cornelia Wrzus, "Advancing a Three-Tier Personality Framework for Posttraumatic Growth," *European Journal of Personality* 36, no. 4 (2022): 704–725.
15. Brady and Jayawickreme, "A Philosophical Approach to Improving Empirical Research."
16. Christopher J. Soto and Oliver P. John, "The Next Big Five Inventory (BFI-2): Developing and Assessing a Hierarchical Model with 15 Facets to Enhance Bandwidth, Fidelity, and Predictive Power," *Journal of Personality and Social Psychology* 113, no. 1 (2017): 117–143.
17. William Fleeson and Eranda Jayawickreme, "Whole Traits: Revealing the Social-Cognitive Mechanisms Constituting Personality's Central Variable," in *Advances in Experimental Social Psychology*, vol. 63, ed. James M. Olson (Academic Press, 2021), 69–128.
18. Jayawickreme and Blackie, "Post-Traumatic Growth as Positive Personality Change"; Howard Tennen and Glenn Affleck, "Personality and Change in the Face of Adversity," in *Posttraumatic Growth: Positive Changes in the Aftermath of Crisis*, ed. Richard G. Tedeschi, Crystal L. Park, and Lawrence G. Calhoun (Lawrence Erlbaum Associates, 1998), 65–98.
19. Tedeschi and Calhoun, *The Posttraumatic Growth Inventory* (1996).
20. McAdams, *The Stories We Live By*.
21. McAdams, *The Stories We Live By*.
22. Weststrate, Jayawickreme, and Wrzus, "Advancing a Three-Tier Personality Framework for Posttraumatic Growth."
23. Weststrate, Jayawickreme, and Wrzus, "Advancing a Three-Tier Personality Framework for Posttraumatic Growth."
24. Jayawickreme and Blackie, "Post-Traumatic Growth as Positive Personality Change."
25. William Fleeson and Eranda Jayawickreme, "Whole Trait Theory," *Journal of Research in Personality* 56 (2015): 82–92.
26. Adler et al., "Variation in Narrative Identity."
27. For a meta-analytic summary of similar studies, see Judith Mangelsdorf, Michael Eid, and Maike Luhmann, "Does Growth Require Suffering? A Systematic Review and Meta-Analysis on Genuine Posttraumatic and Postecstatic Growth," *Psychological Bulletin* 145, no. 3 (2019): 302–338.
28. Jayawickreme et al., "Examining Associations Between Major Negative Life Events."
29. Fleeson and Jayawickreme, "Whole Traits."
30. Frank J. Infurna and Suniya S. Luthar, "Resilience to Major Life Stressors Is Not as Common as Thought," *Perspectives on Psychological Science* 11, no. 2 (2016): 175–194.
31. Chopik et al., "Development of Character Strengths."
32. See also Jayawickreme et al., "Post-Traumatic Growth as Positive Personality Change."
33. Jayawickreme et al., "Post-Traumatic Growth as Positive Personality Change."
34. Gene H. Brody, Tianyi Yu, Edith Chen, Gregory E. Miller, Steven M. Kogan, and Steven R. H. Beach, "Is Resilience Only Skin Deep? Rural African Americans' Socioeconomic Status–Related Risk and Competence in Preadolescence and Psychological Adjustment and Allostatic Load at Age 19," *Psychological Science* 24, no. 7 (2013): 1285–1293.
35. Blackie and Jayawickreme, "Post-Traumatic Growth as Positive Personality Change."
36. Alexandra O'Neill, Nuwan Jayawickreme, Laura E. R. Blackie, A. Demaske, Michelle A. Goonasekera, and Eranda Jayawickreme, "Knowing When Someone Is Resilient: Development and Validation of a Measure of Adaptive Functioning among War-Affected Sri Lankan Tamils," *SSM–Mental Health* 1 (2021): 100026.
37. Seery, Holman, and Silver, "Whatever Does Not Kill Us."

38. Stephanie A. Bossert, Eranda Jayawickreme, Laura E. R. Blackie, and Veronica T. Cole, "Further Exploring the Impact of Cumulative Lifetime Adversity on Life Satisfaction, Psychological Flourishing, and Depressive Symptoms," *Journal of Research in Personality* 110 (2024): 104488.
39. For a similar discussion, see Panchuk, 2024b.
40. Johanna R. Vollhardt and Ervin Staub, "Inclusive Altruism Born of Suffering: The Relationship between Adversity and Prosocial Attitudes and Behavior Toward Disadvantaged Outgroups," *American Journal of Orthopsychiatry* 81, no. 3 (2011): 307–315.
41. Johanna Ray Vollhardt, "Altruism Born of Suffering and Prosocial Behavior Following Adverse Life Events: A Review and Conceptualization," *Social Justice Research* 22, no. 1 (2009): 53–97.
42. Brady and Jayawickreme, "A Philosophical Approach to Improving Empirical Research."
43. Daniel Lim and David DeSteno, "Suffering and Compassion: The Links Among Adverse Life Experiences, Empathy, Compassion, and Prosocial Behavior," *Emotion* 16, no. 2 (2016): 175–182.
44. Daniel Lim and David DeSteno. "Past Adversity Protects Against the Numeracy Bias in Compassion." *Emotion* 20, no. 8 (2020): 1344.
45. Daniel Lim and David DeSteno, "Guilt Underlies Compassion Among Those Who Have Suffered Adversity," *Emotion* 23, no. 3 (2023): 613–621.
46. Daniel Lim, Michael J. Poulin, C. Dale Shaffer-Morrison, Lauren M. Ministero, and Roxane Cohen Silver, "Investigating the Role of Adversity and Benevolence Beliefs in Predicting Prosociality," *Journal of Personality* 93, no. 3 (2025): 670–682.
47. Lim and DeSteno, "Guilt Underlies Compassion."
48. Brady and Jayawickreme, "A Philosophical Approach to Improving Empirical Research."
49. Fleeson and Jayawickreme, 2015, 2021, 2025; Jayawickreme et al., 2019. Fleeson and Jayawickreme, "Whole Trait Theory"; Fleeson and Jayawickreme, "Whole Traits"; William Fleeson and Eranda Jayawickreme, "Getting from States to Traits: Whole Trait Theory's Explanatory and Developmental Engine," *European Journal of Personality* (2024): 1–18, https://doi.org/10.1177/08902070251366709; Eranda Jayawickreme, Corinne E. Zachry, and William Fleeson, "Whole Trait Theory: An Integrative Approach to Examining Personality Structure and Process," *Personality and Individual Differences* 136 (2019): 2–11.
50. Going back to our discussion of the three-tier personality framework, here traits would be characterized as Trait_DES, while both characteristic adaptations and narrative identity would be included under Trait_EXP.
51. Brady and Jayawickreme, "A Philosophical Approach to Improving Empirical Research on Posttraumatic Growth."
52. For a similar discussion, see Jennifer Cole Wright, Michael T. Warren, and Nancy E. Snow, *Understanding Virtue: Theory and Measurement* (Oxford University Press, 2020).
53. Hayley Campbell, "Nick Cave Talks Grief, Joy, and 'Wild God,'" *GQ Magazine*, August 30, 2024.
54. Eranda Jayawickreme, Eli Tsukayama, and Laura E. R. Blackie, "Examining the Impact of Major Life Events on the Frequency and Experience of Daily Social Events," *Journal of Personality* 92, no. 1 (2024): 147–161.
55. Laura E. R. Blackie, Ann Marie Roepke, Marie J. C. Forgeard, Eranda Jayawickreme, and William Fleeson, "Act Well to Be Well: The Promise of Changing Personality States to Promote Well-Being," in *The Wiley Blackwell Handbook of Positive Psychological Interventions*, ed. Acacia C. Parks and Stephen M. Schueller (Wiley Blackwell, 2014), 462–474.
56. Jayawickreme and Blackie, "Post-Traumatic Growth as Positive Personality Change."
57. McLean, *Why Change Is Hard.*
58. van der Lugt, Dark Matters: Pessimism and the Problem of Suffering.

Chapter 7

1. I'm grateful to Ann Marie Roepke for the thoughtful comments she provided on this chapter.
2. James W. Pennebaker, "Writing About Emotional Experiences as a Therapeutic Process," *Psychological Science* 8, no. 3 (1997): 162–166.
3. Michael White and David Epston, *Narrative Means to Therapeutic Ends* (W. W. Norton & Company, 1990).
4. Robert A. Neimeyer, *Meaning Reconstruction & the Experience of Loss* (American Psychological Association, 2001).
5. Edna B. Foa and Barbara Olasov Rothbaum, *Treating the Trauma of Rape: Cognitive-Behavioral Therapy for PTSD* (Guilford Press, 2001).

6. Patricia A. Resick and Monica Schnicke, *Cognitive Processing Therapy for Rape Victims: A Treatment Manual*, vol. 4 (Sage, 1993).
7. Steven C. Hayes, Kirk D. Strosahl, and Kelly G. Wilson, *Acceptance and Commitment Therapy: The Process and Practice of Mindful Change* (Guilford Press, 2011).; Jason B. Luoma, Steven C. Hayes, and Robyn D. Walser, *Learning ACT: An Acceptance and Commitment Therapy Skills Training Manual for Therapists* (New Harbinger Publications, 2017).
8. Ann Marie Roepke, "Psychosocial Interventions and Posttraumatic Growth: A Meta-Analysis," *Journal of Consulting and Clinical Psychology* 83, no. 1 (2015): 129–142.
9. Pennebaker, "Writing About Emotional Experiences as a Therapeutic Process."
10. White and Epston, *Narrative Means to Therapeutic Ends.*
11. Neimeyer, *Meaning Reconstruction & the Experience of Loss.*
12. Resick and Schnicke, *Cognitive Processing Therapy for Rape Victims.*
13. Foa and Rothbaum, *Treating the Trauma of Rape.*
14. Hayes, Strosahl, and Wilson, *Acceptance and Commitment Therapy.*
15. Luoma, Hayes, and Walser, *Learning ACT.*
16. Jon Kabat-Zinn and Thich Nhat Hanh, *Full Catastrophe Living: Using the Wisdom of Your Body and Mind to Face Stress, Pain, and Illness* (Delta, 2009).
17. Zindel Segal, Mark Williams, and John Teasdale, *Mindfulness-Based Cognitive Therapy for Depression* (Guilford Press, 2012).
18. Susan Folkman and Judith Tedlie Moskowitz, "Positive Affect and the Other Side of Coping," *American Psychologist* 55, no. 6 (2000): 647–654.; Helzer and Jayawickreme, "Control and the 'Good Life.'"
19. Roepke et al., "Randomized Controlled Trial of SecondStory."
20. Roepke et al., "Randomized Controlled Trial of SecondStory."
21. Mendonça et al., "Randomized Controlled Trial of COMPASS."
22. Roepke et al., "Randomized Controlled Trial of SecondStory."
23. Russ Harris, *ACT Made Simple: An Easy-to-Read Primer on Acceptance and Commitment Therapy* (New Harbinger Publications, 2019).
24. Gabriele Oettingen, Marion Wittchen, and Peter M. Gollwitzer, "Regulating Goal Pursuit through Mental Contrasting with Implementation Intentions," in *New Developments in Goal Setting and Task Performance*, 523–548 (Routledge, 2013).
25. Aaron T. Beck, "Cognitive Therapy: Nature and Relation to Behavior Therapy," *Behavior Therapy* 1, no. 2 (1970): 184–200.; Milton H. Erickson, "Pseudo-Orientation in Time as an Hypnotherapeutic Procedure," *International Journal of Clinical and Experimental Hypnosis* 2, no. 4 (1954): 261–283.; Scott D. Miller and Insoo Kim Berg, *The Miracle Method: A Radically New Approach to Problem Drinking* (W. W. Norton & Company, 1995).
26. Lisa Najavits, *Seeking Safety: A Treatment Manual for PTSD and Substance Abuse* (Guilford Publications, 2002).
27. Maxine Harris and Roger D. Fallot, *Using Trauma Theory to Design Service Systems* (Jossey-Bass/Wiley, 2001).
28. Frank Neuner, Margarete Schauer, Christine Klaschik, Unni Karunakara, and Thomas Elbert, "A Comparison of Narrative Exposure Therapy, Supportive Counseling, and Psychoeducation for Treating Posttraumatic Stress Disorder in an African Refugee Settlement," *Journal of Consulting and Clinical Psychology* 72, no. 4 (2004): 579–587.
29. Maggie Herzig and Laura Chasin, *Fostering Dialogue Across Divides: A Nuts and Bolts Guide from the Public Conversations Project* (Public Conversations Project, 2006).
30. David O. Avruch and Wendy E. Shaia, "Macro MI: Using Motivational Interviewing to Address Socially-Engineered Trauma," *Journal of Progressive Human Services* 33, no. 2 (2022): 176–204.
31. Annemiek Richters, Cora Dekker, and Willem F. Scholte, "Community Based Sociotherapy in Byumba, Rwanda," *Intervention: Journal of Mental Health and Psychosocial Support in Conflict Affected Areas* 6, no. 2 (2008): 100–116.
32. Elaine Miller-Karas, *Building Resilience to Trauma: The Trauma and Community Resiliency Models* (Routledge, 2015).
33. Williamson, "Towards a Theory of Collective Posttraumatic Growth"; Williamson, "Posttraumatic Growth and Religion in Rwanda."
34. Williamson, "Posttraumatic Growth and Religion in Rwanda," 953–954.
35. Jayawickreme, Brady, and Jayawickreme, "Multidisciplinary Recommendations for Improving the Credibility of Research on Post-Traumatic Growth"; Ahilan Kadirgamar, "Co-existence,"

Daily Mirror, July 15, 2019, https://www.dailymirror.lk/opinion/Co-existence/172-170272; Mahendran Thiruvarangan, "Intellectual Responsibility Amidst Nationalist Uproar: Reflections from Northern Sri Lanka" (Colloquium presentation, Wake Forest University, Winston-Salem, NC, United States, 2025).

36. Zapffe et al., "What Does It Mean to Flourish, Languish, and Grow?"
37. For an interesting perspective, see the economist and blogger Noah Smith: Noah Smith, "Toward a Shallower Future," Noahpinion (blog), January 3, 2024, https://www.noahpinion.blog/p/toward-a-shallower-future.
38. Ami Harbin, "Prescribing Posttraumatic Growth," *Bioethics* 29, no. 9 (2015): 671–679.; Howard Tennen, "Positive Change Following Trauma: Controversies and New Directions" (paper presented at the 29th Annual Meeting of the International Society of Traumatic Stress Studies, Philadelphia, 2013).
39. Blackie et al., "Post-Traumatic Growth as Positive Personality Change."
40. Adam B. Cohen, "Many Forms of Culture," *American Psychologist* 64, no. 3 (2009): 194–204.
41. Brady and Jayawickreme, "A Philosophical Approach to Improving Empirical Research."
42. Seery, Holman, and Silver, "Whatever Does Not Kill Us."
43. Wilhelm Hofmann, Cornelia Betsch, Robert Böhm, Denise de Ridder, Stefan Drews, Benjamin Ewert, Ralph Hertwig, Falko F. Sniehotta, and Jutta Mata, "Rethinking Behaviour Change Interventions in Policymaking," *Nature Human Behaviour* no. 9 (2025): 1765–1767.

Chapter 8

1. Davis (2025) offers a clear and thoughtful description and analysis of the *aragalaya*. My colleagues and I discuss some possible paths forward in Jayawickreme et al. (2025)
2. I should note here that I was fortunate to have a middle-class upbringing that (along with my age) thankfully shielded me from being a direct target of political violence.
3. Van der Lugt, *Dark Matters*, 402.
4. Van der Lugt, *Dark Matters*, 402. See also D. J. Smail, "Power Interest and Psychology," in *Elements of a Social Materialist Understanding of Distress* (PCCS Books, 2005).
5. Anya Kamenetz, *The Stolen Year: How COVID Changed Children's Lives, and Where We Go Now* (Hachette UK, 2022), 334.
6. Benjamin A. Rogers, Herrison Chicas, John Michael Kelly, Emily Kubin, Michael S. Christian, Frank J. Kachanoff, Jonah Berger, Curtis Puryear, Dan P. McAdams, and Kurt Gray, "Seeing Your Life Story as a Hero's Journey Increases Meaning in Life," *Journal of Personality and Social Psychology* 125, no. 4 (2023): 752–778.
7. Brady and Jayawickreme, "A Philosophical Approach to Improving Empirical Research."
8. Schwaba et al., "Subjective Experiences of Life Events."
9. Infurna and Jayawickreme, "Fixing the Growth Illusion."
10. Shweder et al., "The 'Big Three' of Morality."
11. Adler and Schwaba, "Beyond 'Post,' 'Traumatic,' 'Growth,' and Prediction."
12. Van der Lugt, *Dark Matters.*
13. Adler and Schwaba, "Beyond 'Post,' 'Traumatic,' 'Growth,' and Prediction."
14. Jayawickreme et al., "Multidisciplinary Recommendations for Improving the Credibility of Research on Post-Traumatic Growth."
15. Anna Ortega-Williams, Tricia Stephens, and Zuleka Henderson, "Black Intergenerational Healing and Well-Being: Reimagining Posttraumatic Growth," *American Psychologist* 79, no. 8 (2024): 1171–1184.
16. Mary Beth Werdel, *The Paradox of Trauma and Growth in Pastoral and Spiritual Care* (Lexington Books, 2023).
17. Werdel, *The Paradox of Trauma and Growth in Pastoral and Spiritual Care*, 87.
18. Many thanks to Robert Wicks for drawing my attention to Werdel's thoughtful work on post-traumatic growth.
19. Kieran Setiya, *Life Is Hard: How Philosophy Can Help Us Find Our Way* (Penguin, 2023).
20. Setiya, *Life Is Hard*, 179.
21. Lori Gottlieb, "Ask a Therapist: I Hate How My Sister's Husband Treats Her. Can I Intervene?," *The New York Times*, August 14, 2025, https://www.nytimes.com/2025/08/14/well/mind/ask-therapist-lazy-father-husband.html

References

Adichie, Chimamanda Ngozi. "The Danger of a Single Story." TED Talk. TEDGlobal 2009, July 2009. Video, 18:33. https://www.youtube.com/watch?v=D9Ihs241zeg.

Adler, Jonathan M., Ariana F. Turner, Kathryn M. Brookshier, Casey Monahan, Ilana Walder-Biesanz, Luke H. Harmeling, Michelle Albaugh, Dan P. McAdams, and Thomas F. Oltmanns. "Variation in Narrative Identity Is Associated with Trajectories of Mental Health over Several Years," *Journal of Personality and Social Psychology* 108, no. 3 (2015): 476.

Adler, Jonathan M., and Ted Schwaba. "Beyond 'Post,' 'Traumatic,' 'Growth,' and Prediction in Research on Posttraumatic Growth," *American Psychologist* 79, no. 8 (2024): 1227–1240.

Affleck, Glenn, Howard Tennen, Sydney Croog, and Sol Levine. "Causal Attribution, Perceived Benefits, and Morbidity After a Heart Attack: An 8-Year Study," *Journal of Consulting and Clinical Psychology* 55, no. 1 (1987): 29–35.

Aikin, Scott, and William O. Stephens. *Epictetus's Encheiridion: A New Translation and Guide to Stoic Ethics.* Bloomsbury Publishing, 2023.

Al-ǧauzīya, Ibn-Qaiyim, Muḥammad Ibn-Abī-Bakr, and Nāṣir-ad-Dīn Al Ḫaṭṭāb. "Patience and Gratitude: An Abridged Translation of "Uddat as-sabirin wa dhakhirat ash-shakirin"" Ta-Ha Publishers, 1997.

Amarasuriya, Santushi Devini, Maria Guadalupe C. Salanga, Charisse T. Llorin, Marie Rose H. Morales, Eranda Jayawickreme, and Igor Grossmann. "Deconstructing Wisdom Through a Cultural Lens: Folk Understandings of Wisdom and Its Ontology in the Philippines and Sri Lanka," *Transcultural Psychiatry* 61, no. 5 (2024): 767–782.

Aquinas, Saint Thomas. *The Summa Theologica: Complete Edition.* Catholic Way Publishing, 2014.

Aristotle. *Nicomachean Ethics.* Translated by W. D. Ross. Clarendon Press, 1925.

Aurelius, Marcus. *Meditations.* Penguin, 2015.

Avruch, David O., and Wendy E. Shaia. "Macro MI: Using Motivational Interviewing to Address Socially-Engineered Trauma," *Journal of Progressive Human Services* 33, no. 2 (2022): 176–204.

Bakan, David. *The Duality of Human Existence: An Essay on Psychology and Religion*, Rand McNally. 1966.

Badawia, Tarek. "Islamic Practical Theology: Waqf and Zakāt as Theological Foundations." In *Exploring Islamic Social Work: Between Community and the Common Good.* ed. Hansjörg Schmid and Amir Sheikhzadegan. Springer International Publishing, 2022.

Balkaya-Ince, Merve, Madiha Tahseen, Osman Umarji, and Sarah A. Schnitker. "Does Ramadan Serve as a Naturalistic Intervention to Promote Muslim American Adolescents' Daily Virtues? Evidence from a Three Wave Experience Sampling Study," *The Journal of Positive Psychology* 19, no. 5 (2024): 801–816.

Barnes, Elizabeth. "Social Identities and Transformative Experience," *Res Philosophica* 92, no. 2 (2015): 171–187.

Baumel, Judith Tydor. "Women's Agency and Survival Strategies During the Holocaust." *Women's Studies International Forum*, 22, no. 3 (1999): 329–347.

Beck, Aaron T. "Cognitive Therapy: Nature and Relation to Behavior Therapy," *Behavior Therapy* 1, no. 2 (1970): 184–200.

Becker, Gay. *Disrupted Lives: How People Create Meaning in a Chaotic World.* University of California Press, 1997.

Berḳovits, Eliʿezer. *Faith after the Holocaust.* Ktav Publishing House, 1973.

Blackie, Laura E. R., Ann Marie Roepke, Marie J. C. Forgeard, Eranda Jayawickreme, and William Fleeson. "Act Well to Be Well: The Promise of Changing Personality States to Promote Well-Being." In *The Wiley Blackwell Handbook of Positive Psychological Interventions,* ed. Acacia C. Parks and Stephen M. Schueller (2014): 462–474.

Blackie, Laura E. R., and Eranda Jayawickreme. "Promoting Change in Post-Traumatic Growth Research: Response to Commentaries," *European Journal of Personality* 28, no. 4 (2014): 351–361.

Blackie, Laura E. R., Eranda Jayawickreme, Erik G. Helzer, Marie J. C. Forgeard, and Ann Marie Roepke. "Investigating the Veracity of Self-Perceived Posttraumatic Growth: A Profile Analysis Approach to Corroboration," *Social Psychological and Personality Science* 6, no. 7 (2015): 788–796.

Blackie, Laura E. R., Eranda Jayawickreme, Eli Tsukayama, Marie J. C. Forgeard, Ann Marie Roepke, and William Fleeson. "Post-Traumatic Growth as Positive Personality Change: Developing a Measure to Assess Within-Person Variability," *Journal of Research in Personality* 69 (2017): 22–32.

Blackie, Laura E. R., and Kate C. McLean. "Examining the Longitudinal Associations Between Repeated Narration of Recent Transgressions Within Individuals' Romantic Relationships and Character Growth in Empathy, Humility, and Compassion," *European Journal of Personality* 36, no. 4 (2022): 507–528.

Blackie, Laura E. R., N. Somasundaram, Victoria Britt, and Eranda Jayawickreme. "Narratives of Redemption Among a Sample of Tamil War-Affected Women in Eastern Sri Lanka," Manuscript in preparation, 2025.

Blackie, Laura E. R., Eranda Jayawickreme, Nicki Hitchcott, and Stephen Joseph. "Distinguishing Post-Traumatic Growth from Psychological Adjustment Among Rwandan Genocide Survivors." In *Varieties of Virtue Ethics. ed.* David Carr, James Arthur, and Kristján Kristjánsson. Palgrave Macmillan UK (2016): 299–317.

Boals, Adriel. "Illusory Posttraumatic Growth Is Common, but Genuine Posttraumatic Growth Is Rare: A Critical Review and Suggestions for a Path Forward," *Clinical Psychology Review* 103 (2023): 102301.

Boals, Adriel, Eranda Jayawickreme, and Crystal L. Park. "Advantages of Distinguishing Perceived and Veridical Growth: Recommendations for Future Research on Both Constructs," *The Journal of Positive Psychology* 18, no. 5 (2023): 773–783.

Bonanno, George A., Sandro Galea, Angela Bucciarelli, and David Vlahov. "Psychological Resilience After Disaster: New York City in the Aftermath of the September 11th Terrorist Attack," *Psychological Science* 17, no. 3 (2006): 181–186.

Bonanno, George A., Samuel M. Y. Ho, Jane C. K. Chan, Rosalie S. Y. Kwong, Celia K. Y. Cheung, Claudia P. Y. Wong, and Vivian C. W. Wong. "Psychological Resilience and Dysfunction Among Hospitalized Survivors of the SARS Epidemic in Hong Kong: A Latent Class Approach," *Health Psychology* 27, no. 5 (2008): 659–667.

Bonanno, George A., Camille B. Wortman, Darrin R. Lehman, Roger G. Tweed, Michelle Haring, John Sonnega, Deborah Carr, and Randolph M. Nesse. "Resilience to Loss and Chronic Grief: A Prospective Study from Preloss to 18-Months Postloss," *Journal of Personality and Social Psychology* 83, no. 5 (2002): 1150–1164.

Bossert, Stephanie A., Eranda Jayawickreme, Laura ER Blackie, and Veronica T. Cole. "Further Exploring the Impact of Cumulative Lifetime Adversity on Life Satisfaction, Psychological Flourishing, and Depressive Symptoms," *Journal of Research in Personality* 110 (2024): 104488.

Brady, Michael S. "Group Emotion and Group Understanding," *The Epistemic Life of Groups: Essays in the Epistemology of Collectives*, ed. Michael S. Brady and Miranda Fricker. Oxford University Press (2016): 95–110.

Brady, Michael S. *Suffering and Virtue.* Oxford University Press, 2018.

Brady, Michael, and Eranda Jayawickreme. "A Philosophical Approach to Improving Empirical Research on Posttraumatic Growth," *Philosophical Psychology* 38, no. 2 (2025): 796–819.

Brody, Gene H., Tianyi Yu, Edith Chen, Gregory E. Miller, Steven M. Kogan, and Steven R. H. Beach. "Is Resilience Only Skin Deep? Rural African Americans' Socioeconomic Status–Related Risk and Competence in Preadolescence and Psychological Adjustment and Allostatic Load at Age 19," *Psychological Science* 24, no. 7 (2013): 1285–1293.

Bronk, Kendall Cotton, Zach T. Swanson, William B. Whitney, Merve Balkaya-Ince, and Sarah Schnitker. "Exploring Conceptions of Patience Among a Sample of Muslim, Buddhist, Christian, and Nonreligious Young Adults," *Psychology of Religion and Spirituality* 17, no. 3, (2025): 270–281.

Calhoun, Lawrence G., and Richard G. Tedeschi. "The Foundations of Posttraumatic Growth: An Expanded Framework." In *Handbook of Posttraumatic Growth*, ed. Lawrence G. Calhoun and Richard G. Tedeschi. Routledge (2014): 3–23.

Callard, Agnes. "The Philosophy of Anger," *Boston Review* 16, no. 04 (2020).

Campbell, Hayley. "Nick Cave Talks Grief, Joy, and 'Wild God.'" *GQ Magazine*, August 30, 2024.

Carnelley, Katherine B., Camille B. Wortman, Niall Bolger, and Christopher T. Burke. "The Time Course of Grief Reactions to Spousal Loss: Evidence from a National Probability Sample," *Journal of Personality and Social Psychology* 91, no. 3 (2006): 476–492.

Cave, Nick. *The Red Hand Files, Issue# 248.* 2023.

Cave, Nick, and Sean O'Hagan. *Faith, Hope and Carnage: Sunday Times Bestseller.* Canongate Books, 2022.

Chambers, Chris. *The Seven Deadly Sins of Psychology: A Manifesto for Reforming the Culture of Scientific Practice.* Princeton University Press, 2017.

Chan, Rebecca. "Transformative Experience." In *The Stanford Encyclopedia of Philosophy* (Spring 2024 Edition), edited by Edward N. Zalta and Uri Nodelman. https://plato.stanford.edu/archives/spr2024/entries/transformative-experience/

Chang, Edward C. "An Appraisal of Nietzsche's Philosophical Concept of Amor Fati: A Potentially Useful Psychological Construct in the Study of Positive Human Existence?," *The Humanistic Psychologist* 53, no. 2 (2024): 183–196.

Chödrön, Pema. *When Things Fall Apart: Heart Advice for Difficult Times.* Shambhala Publications, 2000.

Chopik, William J., Whitney L. Kelley, Loryana L. Vie, Jeewon Oh, Douglas G. Bonett, Richard E. Lucas, and Martin EP Seligman. "Development of Character Strengths Across the Deployment Cycle Among US Army Soldiers," *Journal of Personality* 89, no. 1 (2021): 23–34.

Clinton, William J. "Address Accepting the Presidential Nomination at the Democratic National Convention in New York." Speech, *Madison Square Garden, New York, NY,* July 16, 1992. Accessed at https://www.presidency.ucsb.edu/documents/address-accepting-the-presidential-nomination-the-democratic-national-convention-new-york

Cohen, Adam B. "Many Forms of Culture," *American Psychologist* 64, no. 3 (2009): 194–204.

Davis, Christina P. "The Language Politics of Aragalaya: A Multilingual Protest Movement in Postwar Sri Lanka," *Anthropological Quarterly* 98, no. 2 (2025): 237–272.

Denson, Thomas F., Grant N. Marshall, Terry L. Schell, and Lisa H. Jaycox. "Predictors of Posttraumatic Distress 1 Year After Exposure to Community Violence: The Importance of Acute Symptom Severity," *Journal of Consulting and Clinical Psychology* 75, no. 5 (2007): 683.

DeVotta, Neil. *Blowback: Linguistic Nationalism, Institutional Decay, and Ethnic Conflict in Sri Lanka.* Stanford University Press, 2004.

Dorfman, Anna, David A. Moscovitch, William J. Chopik, and Igor Grossmann. "None the Wiser: Year-long Longitudinal Study on Effects of Adversity on Wisdom," *European Journal of Personality* 36, no. 4 (2022): 559–575.

Dunlop, William L., and Jessica L. Tracy. "Sobering Stories: Narratives of Self-Redemption Predict Behavioral Change and Improved Health Among Recovering Alcoholics," *Journal of Personality and Social Psychology* 104, no. 3 (2013): 576–590.

Epictetus. *Discourses: Book 1–2.* Dover Publications, 2004.

Ehrenreich, Barbara. *Bright-Sided: How Positive Thinking Is Undermining America.* Metropolitan Books, 2009.

Erickson, Milton H. "Pseudo-Orientation in Time as an Hypnotherapeutic Procedure," *International Journal of Clinical and Experimental Hypnosis* 2, no. 4 (1954): 261–283.

Fleeson, William, and Eranda Jayawickreme. "Whole Trait Theory," *Journal of Research in Personality* 56 (2015): 82–92.

Fleeson, William, and Eranda Jayawickreme. "Whole Traits: Revealing the Social-Cognitive mechanisms constituting Personality's Central Variable." *Advances in Experimental Social Psychology*, 63 (2021): 69–128.

Fleeson, William, and Eranda Jayawickreme. "Getting from States to Traits: Whole Trait Theory's Explanatory and Developmental Engine," *European Journal of Personality* (2024): 08902070251366709.

Foa, Edna B., and Barbara Olasov Rothbaum. *Treating the Trauma of Rape: Cognitive-Behavioral Therapy for PTSD.* Guilford Press, 2001.

Folkman, Susan, and Judith Tedlie Moskowitz. "Positive Affect and the Other Side of Coping," *American Psychologist* 55, no. 6 (2000): 647–654.

Ford, Julian D., Howard Tennen, and David Albert. "A Contrarian View of Growth Following Adversity," In *Trauma, Recovery, and Growth: Positive Psychological Perspectives on Posttraumatic Stress,* ed. Stephen Joseph and P. Alex Linley. Wiley (2008): 295–324.

Forgeard, Marie J. C., Anne C. Mecklenburg, Justin J. Lacasse, and Eranda Jayawickreme. "Bringing the Whole Universe to Order: Creativity, Healing, and Posttraumatic Growth," In *Creativity and Mental Illness,* ed. J.C. Kaufman. Cambridge University Press (2014): 321–342.

Francis, Krishan. "A Wartime Mass Grave in Sri Lanka Yields a Baby Bottle, Children's Clothes and 141 Skeletons," *AP News*, August 21, 2025. https://apnews.com/article/sri-lanka-grave-jaffna-chemmani-tamils-civil-war-d570beb78890405c73bd0ee75c059e69

Frankl, Viktor E. *Man's Search for Meaning.* Simon & Schuster, 1985.

Frazier, Patricia, Amy Conlon, and Theresa Glaser. "Positive and Negative Life Changes Following Sexual Assault," *Journal of Consulting and Clinical Psychology* 69, no. 6 (2001): 1048–1055.

Frazier, Patricia, James C. Coyne, and Howard Tennen. "Post-traumatic Growth: A Call for Less, but Better, Research." *European Journal of Personality* 28, no. 4 (2014): 337–338.

Frazier, Patricia, Howard Tennen, Margaret Gavian, Crystal Park, Patricia Tomich, and Ty Tashiro. "Does Self-Reported Posttraumatic Growth Reflect Genuine Positive Change?," *Psychological Science* 20, no. 7 (2009): 912–919.

Frazier, Patricia, Christiaan Greer, Susanne Gabrielsen, Howard Tennen, Crystal Park, and Patricia Tomich. "The Relation Between Trauma Exposure and Prosocial Behavior," *Psychological Trauma: Theory, Research, Practice, and Policy* 5, no. 3 (2013): 286–294.

Fredrickson, Barbara L., Michele M. Tugade, Christian E. Waugh, and Gregory R. Larkin. "What Good Are Positive Emotions in Crisis? A Prospective Study of Resilience and Emotions Following the Terrorist Attacks on the United States on September 11th, 2001," *Journal of Personality and Social Psychology* 84, no. 2 (2003): 365–376.

Fricker, Miranda. *Epistemic Injustice: Power and the Ethics of Knowing.* Oxford University Press, 2007.

Galatzer-Levy, Isaac R., Anita Madan, Thomas C. Neylan, Clare Henn-Haase, and Charles R. Marmar. "Peritraumatic and Trait Dissociation Differentiate Police Officers with Resilient Versus Symptomatic Trajectories of Posttraumatic Stress Symptoms," *Journal of Traumatic Stress* 24, no. 5 (2011): 557–565.

Ganeshananthan, V. V. *Brotherless Night: A Novel.* Random House, 2023.

Gangel, Meghan J., Rowan Kemmerly, Lindsey Wilson, Sydney Glickson, Patricia A. Frazier, Howard Tennen, and Eranda Jayawickreme. "Does Perceived Posttraumatic Growth Predict Observed Changes in Current-Standing and State Posttraumatic Growth?," *Clinical Psychological Science* 12, no. 3 (2024): 505–516.

Gosetti-Ferencei, Jennifer Anna. *On Being and Becoming: An Existentialist Approach to Life.* Oxford University Press, 2020.

Gottlieb, Lori. "Ask a Therapist: I Hate How My Sister's Husband Treats Her. Can I Intervene?," *New York Times*, August 14, 2025. https://www.nytimes.com/2025/08/14/well/mind/ask-therapist-lazy-father-husband.html

Grant, Amaris I., R. Michael Furr, and Eranda Jayawickreme. "Assessing the Response Process Validity of the Posttraumatic Growth Inventory Using Cognitive Interviews." *Journal of Personality Assessment* (2026): 1–12.

Green, John. *Everything Is Tuberculosis: The History and Persistence of Our Deadliest Infection.* Random House, 2025.

Gunaratna, V. F. *The Significance of the Four Noble Truths.* Buddhist Publication Society, 1968.

Habermas, Tilmann, and Susan Bluck. "Getting a Life: The Emergence of the Life Story in Adolescence," *Psychological Bulletin* 126, no. 5 (2000): 748–769.

Haidt, Jonathan. *The Happiness Hypothesis: Finding Modern Truth in Ancient Wisdom.* Basic Books, 2006.

Hanh, Thich Nhat. *Interbeing: The 14 Mindfulness Trainings of Engaged Buddhism.* Parallax Press, 2020.

Harbin, Ami. "Prescribing Posttraumatic Growth," *Bioethics* 29, no. 9 (2015): 671–679.

Harris, Russ. *ACT Made Simple: An Easy-to-Read Primer on Acceptance and Commitment Therapy.* New Harbinger Publications, 2019.

Harris, Maxine Ed, and Roger D. Fallot. *Using Trauma Theory to Design Service Systems.* Jossey-Bass/Wiley, 2001.

Harrison, Frances. *Still Counting the Dead: Survivors of Sri Lanka's Hidden War.* Portobello Books, 2012.

Hayes, Steven C., Kirk D. Strosahl, and Kelly G. Wilson. *Acceptance and Commitment Therapy: The Process and Practice Of Mindful Change.* Guilford Press, 2011.

Hechtlinger, Shahar, Christin Schulze, Christina Leuker, and Ralph Hertwig. "The Psychology of Life's Most Important Decisions," *American Psychologist* (2024).

Helgeson, Vicki S. "Corroboration of Growth Following Breast Cancer: Ten Years Later," *Journal of Social and Clinical Psychology* 29, no. 5 (2010): 546–574.

Helgeson, Vicki S., Kerry A. Reynolds, and Patricia L. Tomich. "A Meta-Analytic Review of Benefit-Finding and Growth," *Journal of Consulting and Clinical Psychology* 74, no. 5 (2006): 797–816.

Helzer, Erik G., and Eranda Jayawickreme. "Control and the "Good Life": Primary and Secondary Control as Distinct Indicators of Well-Being," *Social Psychological and Personality Science* 6, no. 6 (2015): 653–660.

Herzig, Maggie, and Laura Chasin. *Fostering Dialogue Across Divides: A Nuts and Bolts Guide from the Public Conversations Project.* Public Conversations Project, 2006.

Hick, John. *Evil and the God of Love.* Palgrave Macmillan, 2010.

Hobfoll, Stevan E., Patrick A. Palmieri, Robert J. Johnson, Daphna Canetti-Nisim, Brian J. Hall, and Sandro Galea. "Trajectories of Resilience, Resistance, and Distress During Ongoing Terrorism: The Case of Jews and Arabs in Israel," *Journal of Consulting and Clinical psychology* 77, no. 1 (2009): 138.

Hofmann, Wilhelm, Cornelia Betsch, Robert Böhm, Denise de Ridder, Stefan Drews, Benjamin Ewert, Ralph Hertwig, Falko F. Sniehotta, and Jutta Mata. "Rethinking Behaviour Change Interventions in Policymaking," *Nature Human Behaviour*, no 9 (2025): 1765–1767.

Hoole, Rajan, Kopalasingam Sritharan, Daya Somasundaram, and Rajani Thiranagama. *The Broken Palmyra: The Tamil Crisis in Sri Lanka—An Inside Account.* Sri Lanka Studies Institute, 1990.

Holgersen, Katrine Høyer, Hans Jakob Boe, and Are Holen. "Long-Term Perspectives on Posttraumatic Growth in Disaster Survivors," *Journal of Traumatic Stress* 23, no. 3 (2010): 413–416.

Ignatieff, Michael. *On Consolation: Finding Solace in Dark Times.* Metropolitan Books, 2021.

Infurna, Frank J., and Eranda Jayawickreme. "Fixing the Growth Illusion: New Directions for Research in Resilience and Posttraumatic Growth," *Current Directions in Psychological Science* 28, no. 2 (2019): 152–158.

Infurna, Frank J., and Suniya S. Luthar. "Resilience to Major Life Stressors Is Not as Common as Thought," *Perspectives on Psychological Science* 11, no. 2 (2016): 175–194.

Infurna, Frank J., and Suniya S. Luthar. "Re-Evaluating the Notion That Resilience Is Commonplace: A Review and Distillation of Directions for Future Research, Practice, and Policy," *Clinical Psychology Review* 65 (2018): 43–56.

Irvine, William B. *The Stoic Challenge: A Philosopher's Guide to Becoming Tougher, Calmer, and More Resilient.* WW Norton & Company, 2019.

Janoff-Bulman, Ronnie. *Shattered Assumptions: Towards a New Psychology of Trauma.* Free Press, 1992.

Jaspers, Karl. *Psychologie der Weltanschauungen.* Max Niemeyer Verlag, 1925.

Jayawickreme, Eranda. "Is Redemption Redeeming?" *Psychology Today*, November 8, 2022. https://www.psychologytoday.com/us/blog/pathways-flourishing/202211/is-redemption-redeeming

Jayawickreme, Eranda, and Laura ER Blackie. "Post-Traumatic Growth as Positive Personality Change: Evidence, Controversies and Future Directions," *European Journal of Personality* 28, no. 4 (2014): 312–331.

Jayawickreme, Eranda, and Laura ER Blackie. *Exploring the Psychological Benefits of Hardship: A Critical Reassessment of Posttraumatic Growth.* Springer, 2016.

Jayawickreme, Eranda, Laura ER Blackie, Marie Forgeard, Ann Marie Roepke, and Eli Tsukayama. "Examining Associations Between Major Negative Life Events, Changes in Weekly Reports of Post-Traumatic Growth and Global Reports of Eudaimonic Well-Being," *Social Psychological and Personality Science* 13, no. 4 (2022): 827–838.

Jayawickreme, Eranda, Eli Tsukayama, and Laura ER Blackie. "Examining the Impact of Major Life Events on the Frequency and Experience of Daily Social Events," *Journal of Personality* 92, no. 1 (2024): 147–161.

Jayawickreme, Eranda, Frank J. Infurna, Kinan Alajak, Laura ER Blackie, William J. Chopik, Joanne M. Chung, Anna Dorfman, et al. "Post-Traumatic Growth as Positive Personality Change: Challenges, Opportunities, and Recommendations," *Journal of personality* 89, no. 1 (2021): 145–165.

Jayawickreme, Eranda, Nuwan Jayawickreme, and Elise Miller. "Triumphalism, Fear and Humiliation: The Psychological Legacy of Sri Lanka's Civil War," *Dynamics of Asymmetric Conflict* 3, no. 3 (2010): 208–222.

Jayawickreme, Eranda, Michael Brady, and Nuwan Jayawickreme. "Multidisciplinary Recommendations for Improving the Credibility of Research on Post-Traumatic Growth," Manuscript under review, 2025.

Jayawickreme, Eranda, Corinne E. Zachry, and William Fleeson. "Whole Trait Theory: An Integrative Approach to Examining Personality Structure and Process," *Personality and Individual Differences* 136 (2019): 2–11.

Jayawickreme, Nuwan, Eranda Jayawickreme, Amy Z. McCaffrey, and Mahendran Thiruvarangan. "Mental Health Futures in Post-War Sri Lanka: Resilience, Relational Pluralism, and Implementation Pathways," *SSM-Mental Health* 7 (2025): 100465.

Joseph, Stephen. *What Doesn't Kill Us: The New Psychology of Posttraumatic Growth.* Basic Books, 2013.

Joseph, Stephen, and P. Alex Linley. "Positive Adjustment to Threatening Events: An Organismic Valuing Theory of Growth Through Adversity," *Review of General Psychology* 9, no. 3 (2005): 262–280.

Jost, John T., Brian A. Nosek, and Samuel D. Gosling. "Ideology: Its Resurgence in Social, Personality, and Political Psychology," *Perspectives on Psychological Science* 3, no. 2 (2008): 126–136.

Junger, Sebastian. *Tribe: On Homecoming and Belonging*. Twelve, 2016.

Kabat-Zinn, Jon, and Thich Nhat Hanh. *Full Catastrophe Living: Using the Wisdom of Your Body and Mind to Face Stress, Pain, and Illness*. Delta, 2009.

Kadirgamar, Ahilan. "Polarization, Civil War, and Persistent Majoritarianism in Sri Lanka," *Political Polarization in South and Southeast Asia: Old Divisions, New Dangers*, ed. Thomas Carothers and Andrew O'Donohue. Carnegie Endowment for International Peace (2020): 53–66.

Kadirgamar, Ahilan. "Co-existence," *Daily Mirror*, July 15, 2019. https://www.dailymirror.lk/opinion/Co-existence/172-170272

Kamenetz, Anya. *The Stolen Year: How COVID Changed Children's Lives, and Where We Go Now*. Hachette UK, 2022.

Karunatilaka, Shehan. *The Seven Moons of Maali Almeida: Winner of the Booker Prize 2022*. Sort of Books, 2022.

Kemmerly, Rowan, Howard Tennen, and Eranda Jayawickreme. "An Agenda for the Next Generation of Posttraumatic Growth Research." In *The Routledge International Handbook of Posttraumatic Growth*, ed. Roni Berger. Routledge (2023): 67–80

Kidd, Ian James. "Adversity, Wisdom, and Exemplarism," *The Journal of Value Inquiry* 52, no. 4 (2018): 379–393.

Klaas, Brian. *Fluke: Chance, Chaos, and Why Everything We Do Matters*. Simon and Schuster, 2024.

Klodawsky, H. No *More Tears Sister: Anatomy of Hope and Betrayal* [video recording]. National Film Board of Canada, 2005.

Kraemer, Lia M., Annette L. Stanton, Beth E. Meyerowitz, Julia H. Rowland, and Patricia A. Ganz. "A Longitudinal Examination of Couples' Coping Strategies as Predictors of Adjustment to Breast Cancer," *Journal of Family Psychology* 25, no. 6 (2011): 963–972.

Kushner, Harold S. *When Bad Things Happen to Good People*. Vintage, 1981.

Lam, Wendy WT, George A. Bonanno, Anthony D. Mancini, Samuel Ho, Miranda Chan, Wai Ka Hung, Amy Or, and Richard Fielding. "Trajectories of Psychological Distress Among Chinese Women Diagnosed with Breast Cancer," *Psycho-Oncology* 19, no. 10 (2010): 1044–1051.

Lambert, Alan J., John P. Schott, and Laura Scherer. "Threat, Politics, and Attitudes: Toward a Greater Understanding of Rally-'Round-the-Flag Effects," *Current Directions in Psychological Science* 20, no. 6 (2011): 343–348.

Laurance, Jeremy. "The Danger of Stoicism," *The Lancet* 376, no. 9747 (2010): 1137.

Lemon, Geoff. *The Comeback Summer*. Hardie Grant Publishing, 2020.

Landau, Mark J., Aaron C. Kay, and Jennifer A. Whitson. "Compensatory Control and the Appeal of a Structured World," *Psychological Bulletin* 141, no. 3 (2015): 694–722.

Lewis, Clive Staples. *A Grief Observed*. Zondervan, 2001.

Lim, Daniel, and David DeSteno. "Suffering and Compassion: The Links Among Adverse Life Experiences, Empathy, Compassion, and Prosocial Behavior," *Emotion* 16, no. 2 (2016): 175.

Lim, Daniel, and David DeSteno. "Past Adversity Protects Against the Numeracy Bias in Compassion," *Emotion* 20, no. 8 (2020): 1344–1356.

Lim, Daniel, and David DeSteno. "Guilt Underlies Compassion Among Those Who Have Suffered Adversity," *Emotion* 23, no. 3 (2023): 613–621.

Lim, Daniel, Michael J. Poulin, C. Dale Shaffer-Morrison, Lauren M. Ministero, and Roxane Cohen Silver. "Investigating the Role of Adversity and Benevolence Beliefs in Predicting Prosociality," *Journal of Personality* 93, no. 3 (2025): 670–682.

Luoma, Jason B., Steven C. Hayes, and Robyn D. Walser. *Learning ACT: An Acceptance and Commitment Therapy Skills Training Manual for Therapists.* New Harbinger Publications, 2017.

Maercker, Andreas, and Tanja Zoellner. "The Janus Face of Self-Perceived Growth: Toward a Two-Component Model of Posttraumatic Growth," *Psychological Inquiry* 15, no. 1 (2004): 41–48.

Mancini, Anthony D., George A. Bonanno, and Andrew E. Clark. "Stepping Off the Hedonic Treadmill: Individual Differences in Response to Major Life Events," *Journal of Individual Differences* 32, no. 3(2011): 144–152.

Mangelsdorf, Judith, Michael Eid, and Maike Luhmann. "Does Growth Require Suffering? A Systematic Review and Meta-Analysis on Genuine Posttraumatic and Postecstatic Growth," *Psychological Bulletin* 145, no. 3 (2019): 302–338.

Maslin, Abby. *Love You Hard: A Memoir of Marriage, Brain Injury, and Reinventing Love.* Dutton, 2019.

McAdams, Dan P. *The Stories We Live By: Personal Myths and the Making of the Self.* Guilford Press, 1993.

McAdams, Dan P. "Personality, Modernity, and the Storied Self: A Contemporary Framework for Studying Persons," *Psychological Inquiry* 7, no. 4 (1996): 295–321.

McAdams, Dan P. "The Psychology of Life Stories," *Review of General Psychology* 5, no. 2 (2001): 100–122.

McAdams, Dan P. "First We Invented Stories, Then They Changed Us: The Evolution of Narrative Identity," *Evolutionary Studies in Imaginative Culture* 3, no. 1 (2019): 1–18.

McAdams, Dan P., E. D. de St Aubin, and Regina L. Logan. "Generativity Among Young, Midlife, and Older Adults," *Psychology and Aging* 8, no. 2 (1993): 221–230.

McAdams, Dan P., and Kate C. McLean. "Narrative Identity," *Current Directions in Psychological Science* 22, no. 3 (2013): 233–238.

McAdams, Dan P., and Bradley D. Olson. "Personality Development: Continuity and Change over the Life Course," *Annual Review of Psychology* 61 (2010): 517–542.

McAdams, Dan P., and Jennifer L. Pals. "A New Big Five: Fundamental Principles for an Integrative Science of Personality," *American Psychologist* 61, no. 3 (2006): 204–217.

McAdams, Dan P., Jennifer Reynolds, Mara Lewis, A. H. Patten, and Philip J. Bowman. "When Bad Things Turn Good and Good Things Turn Bad: Sequences of Redemption and Contamination in Life Narrative and Their Relation to Psychosocial Adaptation in Midlife Adults and in Students," *Personality and Social Psychology Bulletin* 27, no. 4 (2001): 474–485.

McChesney, Robert W. *The Soul Also Keeps the Score: A Trauma-Informed Companion to the Spiritual Exercises of St. Ignatius.* Liturgical Press, 2025.

McFarland, Cathy, and Celeste Alvaro. "The Impact of motivation on Temporal Comparisons: Coping with Traumatic Events by Perceiving Personal Growth," *Journal of Personality and Social Psychology* 79, no. 3 (2000): 327–343.

McLean, Kate C. *Why Change Is Hard: The Power of Master Narratives over Self and Society*. Oxford University Press, 2024.

McLean, Kate C., and Moin Syed. "Personal, Master, and Alternative Narratives: An Integrative Framework for Understanding Identity Development in Context," *Human Development* 58, no. 6 (2016): 318–349.

McLean, Kate C., Jillian Fish, Leoandra Onnie Rogers, and Moin Syed. "Integrating Systems of Power and Privilege in the Study of Resilience," *American Psychologist* 79, no. 8 (2024): 999–1011.

McLean, Kate C., Brianna C. Delker, William L. Dunlop, Rowan Salton, and Moin Syed. "Redemptive Stories and Those Who Tell Them Are Preferred in the US," *Collabra: Psychology* 6, no. 1 (2020): 39.

McMillen, J. Curtis, and Cynthia Loveland Cook. "The Positive By-Products of Spinal Cord Injury and Their Correlates," *Rehabilitation Psychology* 48, no. 2 (2003): 77–85.

McMillen, J. Curtis, Elizabeth M. Smith, and Rachel H. Fisher. "Perceived Benefit and Mental Health After Three Types of Disaster," *Journal of Consulting and Clinical Psychology* 65, no. 5 (1997): 733–739.

McRae, Emily. "Suffering and the Six Perfections: Using Adversity to Attain Wisdom in Mahāyāna Buddhist Ethics," *The Journal of Value Inquiry* 52, no. 4 (2018): 395–410.

Mendonça, Sara Etz, Ann Marie Roepke, Eli Tsukayama, Amaris Grant, and Eranda Jayawickreme. "Randomized Controlled Trial of COMPASS, an Online Psychosocial Intervention Targeting Posttraumatic Growth: Addressing Acceptability and Feasibility," *The Journal of Positive Psychology* 20, no. 5 (2025): 774–790.

Mendonça, Sara Etz, Michael Brady, and Eranda Jayawickreme. "Can Exemplars Promote Character Development in the Wake of Adversity?." In *The Routledge International Handbook of Multidisciplinary Perspectives on Character Development, Volume II*. ed. Michael D. Matthews and Richard M. Lerner. Routledge (2024): 165–176.

Miller, Christian B. "A Satisfactory Definition of 'Post-Traumatic Growth' Still Remains Elusive." *European Journal of Personality* 28, no. 4 (2014): 344–346.

Miller-Karas, Elaine. *Building Resilience to Trauma: The Trauma and Community Resiliency Models*. Routledge, 2015.

Miller, Scott D., and Insoo Kim Berg. *The Miracle Method: A Radically New Approach to Problem Drinking*. WW Norton & Company, 1995.

Najavits, Lisa. *Seeking Safety: A Treatment Manual for PTSD and Substance Abuse*. Guilford Publications, 2002.

Neimeyer, Robert A. *Meaning Reconstruction & the Experience of Loss*. American Psychological Association, 2001.

Neuner, Frank, Margarete Schauer, Christine Klaschik, Unni Karunakara, and Thomas Elbert. "A Comparison of Narrative Exposure Therapy, Supportive Counseling, and Psychoeducation for Treating Posttraumatic Stress Disorder in an African Refugee Settlement," *Journal of Consulting and Clinical Psychology* 72, no. 4 (2004): 579–587.

Newberry, Laura. "Is It True That 'What Doesn't Kill You Makes You Stronger'? Exploring the Idea of Post-Traumatic Growth," *Los Angeles Times*, May 9, 2023. https://www.latimes.com/california/newsletter/2023-05-09/burnout-post-traumatic-growth-group-therapy

Nietzsche, Friedrich Wilhelm. *Beyond Good and Evil: Prelude to a Philosophy of the Future*. Translated by R. J. Hollingdale. London: Penguin Books, 1990.

Nietzsche, Friedrich. *Twilight of the Idols*. Translated by Duncan Large. Oxford: Oxford University Press, 1998.

Nolen-Hoeksema, Susan, and Jannay Morrow. "A Prospective Study of Depression and Posttraumatic Stress Symptoms After a Natural Disaster: The 1989 Loma Prieta Earthquake," *Journal of Personality and Social Psychology* 61, no. 1 (1991): 115–121.

Norris, Fran H., Melissa Tracy, and Sandro Galea. "Looking for Resilience: Understanding the Longitudinal Trajectories of Responses to Stress," *Social Science & Medicine* 68, no. 12 (2009): 2190–2198.

Nussbaum, Martha C. *Anger and Forgiveness: Resentment, Generosity, Justice.* Oxford University Press, 2016.

Oettingen, Gabriele, Marion Wittchen, and Peter M. Gollwitzer. "Regulating Goal Pursuit Through Mental Contrasting with Implementation Intentions," In *New Developments in Goal Setting and Task Performance*, ed. E. A. Locke and G. P. Latham. Routledge/Taylor & Francis Group (2013): 523–548.

Oishi, Shigehiro, Ayano Yagi, Asuka Komiya, Florian Kohlbacher, Takashi Kusumi, and Keiko Ishii. "Does a Major Earthquake Change Job Preferences and Human Values?," *European Journal of Personality* 31, no. 3 (2017): 258–265.

O'Neill, Alexandra, Nuwan Jayawickreme, Laura ER Blackie, A. Demaske, Michelle A. Goonasekera, and Eranda Jayawickreme. "Knowing When Someone Is Resilient: Development and Validation of a Measure of Adaptive Functioning Among War-Affected Sri Lankan Tamils," *SSM-Mental Health* 1 (2021): 100026.

Ortega-Williams, Anna, Tricia Stephens, and Zuleka Henderson. "Black Intergenerational Healing and Well-Being: Reimagining Posttraumatic Growth," *American Psychologist* 79, no. 8 (2024): 1171–1184.

Owenz, Meghan, and Blaine J. Fowers. "Perceived Post-Traumatic Growth May Not Reflect Actual Positive Change: A Short-Term Prospective Study of Relationship Dissolution," *Journal of Social and Personal Relationships* 36, no. 10 (2019): 3098–3116.

Oyserman, Daphna. "Culturally Fluent Theories, Metascience, and Scientific Progress: A Case Example: Commentary on Macnamara and Burgoyne (2023) and Burnette et al. (2023)." *Psychological Bulletin* 149, no. 3–4 (2023): 220–228.

Pagels, Elaine H. *Why Religion?: A Personal Story.* HarperLuxe, an imprint of HarperCollins Publishers, 2018.

Pagels, Elaine. *Miracles and Wonder: The Historical Mystery of Jesus.* Doubleday, 2025.

Panchuk, Michelle. "Distorting Concepts, Obscured Experiences: Hermeneutical Injustice in Religious Trauma and Spiritual Violence," *Hypatia* 35, no. 4 (2020): 607–625.

Panchuk, Michelle. "What Doesn't Kill Me Makes Me Stronger? Post-Traumatic Growth and the Problem of Suffering," Religious Studies 60, no. 3 (2024a): 428–444.

Panchuk, Michelle. *Religious Trauma.* Cambridge University Press, 2024b.

Park, Crystal L., Lawrence H. Cohen, and Renee L. Murch. "Assessment and Prediction of Stress-Related Growth," *Journal of Personality* 64, no. 1 (1996): 71–105.

Paul, L.A. *Transformative Experience.* Oxford University Press, 2014.

Pennebaker, James W. "Writing About Emotional Experiences as a Therapeutic Process." *Psychological Science* 8, no. 3 (1997): 162–166.

Pigliucci, Massimo, and Gregory Lopez. *A Handbook for New Stoics: How to Thrive in a World out of Your Control—52 Week-by-Week Lessons.* The Experiment, 2019.

Porter, Tenelle. "Jingle-Jangle Fallacies in Intellectual Humility Research," *The Journal of Positive Psychology* 18, no. 2 (2023): 221–223.

Raphael, Melissa R. "The Price of (Masculine) Freedom and Becoming: A Jewish Feminist Response to Eliezer Berkovits's Post-Holocaust Free Will Defence of God's

Non-Intervention in Auschwitz," in *Feminist Philosophy of Religion: Critical Readings*, ed. Pamela Sue Anderson and Beverley Clack. Routledge (2004): 136–150.

Rendon, Jim. *Upside: The New Science of Post-Traumatic Growth*. Simon and Schuster, 2015.

Resick, Patricia A., and Monica Schnicke. *Cognitive Processing Therapy for Rape Victims: A Treatment Manual, Vol. 4*. Sage, 1993.

Reynolds, Caleb J., Laura ER Blackie, R. Michael Furr, A. Demaske, Ann Marie Roepke, Marie Forgeard, and Eranda Jayawickreme. "Investigating corroboration of Self-Perceived Posttraumatic Growth Among Sri Lankan Tamil Survivors of Ethnopolitical Warfare Through Trait, Domain, and Profile Agreement Approaches," *Psychological Assessment* 34, no. 12 (2022): 1155–1165.

Richters, Annemiek, Cora Dekker, and Willem F. Scholte. "Community Based Sociotherapy in Byumba, Rwanda," *Intervention Journal of Mental Health and Psychosocial Support in Conflict Affected Areas* 6, no. 2 (2008): 100–116.

Roberts, Brent W. "Back to the Future: Personality and Assessment and Personality Development," *Journal of Research in Personality* 43, no. 2 (2009): 137–145.

Robson, David. "The Complicated Truth of Post-Traumatic Growth," *BBC News*, March 14, 2022.

Roepke, Ann Marie. "Psychosocial Interventions and Posttraumatic Growth: A Meta-Analysis," *Journal of Consulting and Clinical Psychology* 83, no. 1 (2015): 129–142.

Roepke, Ann Marie, Eli Tsukayama, Marie Forgeard, Laura Blackie, and Eranda Jayawickreme. "Randomized Controlled Trial of SecondStory, an Intervention Targeting Posttraumatic Growth, with Bereaved Adults," *Journal of Consulting and Clinical Psychology* 86, no. 6 (2018): 518–532.

Rogers, Benjamin A., Herrison Chicas, John Michael Kelly, Emily Kubin, Michael S. Christian, Frank J. Kachanoff, Jonah Berger, Curtis Puryear, Dan P. McAdams, and Kurt Gray. "Seeing Your Life Story as a Hero's Journey Increases Meaning in Life," *Journal of Personality and Social Psychology* 125, no. 4 (2023): 752–778.

Salgado, Minoli. *Twelve Cries from Home: In Search of Sri Lanka's Disappeared*. Repeater, 2022.

Sarner, Moya. "Post-Traumatic Growth: The Woman Who Learned to Live a Profoundly Good Life After Loss." The Guardian, May 11, 2021.

Samuelson, Scott. *Seven Ways of Looking at Pointless Suffering: What Philosophy Can Tell Us About the Hardest Mystery of All*. University of Chicago Press, 2018.

Schwaba, Ted, Jaap J. A. Denissen, Maike Luhmann, Christopher J. Hopwood, and Wiebke Bleidorn. "Subjective Experiences of Life Events Match Individual Differences in Personality Development," *Journal of Personality and Social Psychology* 125, no. 5 (2023): 1136–1156.

Sears, Sharon R., Annette L. Stanton, and Sharon Danoff-Burg. "The Yellow Brick Road and the Emerald City: Benefit-Finding, Positive Reappraisal Coping and Posttraumatic Growth in Women with Early-Stage Breast Cancer," *Health Psychology* 22, no. 5 (2003): 487–497.

Seery, Mark D., E. Alison Holman, and Roxane Cohen Silver. "Whatever Does Not Kill Us: Cumulative Lifetime Adversity, Vulnerability, and Resilience," *Journal of Personality and Social Psychology* 99, no. 6 (2010): 1025–1041.

Segal, Zindel, Mark Williams, and John Teasdale. *Mindfulness-Based Cognitive Therapy for Depression*. Guilford Press, 2012.

Sen, Amartya. *Home in the World: A Memoir*. Liveright Publishing, 2021.

Setiya, Kieran. *Life Is Hard: How Philosophy Can Help Us Find Our Way*. Penguin, 2023.

Shakespeare-Finch, Jane, and Tracey Enders. "Corroborating Evidence of Posttraumatic Growth," *Journal of Traumatic Stress: Official Publication of The International Society for Traumatic Stress Studies* 21, no. 4 (2008): 421–424.

Sherman, Nancy. *Stoic Wisdom: Ancient Lessons for Modern Resilience*. Oxford University Press, 2021.

Shweder, Richard A., Nancy C. Much, Manamohan Mahapatra, and Lawrence Park. 1997. "The 'Big Three' of Morality (Autonomy, Community, Divinity) and the 'Big Three' Explanations of Suffering." In *Morality and Health*, edited by Allan Brandt and Paul Rozin, 119–169. New York: Routledge.

Smail, D. J. *Power Interest and Psychology*: Elements of a Social Materialist Understanding of Distress. PCCS Books, 2005.

Smith, Noah. "Toward a Shallower Future." Noahpinion (blog), January 3, 2024. https://www.noahpinion.blog/p/toward-a-shallower-future.

Snowden, Frank M. *Epidemics and Society: From the Black Death to the Present*. Yale University Press, 2019.

Somasundaram, Daya. *Scarred Communities: Psychosocial Impact of Man-Made and Natural Disasters on Sri Lankan Society*. SAGE Publications, 2014.

Soto, Christopher J., and Oliver P. John. "The Next Big Five Inventory (BFI-2): Developing and Assessing a Hierarchical Model with 15 Facets to Enhance Bandwidth, Fidelity, and Predictive Power," *Journal of Personality and Social Psychology* 113, no. 1 (2017): 117–143.

Specht, Jule, Boris Egloff, and Stefan C. Schmukle. "Stability and Change of Personality Across the Life Course: The Impact of Age and Major Life Events on Mean-Level and Rank-Order Stability of the Big Five," *Journal of Personality and Social Psychology* 101, no. 4 (2011): 862–882.

Spiro, Avron, Paula P. Schnurr, and Carolyn M. Aldwin. "Combat-Related Posttraumatic Stress Disorder Symptoms in Older Men," *Psychology and Aging* 9, no. 1 (1994): 17–26.

Stockdale, Katie. *Hope Under Oppression*. Oxford University Press, 2021.

Stump, Eleonore. *Wandering in Darkness: Narrative and the Problem of Suffering*. Oxford University Press, 2010.

Subramanian, Samanth. *This Divided Island: Stories from the Sri Lankan War*. Atlantic Books Ltd, 2015.

Táíwò, Olúfẹ́mi O. *Elite Capture: How the Powerful Took Over Identity Politics (and Everything Else)*. Haymarket Books, 2022.

Taylor, Shelley E., and David A. Armor. "Positive Illusions and Coping with Adversity," *Journal of Personality* 64, no. 4 (1996): 873–898.

Tedeschi, Richard G., and Lawrence G. Calhoun. "The Posttraumatic Growth Inventory: Measuring the Positive Legacy of Trauma," *Journal of Traumatic Stress* 9, no. 3 (1996): 455–471.

Tennen, Howard. "Positive Change Following Trauma: Controversies and New Directions." In *Comments Presented at the 29th Annual Meeting of International Society of Traumatic Stress Studies, Philadelphia*. 2013.

Tennen, Howard, and Glenn Affleck. "Personality and Change in the Face of Adversity." In *Posttraumatic Growth: Positive Changes in the Aftermath of Crisis*, edited by Richard G. Tedeschi, Crystal L. Park, and Lawrence G. Calhoun. Lawrence Erlbaum Associates, 1998.

Tennen, Howard, and Glenn Affleck. "Assessing Positive Life Change: In Search of Meticulous Methods." In *Medical Illness and Positive Life Change: Can Crisis Lead to Personal Change?*, edited by Crystal L. Park, Susan C. Lechner, Michael H. Antoni, and Annette L. Stanton. American Psychological Association, 2009.

"The Moral of 'The Salt Path,' an Embellished Bestseller," *The Economist*, August 16, 2025. https://www.economist.com/britain/2025/08/16/the-moral-of-the-salt-path-an-embellished-bestseller

Thiruvarangan, Mahendran. "Intellectual Responsibility Amidst Nationalist Uproar: Reflections from Northern Sri Lanka," Colloquium presentation, Wake Forest University, Winston-Salem, NC, United States, 2025.

Tiberius, Valerie. "Growth and the Multiple Dimensions of Well-Being: A Philosopher's Take on the Idea of Post-Traumatic Growth." In *Redesigning Research on Post-Traumatic Growth: Challenges, Pitfalls, and New Directions*, edited by Frank J. Infurna and Eranda Jayawickreme. Oxford University Press, 2021.

U.S. Agency for International Development. *Rebuilding Postwar Rwanda: The Role of the International Community (A.I.D. Evaluation Special Study Report No. 76)*. Washington, DC: U.S. Agency for International Development, 1996.

Updegraff, John A., Roxane Cohen Silver, and E. Alison Holman. "Searching for and Finding Meaning in Collective Trauma: Results from a National Longitudinal Study of the 9/11 Terrorist Attacks," *Journal of Personality and Social Psychology* 95, no. 3 (2008): 709–722.

Van der Lugt, Mara. *Dark Matters: Pessimism and the Problem of Suffering*. Princeton University Press, 2021.

van Deurzen, Emmy. *Existential Counselling and Psychotherapy in Practice*. Sage, 2008.

Van Tongeren, Daryl R., and Sara A. Showalter Van Tongeren. *The Courage to Suffer: A New Clinical Framework for Life's Greatest Crises*. Templeton Foundation Press, 2020.

Vedantam, Shankar. "What We Gain from Pain," *Hidden Brain*. Podcast audio. Hidden Brain Media, July 31, 2023.

Vollhardt, Johanna Ray. "Altruism Born of Suffering and Prosocial Behavior Following Adverse Life Events: A Review and Conceptualization," *Social Justice Research* 22, no. 1 (2009): 53–97.

Vollhardt, Johanna R., and Ervin Staub. "Inclusive Altruism Born of Suffering: The Relationship Between Adversity and Prosocial Attitudes and Behavior Toward Disadvantaged Outgroups," *American Journal of Orthopsychiatry* 81, no. 3 (2011): 307–315.

Vos, Joel. "Meaning and Existential Givens in the Lives of Cancer Patients: A Philosophical Perspective on Psycho-Oncology," *Palliative & Supportive Care* 13, no. 4 (2015): 885–900.

Wang, Robin R. "Understanding of Yin Yang," *Religion Compass* 7, no. 6 (2013): 214–224.

Werdel, Mary Beth. *The Paradox of Trauma and Growth in Pastoral and Spiritual Care*. Lexington Books, 2023.

Weststrate, Nic M., Eranda Jayawickreme, and Cornelia Wrzus. "Advancing a Three-Tier Personality Framework for Posttraumatic Growth," *European Journal of Personality* 36, no. 4 (2022): 704–725.

White, Michael, and David Epston. *Narrative Means to Therapeutic Ends*. WW Norton & Company, 1990.

Wickrematunge, Lasantha. "And Then They Came for Me," *The Sri Lanka Reader: History, Culture, Politics*, ed. John Clifford Holt. Duke University Press (2011): 715–720.

Williamson, Caroline. "Towards a Theory of Collective Posttraumatic Growth in Rwanda: The pursuit of Agency and Communion," *Traumatology: An International Journal* 20, no. 2 (2014a): 91–102.

Williamson, Caroline. "Posttraumatic Growth and Religion in Rwanda: Individual Well-Being vs. Collective False Consciousness," *Mental Health, Religion & Culture* 17, no. 9 (2014b): 946–955.

Wolpe, Rabbi David. *Making Loss Matter: Creating Meaning in Difficult Times*. Penguin, 2000.

Wright, Jennifer Cole, Michael T. Warren, and Nancy E. Snow. *Understanding Virtue: Theory and Measurement*. Oxford University Press, 2020.

Wu, Xiaoli, Atipatsa C. Kaminga, Wenjie Dai, Jing Deng, Zhipeng Wang, Xiongfeng Pan, and Aizhong Liu. "The Prevalence of Moderate-to-High Posttraumatic Growth: A Systematic Review and Meta-Analysis," *Journal of Affective Disorders* 243 (2019): 408–415.

Yanez, Betina R., Annette L. Stanton, Michael A. Hoyt, Howard Tennen, and Suzanne Lechner. "Understanding Perceptions of Benefit Following Adversity: How Do Distinct Assessments of Growth Relate to Coping and Adjustment to Stressful Events?," *Journal of Social and Clinical Psychology* 30, no. 7 (2011): 699–721.

Zachry, Corinne E., and Eranda Jayawickreme. "Unbelieving Wisdom: Does Critiquing Reports of Perceived Growth Following Adversity Constitute an Epistemic Injustice?" In *Post-Traumatic Growth to Psychological Well-Being: Coping Wisely with Adversity*, ed. Melanie Munroe and Michel Ferrari. Springer International Publishing (2022): 31–42.

Zapffe, Linn, Kaitlyn Hennig, Nuwan Jayawickreme, and Eranda Jayawickreme. "What Does It Mean to Flourish, Languish, and Grow? A Qualitative Analysis of Civilian Interviews from Survivors of the 1994 Rwandan Genocide," *SSM-Mental Health* 4 (2023): 100274.

Zaretsky, Robert. *A Life Worth Living*. Harvard University Press, 2013.

Index

For the benefit of digital users, indexed terms that span two pages (e.g., 52–53) may, on occasion, appear on only one of those pages.

Tables, figures, and boxes are indicated by an italic *t*, *f*, or *b*.